THE LIFE OF A LANCER IN THE WARS OF THE PUNJAUB

OR
SEVEN YEARS IN INDIA, 1843–50

James Gilling, Ninth Lancers

Edited and with an introduction
by John H. Rumsby

Helion & Company Ltd

Helion & Company Limited
26 Willow Road
Solihull
West Midlands
B91 1UE
England
Tel. 0121 705 3393
Fax 0121 711 4075
Email: info@helion.co.uk
Website: www.helion.co.uk
Twitter: @helionbooks
Visit our blog http://blog.helion.co.uk/

Published by Helion & Company 2014

Designed and typeset by Farr out Publications, Wokingham, Berkshire
Cover designed by Farr out Publications, Wokingham, Berkshire
Printed by Lightning Source, Milton Keynes, Buckinghamshire

Introduction, notes and supplementary material © John H. Rumsby
Images © as individually credited
Maps © Helion & Company Limited 2014. Maps designed by George Anderson

ISBN 978 1 909982 23 9

British Library Cataloguing-in-Publication Data.
A catalogue record for this book is available from the British Library.

All rights reserved. No part of this publication may be reproduced, stored in a retrieval system, or transmitted, in any form, or by any means, electronic, mechanical, photocopying, recording or otherwise, without the express written consent of Helion & Company Limited.

Front cover: Private of the Ninth Lancers 1828 (Author's collection). Rear cover: Map of the Battle of Chillianwallah (George Anderson).

For details of other military history titles published by Helion & Company Limited contact the above address, or visit our website: http://www.helion.co.uk.

We always welcome receiving book proposals from prospective authors.

In memory of Jim Cradock,
Ninth Lancers and Army Catering Corps,
who first told me about the Lance Exercise.

Contents

List of illustrations	vii
List of maps	ix
Glossary	x
Acknowledgments	13
Introduction	14
A note on the text	39
Preface to the original edition	40

1 **Enlistment**   41
The Author arrives in London, and enlists in the 9th Lancers – Bodily inspection – His departure for Maidstone – Fatigues.

2 **Voyage to India**   43
Embarkation at Gravesend – Hammocks – "Use is second nature." – Voyage to India – A calm at Sea – Terrific hurricane – An American Whaler – Burial at Sea – Military punishment at Sea – The Culprit released by his comrades – Man overboard – Anchor near the mouth of the Hoogly – The Pariahs – Woman and child on the banks of the Hoogly – Arrived at Calcutta.

3 **First experiences of India**   50
First night in India – Mosquitoes – Barracks at Chinsurah – Indian Hawks – Indian toddy.

4 **Calcutta**   52
Mussulman Festival – Change quarters to Dum Dum – Hindoo burial of banners, &c – Breakfast in India – Barracks at Dum Dum – Visit of the Tars of the *Queen* – Removal to Fort William – Bomb proof Barracks – Cholera – Departure from Calcutta – River storm.

5 **Upriver to Cawnpore**   57
Monghye – Arrival at Benares – Periodical hot winds – Fort Chunar – Eastern Princesses – Escape of the Ranee Chunder – Arrival at Allahabad – Sacred water of the Ganges – Dust Storms – Arrival at Cawnpore – Joins the Regiment.

6 **Life in the Regiment**   61
The novitiate – Rough Riding – Breaking in my Steed – Suicide of a comrade – Trying Season – Drinking in the Army – Sir C. Napier – Desertion of two men – Rumours of war – Half the Regiment in the Hospital.

7 **The Sutlej Campaign**   67
Arrival at Meerut – Attempted despotism of an officer – Insubordination – Punishment – The Sikh Soldiery – March to Sirdhana – The Begum Sumroo – Hindu Superstition – Arrival at Mudki – "Field" of Ferozeshah – Join Sir Hugh Gough's force – Interruption at dinner – Turn out – The Sikh camp – The field tent of Lalla Sing – The Battle of Sobraon.

8   **The Battle of Sobraon**   73
    The "tug of war" – The eve of battle – Combat in the valley of the Sutlej
    – Great victory – Reciprocal kindness of English and native soldiery –
    Remuneration of our Government to worn out soldiers – Return to the
    Camp – Appearance of an English lady on the scene – Praiseworthy
    conduct of the Ladies towards the sick and wounded – The cavalry cross
    the Sutlej – Indifference of the Natives – Departure for Lahore – Arrival
    at Kussor – Return of prisoners from the Sikh camp – Diplomatic mission
    – Goolab Sing – The British camp – View of Lahore – A tremendous
    storm – The Gurkhas – A "flare up" – The Barrack room – Drunkenness.

9   **Military Executions**   89
    Insubordination – A General Court Martial – Capital punishment – The
    flogging system – The Cobra di Capello.

10 **The Punjab Campaign: Ramnuggar**   98
    Conspiracies and intrigues – Harassing marches – Mudki and Ferozeshah
    – Ferozepore – The soldier's "honour and glory" – Brigadier Pope –
    Arrived at Lahore – A Plot – Magnificent Tombs at Agra – The mirage
    – A chase – A glorious victory – Inducements to Sepoys to desert – A perilous situation

11 **Pursuing Shere Singh**   108
    Shere Sing "smells a rat" – Sudden disappearance of the Sikh camp –
    Inhuman treatment of a Sikh soldier – Camp amusements – Letters from home.

12 **The Battle of Chillianwallah**   114
    Chillianwallah – An Engagement – The enemy foiled – Coolness of a
    Gunner – A fearful tragedy – Spartan-like courage – Dreadful conflict –
    Visit to the field after a battle – Jackalls – Burial in the camp.

13 **Battle of Gujerat and Home**   125
    Hairbreadth escapes – Revenge – Anxiety for an engagement – The fall
    of Multan – A narrow escape – A visit to the enemy's evacuated position
    – A sad spectacle – A soldier's motives – Encampment near Lussoorie –
    Accession of troops from Multan – An artillery fight – A Sikh's gratitude
    – Excessive thirst – Surrender of the Sikhs – Obtains his discharge – Return home.

Appendices
I   Military executions at Meerut 1847: Major James Hope Grant's account   141
II   The actions of Pope's Brigade at the Battle of Chillianwallah: Major Grant's report   144
III The actions of the cavalry on the left flank at the Battle of Gujerat: Major-
     General Sir Joseph Thackwell's account.   146

Notes   147
Bibliography   162
Index   168

List of illustrations

Ninth Lancers 1846. A print by Martens and Lynch, showing a mounted sergeant in full dress, with an officer in frock coat; to the left is a trumpeter, and to the right two privates in undress uniform. (Anne S K Brown Military Collection, Brown University Library)   22

Shoulder scales. Worn by lancers and other light cavalry, these brass scales were too flimsy to afford much protection from a Sikh *tulwar*. (By courtesy of the 9th/12th Lancers Museum, Derby)   23

Ninth Lancers in heavy marching order c.1840. A print by Hayes and Lynch. Although this scene is set in Britain, the uniform worn on campaign in Bengal was almost identical, with the addition of white cap covers, and probably plain horse blankets replacing the elaborate embroidered shabraques. (Anne S K Brown Military Collection, Brown University Library)   28

Light Cavalry sword, other ranks' pattern. This sword was approved in 1821, but the Ninth Lancers did not receive theirs until 1831. The blade was not really curved enough to be a good cutting weapon, but was not strong enough for thrusting. This specimen, like many surviving examples, demonstrates the weak scabbard, vulnerable to denting and rusting. (Private collection) 30

Punjab and Indian Mutiny medals of 1303 Private Thomas Derome. Derome, a tailor by trade, enlisted in the Ninth Lancers on 15 June 1843. He was shipped to India in the same draft as James Gilling. He served in India for over fifteen years, being finally discharged in 1860 as a consequence of a fractured wrist. He was also entitled to the Sutlej Medal for Sobraon. (By courtesy of the 9th/12th Lancers Museum, Derby)   45

Medals of Samuel Higginson. No 1076 Private Higginson was born in Brighton, Sussex, and served in the Sixth Dragoon Guards before transferring to the Ninth. His medals are (left to right): Punniar Star, Sutlej (for Sobraon), Punjab, Indian Mutiny, and Long Service and Good Conduct Medal. He was discharged in 1864 after nearly 28 years' service. (By courtesy of the 9th/12th Lancers Museum)   45

Cawnpore. For many cavalry soldiers arriving by *budgerow*, this was the first glimpse of their home for the next year. The exotic nature of their surroundings in Bengal – people, houses, transport and wildlife – was a continuing source of fascination for many soldiers, who often compared the sights to scenes they had read of in the Bible. (Author's collection)   58

Barracks canteen, c. 1850. This scene is probably in England, but canteens in India were similar, with food on offer as well as local liquor and, for those who could afford it, imported English beer. (Author's collection)   60

"Our Moonshee." A satirical depiction of British life in India, from George Atkinson's *Curry and Rice (on Forty Plates)* published in 1853. The *moonshee* was a language teacher, but the officer seems more interested in the bottle being opened by one of his other servants. Note the *punkah* overhead to provide a cooling draught. (Author's collection)   64

"Our Theatricals". Another of Atkinson's well-observed scenes of garrison life; all the parts are played by men. The Sixteenth Lancers had a particularly renowned theatre troupe. (Author's collection)   65

Captured Sikh guns after the Sutlej campaign, 1847. The vast number and great size of the Sikh artillery pieces exceeded anything the British forces had ever faced before in their Indian campaigns. (Author's collection)   78

Sutlej Medal for Sobraon. This medal was awarded to Number 330 Private Cornelius McIneyrey. Although the rim of the medal gives his regiment as the 80th Foot, he earned the medal whilst serving with the Ninth Lancers, transferring to the 80th in July 1847. McIneyrey was born in Clonmel, Co Tipperary, Ireland, and was a labourer when he enlisted in 1829. He was discharged in 1851, whilst holding four good conduct badges. He was also entitled to the Punniar Star. (Private collection)   87

Colonel James Hope Grant (1808-1875). He served in the First China War, the Sutlej and Punjab campaigns, commanded a cavalry brigade in the Indian Mutiny, and commanded the British forces in the Second China War. He ended his career as a Major General and GCB. (Private collection)   92

Captain Richard Freer Thonger c.1860. Thonger, born in Boston, Lincolnshire in 1819, enlisted in the Ninth Lancers in 1841. A man of obvious ability, he rose quickly through the ranks to become a troop sergeant major in 1849, and regimental sergeant major in 1851. He was commissioned in 1857 and retired as a captain in 1865. Here he is wearing mess dress, with the ribbons for the Sutlej, Punjab and Indian Mutiny medals. He died in 1906. (By courtesy of the 9th/12th Lancers Museum, Derby)   93

The Battle of Chillianwallah. The scrubby jungle and pools of water that covered the battlefield, compounded by the low evening light and musket smoke, made it a very unsuitable place for cavalry to deploy. (Anne S K Brown Military Collection, Brown University Library)   116

Sikh 9-pounder cannon, captured at the Battle of Chillianwallah. Cast in the Mogul fashion in about 1800, but with a British style carriage. Its performance would have been equal to those of the British-Indian artillery which confronted it at Chillianwallah. (Copyright Royal Armouries collection, Fort Nelson)   120

The Battle of Gujerat. The British commanders cluster under a tree as an aide-de-camp gallops up with a message. Although fanciful in places, this contemporary print does convey something of the crowded nature of a battle fought with short-range weapons, and the confusion resulting from clouds of gunpowder smoke from cannon and muskets. (Anne S K Brown Military Collection, Brown University Library)   135

The Surrender of the Sikhs. The reverse of the Punjab Medal depicts the scene as Sikhs lay down their firearms, swords and shields at the feet of a British general. (Private collection.)   138

List of maps

Northern India	17
Seat of the Anglo-Sikh Wars	32
The Battle of Chillianwallah	117

Glossary

(Spelling is as used by Gilling, with the more usual spelling where applicable in brackets.)[1]

Abattis	barricade made from felled trees, with the branches sharpened
Akali	ill-disciplined but fanatically brave Sikh foot-soldier, clothed in blue cloth and heavily armed
Attah (ata)	flour
Brahmin	a member of the Hindu priestly caste
Budgerow	a large keel-less river barge powered by sail or tow, often used to transport troops along the Ganges
Charpoy	'The ... bed in common use is a charpoy, or frame of light wood, laced together across with twine, and raised on four legs, about eight inches high.'[2]
Chatty	a pottery vessel for water or other liquids
Chillum chee	a brass basin for washing the hands
Chokedar (chowkedar)	watchman (the first element 'choky' entered into English as a slang word for prison.)
Choppah (chopper)	thatched roof
Chunam	lime plaster used to cover brickwork; it could be polished to a smooth, marble-like finish
Crore	one hundred *lacs* i.e. ten million
Dak (dawk)	system of travel by posting horses or palanquin bearers at regular intervals along a road. The system was especially used for postal services, hence the term came to be used often to mean the post
Dandee (dandy)	boatman on the River Ganges
Dexee	cooking pot (adapted into British army slang as 'dixie,' a large metal pot to carry stew or tea)
Dhooly	a light cot suspended from a bamboo pole: ' ... a conveyance for sick, carried by four men by means of a long pole on the shoulders leaving the body of the dhooly swinging in the centre, not altogether a very pleasant affair to ride in.'[3]
Dinghee (dinghy)	small boat or canoe
Doab	stretch of land between two rivers
Dunree (dumree)	small value copper coin
Epaulment (epaulement)	fortification designed to protect a flank
Fakir	usually used for a Hindu ascetic devotee

---

1 Most of the definitions given for Indian words are derived from H Yule and A C Burnell, *Hobson-Jobson: The Anglo-Indian Dictionary* (London, 1996; first published 1886). One of the authors, Henry Yule, was a brother of Captain Yule of the 9th Lancers.

2 H Lawrence, *The Journals of Honoria Lawrence: India observed 1837-1854* ed J Lawrence and A Woodiwiss (London, 1980) p. 75.

3 National Army Museum (NAM) 7201-45, F Potiphar, Narrative 1857-9, p. 11.

Fascine	a bundle of branches tied together, used to build up and reinforce earth fortifications
Fausse-braze (fausse-braie)	a lower wall in front of, and thus protecting the foot of, the main wall of a fortress
Feringhee	foreigner – usually used pejoratively for the British
Ghaut	landing place or quay on a river
Ghee	clarified butter, used for cooking
Goorchurra	Sikh cavalrymen heavily armed with firearms and edged weapons
Grape (as in grape-shot)	strictly speaking, grape-shot consisted of nine very large bullets wired together, fired from a cannon. The term is however more often used by writers such as Gilling for case-shot, canisters containing large numbers of musket-balls, turning the cannon into a giant shot-gun, with devastating effect against cavalry or infantry at close range[4]
Hackery	simple cart usually drawn by bullocks
Hookah	smoking pipe with a long flexible tube, enabling the flavoured smoke to be drawn through water in a vase
Jagheer	hereditary grant of land and its income
Jin-jowl (gingall)	heavy-calibre musket with a long range, often mounted on fortifications
Kalsa (Khalsa)	originally the religious, social and military entity of Sikhism, but generally used by the British to mean the Sikh army
Lac	one hundred thousand (as in 'a lac of rupees')
Murzir	coat of quilted cotton
Nullah	steep-sided water-course, usually dry
Pagoda	temple, usually used by soldiers in India for a Muslim mosque.
Pajams	loose trousers tied at the waist (hence the English word pyjamas)
Palanquin	a box-shaped litter with a pole projecting from front and rear, carried on the shoulders of four men
Pie (plural pice)	a small low-value copper coin
Pontoon	bridge supported on a string of floating boats. Many bridges in northern India were of this temporary nature due to the huge seasonal rise and fall (and consequent variation in width) of rivers
Pulwar	a river-boat, carrying about 12-15 tons of cargo
Qui hie	English slang for a servant, derived from the phrase used by the British to summon a servant: 'Koi hai?' ('Is anyone there?')
Sepoy	Indian infantry soldier
Seraie	building for the accommodation of travellers and their pack animals, usually in the form of an enclosed courtyard surrounded by small rooms
Sirdar	leader or commander
Tope	a grove or orchard, often of mango trees
Tulwar	the characteristic northern Indian curved sword, used especially

---

4 B P Hughes, *Firepower: Weapons Effectiveness on the Battlefield, 1630-1850* (London, 1974) p. 35.

	by the Sikhs: 'The tulwar or sword of the enemy has a broader back, thicker blade, and keener edge than ours; and the enemy are in the habit of delivering the drawing cut, a most cutting kind of blow.'[5]
Vidette (vedette)	mounted sentries, usually placed in a ring around an army to give advance warning of enemy movements

---

[5] E J Thackwell, *Narrative of the Second Seikh War in 1848-1849* (London, 1851) p. 181.

Acknowledgements

This work would not have been possible without the co-operation of the Library Staff at the National Army Museum, who supplied a copy of the original text of Gilling's book. I must also thank Dr Mike Galer of Derby Museums Service, and Captain Mick Holtby of the Queen's Royal Lancers Archives, for their generosity and hospitality in allowing access to the archives in their care. The staffs at the National Archives at Kew and the British Library were models of quiet efficiency in making their collections available. As always I am indebted to my wife Barbara Smith and other members of the family, and to Sheila and Douglas Robinson, for their support, hospitality and encouragement.

Introduction

The author of *The Life of a Lancer*

James Gilling was not an exceptional soldier. He did not rise to high rank, and rather than spend his full enlistment time of twenty-four years in the cavalry, he bought himself out, at considerable expense. By his own admission, he was not always very brave. When faced, unarmed, with several enraged Sikhs in a village near Lahore, he took the only sensible action and ran away as fast as he could. However, when sent alone on a night-time scouting expedition after Ramnuggar, he resisted the temptation to return with his mission uncompleted, because of the fear that he would lose the respect of his comrades – an incentive to valour that soldiers of all eras would probably recognise. Gilling barely rates any mention in official records, but it is this very ordinariness that makes his account of soldiering in India in the 1840s so valuable.

Gilling was born on 2 September 1822, probably in Worksop, Nottinghamshire.[1] He was the son of John Gilling, a publican. When James grew up he became a hairdresser, but this life obviously palled, and he decided to seek 'the pride, pomp and circumstances of war,' by joining the army. Gilling seems to have had a good education, and no doubt read in newspapers and books about the recent campaigns of the British army in India, such as the Afghan War of 1838-42. According to his own testimony, he did not wait for a recruiting party to visit his home town, but instead travelled to London, the country's main recruiting centre. After consulting with a friend in the Royal Horse Guards, he enlisted in a cavalry regiment, the Ninth Lancers, then serving in Bengal. Following a medical inspection, he was sent to Maidstone, the depot for light cavalry regiments stationed overseas, where he was entered on the rolls from 1 July 1843.[2] Before there was time for anything but the most rudimentary training, he obtained his ambition by being shipped off to join his regiment in Bengal. He certainly experienced the 'circumstances of war,' taking part in the two Anglo-Sikh Wars (1845-6 and 1848-9). By this time he had apparently had enough of soldiering in India, and managed to scrape together enough money to purchase his discharge, which he received on 30 September 1850.[3]

Gilling returned to Worksop, where in 1852 he married Eleanor Moody. However, he was not yet finished with adventure, and in 1853 the couple emigrated to the United States of America. They probably sailed from Liverpool to New York as most emigrants did, but by 1860 they had moved westwards, settling in Lyons City, Clinton County, in the Midwest state of Iowa.[4] Lyons, situated on the west bank of the Mississippi River, had been founded in 1835, and was a well laid out town with a population of just over 3,000, with a ferry-point and various industries such as saw-milling.[5] Many of its citizens were, like the Gillings, immigrants: in 1860 their neighbours included people born in England, Scotland,

---

1. Most of the personal details of Gilling's life are taken from notes supplied by a descendant who sold a copy of his book to Worksop Library in 1968, and which was copied by the National Army Museum.
2. The National Archives (TNA) WO 12/891.
3. TNA WO 12/895.
4. *US Census* (1860).
5. *Iowa State Gazetteer* (c. 1865) pp. 69, 141-4.

Ireland, Canada and Germany as well as many other American states. James took up his old trade as a barber, and the couple owned property worth $1500. They had two daughters, Aida and Florence, both born in Iowa. However, James Gilling died in 1861, leaving his widow and daughters living in reduced circumstances.[6]

Like a select few of his fellow soldiers, James Gilling left us an account of his services in the army. He appears to have written this in the two or three years he spent in Worksop between leaving the army and emigrating. The freshness of his memory at that time, helped by the notebook which he mentions having kept, means that many of the incidents and individuals that he describes can be confirmed from other sources. *The Life of a Lancer in the Wars of the Punjaub, or Seven Years in India* was published in London by Simpkin, Marshall and Co in 1855, after its author had left for the USA, so it is possible that he never saw it in print. Certainly the book is extremely rare, only one copy having been traced in a public collection, although the regimental historian, Major Sheppard, did have access to a copy in the 1930s[7]. Although a number of memoirs by other ranks who served in India in the 1840s have been published, Gilling's appears to be the only one by a member of a lancer regiment, and this gives it particular value, alongside Gilling's frank descriptions of regimental soldiering, and his opinions of the conduct of the campaigns in which he took part.

The Ninth Lancers

By the time James Gilling joined his regiment in India, the Ninth Lancers already had over a hundred years of distinguished service behind it.[8] It was raised in 1715 as Wynne's Dragoons, named, as was the custom, after the Colonel, Major General Owen Wynne. (It gained its number as the Ninth Dragoons in 1719.) Strangely, its first active service was not in some far-flung country, but at Preston, Lancashire, where it was part of a force which attacked and ultimately defeated part of the rebel Scots Jacobite army in November 1715. From 1783 the Ninth was designated as 'light dragoons' with the tasks of skirmishing, scouting ahead and picketing to protect the army from surprise. It made little difference to the actual role of the regiment: despite some changes in uniform, it still consisted of big men, heavily equipped, who could be used as shock troops in a charge on the battlefield if necessary. Its next service was again against rebels: this time in the Irish uprising of 1798, when it fought several bloody skirmishes as well as in larger battles at Carlow, New Ross and Vinegar Hill.

The Revolutionary and Napoleonic Wars saw the regiment sent to more distant regions, and its experiences included fighting the Spanish in South America at Buenos Ayres (1806-7), a shipwreck in Mounts Bay, Cornwall, the disease-ridden expedition to the island of Walcheren in the Low Countries (1809), and a more successful period in the Iberian Peninsula (1811-13). Although not engaged in any major battles during its short stay in the Peninsula, the Ninth distinguished itself in many minor combats, as well as at the surprise of a French force at Arroyo dos Molinos (28 October 1811) when it captured the French general. In the campaigns in Portugal, Spain and France the British light cavalry really learnt its business as the eyes and ears of the army, and when Gilling joined there were still one or two officers serving who had Peninsular experience that they could pass on to the

---

6   *US Census* (1870).
7   E W Sheppard, *The Ninth Queen's Royal Lancers 1715-1936* (Aldershot, 1939) p. 110.
8   F H Reynard, *The Ninth (Queen's Royal) Lancers 1715-1903* (Edinburgh, 1904).

next generation.

The experience of British troops against French and Polish lancers during the Napoleonic Wars prompted the army to form lancer regiments of its own. Rather than raise new regiments (at a time when the army was still in the throes of post-war reductions), in 1816 some existing regiments of light dragoons were selected for conversion to lancers, these being the Ninth, Twelfth, Sixteenth and Twenty-Third (later replaced by the Seventeenth).[9] Groups of officers and men from these regiments were sent successively to the riding establishment at Pimlico to be instructed in the lance exercise by Major R H De Montmorency, Sergeant Major Robert Cooke of the Ninth Lancers, and later by Major J G Peters, a 'presumptuous German' who had nevertheless 'made himself master of the Lance Exercise and he instructed the men well, and taught a very good riding school drill.'[10] Despite the new weapon and some uniform changes, it was to be many years before the men ceased to be referred to as 'dragoons' and the regiment was still occasionally abbreviated to '9th Dragoons' in the 1840s.

The Ninth Lancers saw no more active service for many years, being stationed in various parts of Britain or Ireland. However, in April 1842 the regiment was warned for service in India. It handed over its horses to the Fourth Light Dragoons (regiments never took their horses on the long voyage to India), and embarked at Gravesend in five ships, in May 1842. The various contingents arrived at Calcutta between 25 August and 23 September. Their journey was by no means over, and the regiment was sent off up the River Ganges, reaching their station at Cawnpore in Bengal in January 1843.

British cavalry regiments in Bengal normally moved every five years or so between the two large military stations or cantonments of Cawnpore and Meerut, both strategically placed to defend the north-western flank of British-controlled territory in India. The Ninth were moved to Meerut in October 1845, but thereafter the orderly alternation of stations was disrupted by the Anglo-Sikh Wars, at the end of which it found itself based at Wuzeerabad, until 1857. From that date it was engaged in the long campaign to suppress the Indian Mutiny and uprising, with a base at Umballa until it returned to England in 1859.

Cawnpore was a large station, housing two cavalry regiments (one British, one Indian), three infantry regiments, and several artillery batteries. The military cantonment, some distance from the 'native' town, provided ample space for parades and training, but was very hot and dusty. One visitor in 1837 noted

> Of all the ugly Indian stations I have yet seen, this is the very ugliest and dead flat, of course. But not one single blade of even brown grass to be seen, nothing but loose brown dust, which rises in clouds at the slightest provocation.[11]

Meerut, where the Ninth was stationed from March 1846 to February 1849, had a garrison of similar size to Cawnpore, but was considered a much better posting. The hot season was two or three weeks shorter than at Cawnpore, and for the officers 'society' was

---

9   Marquess of Anglesey, *A History of the British Cavalry 1816 to 1919 Volume 1: 1816 to 1850* (London, 1973) pp. 98-101.

10   Thus described by John Luard of the 16th Lancers, J Lunt, *Scarlet Lancer* (London, 1964) p. 110. The drill devised by Peters is illustrated in D Dighton, *The Lance Exercise, in Three Divisions* (London, 1825). See also R M Collins, 'Lieut Colonel Reymond Hervey De Montmorency.' *JSAHR* 46 (1968) 97-106.

11   F Eden, *Tigers, Durbars and Kings: Fanny Eden's Indian Journals 1837-1838* ed J Dunbar (London, 1988) p. 98.

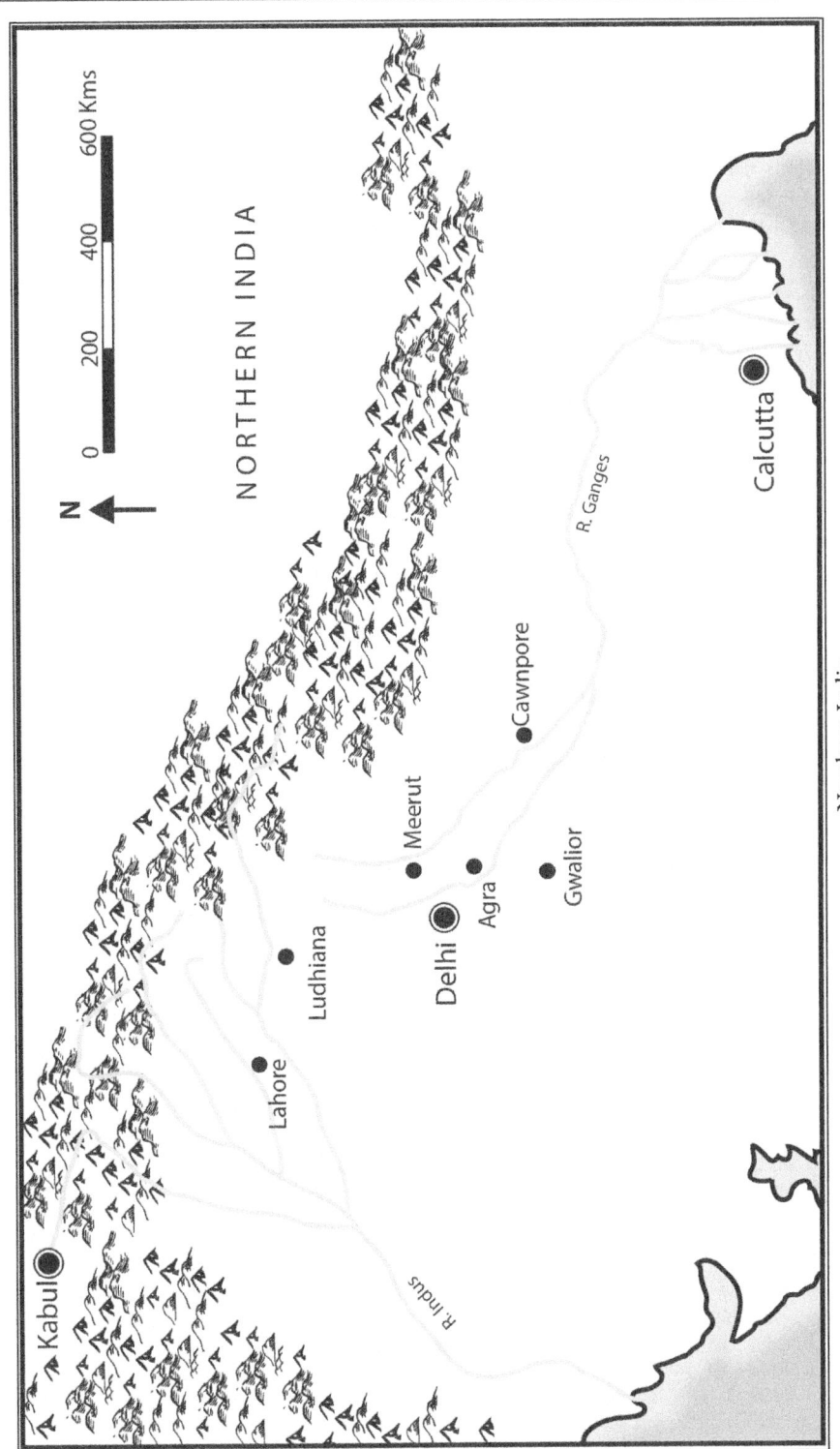

Northern India

much friendlier and more united.[12] For the other ranks, the barracks were superior, with a good hospital for the cavalry.[13] Officers in permanent stations normally lived in bungalows, each within their own gardens; married officers were provided with these, but junior officers had to purchase their own, and consequently usually shared. These bungalows (the word itself is Indian) and the barracks were well adapted to the climate, with thick baked-earth or brick walls and high thatched roofs, and were surrounded by wide verandas to provide shade. In the hot season the verandas were provided with *tatties*, blinds made from *cuscus*, a sweet-smelling grass which was wetted to cool the breezes passing through. The barracks were single-storey, each housing a troop of about seventy to ninety men. The men's *charpoys* (simple bamboo-framed bedsteads) were close together, with bedding consisting of a quilt (*gutteree* – Anglicised by the men as 'guthrie'), which remained unwashed, and was replaced every two years. Each man stored his personal possessions in a chest at the foot of his bed, and his saddle, belts and weapons hung on hooks above the bed. Senior NCOs were given some privacy, being provided with rooms made by partitioning off the ends of the verandas. In Bengal soldiers with families were merely assigned corners of the common barrack-room with curtains hung up for privacy.[14] Sanitation for the men consisted of privies outside the barrack-blocks, the contents of which were removed by Indian 'sweepers' to larger pits, where it was in danger of polluting the water supply.

Most expenses of British troops in India were paid for by the Honorable East India Company, which by this time had ceased to be merely a trading company, and in effect ruled British India on behalf of Britain. The basic soldier's ration was the same as in Britain, with no concession to the local climatic or supply conditions. Each man was issued with 1½ lb of bread and 1 lb of beef.[15] However, this was supplemented (through stoppages from the soldier's pay) by tea or coffee, sugar, rice, salt and vegetables. Therefore a day's fare might consist of fried or boiled meat and tea for breakfast, soup, boiled, roasted or curried meat and vegetables for dinner, and tea for supper, supplemented by whatever a man could afford to buy privately.[16] These meals were prepared by Indian cooks, the men taking their meals at tables in the barracks, provided with table cloths, and 'Europe or China cups and plates,' a civilized arrangement no doubt appreciated by men drawn from the English artisan classes, but viewed with disgust by the Duke of Wellington, who did not approve of table cloths for ordinary soldiers.[17] The table cloths and utensils were purchased from the fund set up from the canteen profits, which was also used to buy library books, and provided donations for men invalided to England, and to widows and orphans of the regiment.[18]

Primitive though these conditions seem to modern eyes, they were generally superior to most barracks in Britain, where, for example, cavalry soldiers lived in rooms directly above the stables. They were also better than the appalling conditions in the fast-expanding

---

12 [A C Lowe], *The Diary of an Officer of the 16th (Queen's) Lancers June 16 1822 to June 16 1840* (Calcutta, 1894) pp. 136, 141, 143.
13 Queen's Royal Lancers Archives (QRLA), J Thomas, Diary 1840s, pp. 5-6.
14 M Trustram, *Women of the Regiment: Marriage and the Victorian Army* (Cambridge, 1984) pp. 69-78.
15 E M Spiers, *The Army and Society 1815-1914* (London, 1980) pp. 58-9; D Smurthwaite, 'A Recipe for Discontent: the Victorian Soldier's Cuisine.' in M Harding (ed), *The Victorian Soldier* (London, 1993); J H Burton, 'The Soldier and the Surgeon.' *Blackwood's Magazine* 84 (1858) p. 6.
16 TNA WO 27/194 Meerut, 1829.
17 TNA WO 27/158 Inspection Report, Sixteenth Lancers, Cawnpore 1823; Derby Museums (DM), Regimental Order Book p. 75, Cawnpore 24 May 1843; WO 3/100/362 Horse Guards Letter 28 Dec 1843.
18 DM, Regimental Order Book pp 102, 119.

industrial towns of the early nineteenth century, with which many of the soldiers were familiar: jerry-built back-to-back houses with little or no sanitation and no safe water supply. One provision made by the East India Company for European soldiers in India was a supply of servants, not just for officers, but for the other ranks as well. A cavalry soldier was provided with a *syce* or groom to care for his horse and harness, and each troop had two barbers, two shoe-blacks, two belt-cleaners and eight *dhobies* (laundrymen).[19] This relieved the men of many of the tedious chores that constituted life in English barracks, and contributed to their sense that in India they were part of the ruling class. Men wrote home delightedly that they were 'all gentlemen' now.[20] This released men for leisure activities, some of which similarly would not have been open to them in Britain. Many soldiers, for example, were able to purchase ponies and fowling guns for hunting expeditions, often combined with sight-seeing tours.[21] Other pastimes indulged in by the other ranks were sports (cricket was especially popular), theatricals (Cawnpore had an impressive theatre), collecting natural history specimens, reading, and writing journals and letters. At Meerut the Regiment had a large swimming bath in its lines, which must have been refreshing in the heat.[22] Pets such as dogs, monkeys, and goats were common, although officially forbidden.[23] Although time in the cantonment could drag, especially in the seemingly endless, energy-sapping hot season, an intelligent and active soldier with a little initiative could find plenty to do, and many men, unlike Gilling, enjoyed the life enough to volunteer to transfer to incoming regiments when their own was sent home. George Farmer of the Eleventh Light Dragoons summed up his life in Meerut in the 1830s thus:

> ... whatever a man's taste might be in reference to his out-of-door pursuits and athletic amusements, here ample opportunity was afforded of indulging them. We had cricket, long-ball, and rackets – there was capital angling in the tanks, all of which swarmed with fine fish. There was shooting of every description ... I have no recollection that the time hung, throughout our sojourn there, heavy on our hands.[24]

Unfortunately, for many men the chief recreation was getting drunk, and this accounted for almost all the disciplinary problems of the army: 'Whilst men drink as they do we must have crime.' as one inspecting officer, Major General Nicolls, succinctly put it.[25] He asserted that in eight out of ten courts martial in Meerut, liquor was a factor.[26] Even one of the regimental historians admitted that 'before many months had passed [the Ninth]

---

19 QRLA, Thomas, Diary 1843-5 p. 9.
20 NAM 6405-61 George Tookey, Letter 17 Dec 1846; T Malcolm, *Barracks and Battlefields in India: or, the Experiences of a Soldier of the 10th Foot – North Lincoln in the Sikh Wars and Sepoy Mutiny* ed C Caine (London, 1891) p. 35.
21 J Pearman, *The Radical Soldier's Tale: John Pearman 1819-1908* ed C Steedman (London, 1988) p. 146; QRLA, Thomas, Diary 1843-5, pp. 2-3; QRLA, Journal of Charles Godward. For soldiers owning ponies and guns, Thackwell, *Narrative* p. 249 and British Library (BL) L/MIL/17/1968 pp. 26-7 General Order 20 February 1821 respectively.
22 R A Yule, Letter Meerut 8 May 1848, 'The Letters of Brevet Lieutenant-Colonel Robert Abercromby Yule.' ed J Fraser *JSAHR* 61 (1983) p. 141.
23 DM, Regimental Order Book p. 114, Umballa 13 Oct 1852.
24 G Farmer, *The Light Dragoon* ed G R Gleig (London, 1844) II pp. 265-6.
25 TNA WO 27/198.
26 D M Peers, 'Imperial Vice: sex, drink and the health of British troops in North Indian cantonments 1800-1858.' in D Killingray and D Omissi (ed), *Guardians of Empire* (Manchester, 1999) p. 41.

had acquired the reputation of being more addicted to strong drink than any Corps in India.'[27] Complaints of drunkenness were frequent in the Regimental Order Book:

> The Commanding Officer having reason to believe that Tipling has been going on in some of the Barrack rooms to a considerable extent, but more particularly in the Tailor's shop, he therefore calls upon the whole of the Non Commissioned Officers at once to put a stop to so injurious a practice, and to confine any Man who may be guilty, of bringing or conniving at spirits being brought into Barracks ... [28]

The men in India were issued with half a pint of rum a day, or its equivalent in the locally-distilled rice spirit, *arrack*. More could be purchased in the regimental canteen or, illicitly, from native bazaars. Whenever men had money in their pockets, such as on pay-day or when the field allowances known as *batta* was issued, officers could expect an outbreak of the 'crime' of drunkenness. The distribution of the six-month *batta* for the Punjab campaign 'led to irregularities, but these ceased with the means of procuring liquor – the men have generally been well behaved in quarters.'[29] Of course, heavy drinking was not confined to the army. It was a feature of working-class life in towns too. However, a brawl in barracks could easily become a deadly encounter when men had their lances, swords and pistols hanging above their beds, and chose in their drunken stupor to resist arrest. Most of the resultant defaulters' parades or courts martial ended in terms of imprisonment in the *congee house* (regimental jail) as described by Gilling. However, more serious or repeated crimes could lead to a flogging with the cat o' nine tails. The capital sentences that Gilling describes being inflicted on men at Meerut in 1847 were wholly exceptional.

Despite his own orders against drunkenness, the Ninth's commanding officer, Lieutenant Colonel Alexander Campbell, was notoriously intemperate, even when he was commanding a brigade at the Battle of Sobraon:

> On the day of the battle, [Campbell] appeared very drunk. He had been taking nips to keep up his spirits. He was drunk before us all; everybody saw it when we were going into action, and a hiss was very audible throughout our ranks. He was utterly useless; he was even incapably nervous, and his behaviour annoyed us all very much.

It must have been difficult for officers and NCOs to enforce sobriety amongst their men when the senior officer set such an example. Major Grant actually tried to place Campbell, his senior, in arrest after Sobraon, but instead Campbell arrested him; after a secret court of enquiry the whole matter was hushed up.[30]

One crime not associated with drunkenness, and which required at least in India careful planning, was desertion. A white soldier separated from his regiment in 1840s Bengal, whether in uniform or not, was likely to be conspicuous, and the chances of getting home were slim. Nevertheless, if Gilling is to be believed, some men were successful. The

---

27 Sheppard, *Ninth Queen's Royal Lancer*, p. 103.
28 DM, Regimental Order Book p. 74, Cawnpore 18 May 1843.
29 TNA WO 27/398 Inspection Report, 9th Lancers, Wuzeerabad, 13 April 1850. There were fourteen courts martial during this half-year, rather fewer than average.
30 H Knollys, *Life of General Sir Hope Grant with selections from his Correspondence* (2 vols, Edinburgh, 1894) pp. 84-92.

two men who escaped on an elephant with the intention of returning to Europe overland, presumably through the Punjab, Afghanistan and Persia, must have had many Kiplingesque adventures, if they survived very long.

The Ninth's uniform at this time consisted of a dark blue double-breasted jacket, with red facings (collar and cuffs), and dark grey trousers ('overalls' in cavalry parlance) with a scarlet stripe down the outer seam.[31] The most distinctive part of the uniform was the cap or *czapka*, worn exclusively by lancers. This was copied from the Polish national headdress and consisted of a black leather skull-cap above which spread a square black cloth top. It was undeniably smart, but impractical: top-heavy, and giving little protection against rain, sunshine or enemy blows. Few concessions on uniform were given to the Indian climate, apart from white cap-covers with curtains to cover the neck, and the substitution of flannel drawers by cotton in 1844.[32] The jackets were made from wool, which was sent out from England as cloth, and made up by the regiment's own Master Tailor, who had been enlisted by 'Special Authority' and had no other duties.[33] Possibly he was helped at busy times by some of the many former tailors in the ranks. These woollen jackets, and the cloaks also provided, were not as impractical in India as might at first seem. Campaigns in Bengal took place in the cool season, roughly equivalent to an English summer, and the weather could be cold at night, and often wet, as Gilling discovered in the dreary weeks after the Battle of Chillianwallah. The men were also issued with a large quantity of other clothing and equipment – more than most of them had probably ever possessed in their lives:

one cap with lines, plume and cover	two towels
one forage cap	one hair comb
one dress jacket	one hair brush
one undress jacket	one razor, brush and soap
two flannel jackets	one clothes brush
four white jackets	two shoe brushes
one pair blue overalls	one knife, fork and spoon
six pairs white overalls	one mess tin and case
two pairs *Settringee* overalls	one turnscrew, worm etc
six shirts	one corn bag
two pairs drawers	one horse brush
six pairs socks	one mane comb
one sash	one horse picker
one pair gloves	one pair scissors
one pair gauntlets	one stock and clasp
one pair braces	one girdle
two pairs braces for white clothing	one buttonstick and brush
one pair boots and spurs	one tin bottle with oil
one pair ankle boots	one lock cover
one hold all for small articles	one valise
one strong box[34]	

---

31 W Y Carman, *Dress Regulations 1846 with a new introduction* (London, 1971) pp. 126-30; Reynard, *The Ninth Lancers*, pp. 34, 38.
32 DM, Regimental Order Book p. 86, Cawnpore 1 Dec 1844.
33 TNA WO 27/342, 376.
34 DM, Regimental Order Book p. 64, 1842. *Settringee* was a type of hard-wearing cotton cloth, often striped,

Ninth Lancers 1846. A print by Martens and Lynch, showing a mounted sergeant in full dress, with an officer in frock coat; to the left is a trumpeter, and to the right two privates in undress uniform. (Anne S K Brown Military Collection, Brown University Library)

Although inspecting generals were vigilant in detecting any deviation from official regulations on parade, on campaign the officers at least sometimes adopted more practical wear. The propensity of Sikh cavalrymen to aim passing cuts at the back of the head in personal combat led many officers to acquire unofficial helmets with neck-flaps, covered with white linen as additional protection against the sun.[35] Captain Yule was one of these, sporting 'a sort of leather helmet covered with cotton & a turban round it. Many officers wear them ... '[36]

The first concern of a cavalry regiment was an adequate supply of good-quality horses. A regiment arriving in India took over the horses of a regiment going home, any shortfalls being made up by purchases made locally or from the East India Company's studs at

---

which was treated with pipe clay and worn when watering the horses and similar duties: Regimental Order Book p. 79, Cawnpore 21 July 1843. The 'turnscrew, worm etc' were tools for maintaining firearms. The 9th Lancers, by regimental custom, did not in fact wear the 'girdle,' which was a decorative belt worn by cavalry: M Barthorp, *British Cavalry Uniforms since 1660* (Poole, 1984) p. 121.
35 Thackwell, *Narrative*, pp. 59-60.
36 Yule, Letter 17 February 1848, *JSAHR* 62 (1984) p. 43.

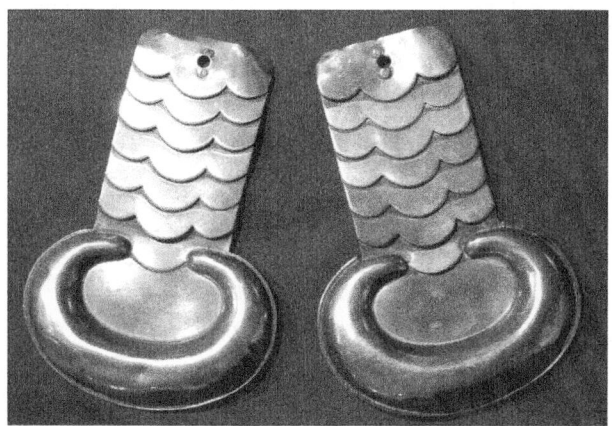

Shoulder scales. Worn by lancers and other light cavalry, these brass scales were too flimsy to afford much protection from a Sikh *tulwar*.
(By courtesy of the 9th/12th Lancers Museum, Derby)

Ghazeepore or Haupper. Officers purchased their own horses. A variety of breeds were used, mainly Arabs, Turcomans and Persians from Afghanistan, 'Walers' from New South Wales, and 'Capes' from South Africa.[37] The relative merits of these breeds were, of course, keenly discussed by officers. The chief anxiety, however, was whether the horses were big and strong enough to carry the men and their weapons and equipment. In the 1830s it was the policy of the Ninth's colonel, Lord Loughborough, not to enlist any men under 5 ft 9 ins in height, and many were six foot or more.[38] Despite the increased demands for men when the regiment went to India, in 1843 the men still averaged 5 ft 10 ins, and with all their equipment, the horses had to carry an average of nineteen stone in weight.[39] Not surprisingly, remarks regularly appeared in the inspection reports that the horses were too small to carry 'Men of such large stature.'[40] At this time it was a long-established army custom that the cavalry only used 'entire' (i.e. ungelded) stallions, which were thought, without much evidence, to be braver and have better stamina than mares and geldings. However, the corollary was that stallions could easily become unmanageable, and many incidents were described by writers of horses throwing and attacking – even killing – their riders in stables or on parade. As George Stent of the Fourteenth Light Dragoons recorded,

> The cavalry, in India, use entire horses only; and if one breaks loose, it sometimes causes an immense deal of trouble – the others fighting, plunging, and endeavouring to break loose as well. One loose horse at a field day will often throw a whole troop into confusion; the horses getting into a fearful state of excitement, rearing, plunging, fighting, and using every effort to throw their riders.[41]

---

37 G Tylden, *Horses and Saddlery* (London, 1965).
38 J A Thomson, *Eighty Years' Reminiscences* (London, 1904) pp. 40, 67.
39 TNA WO 27/327.
40 TNA WO 27/342 December 1845.
41 G C Stent, *Scraps from my Sabretasche, being personal adventures while in the 14th (King's Light) Dragoons* (London, 1882) p. 263.

This might be merely amusing to the onlookers at a field day in cantonments, but if a man's horse became unmanageable on the battlefield, the consequences could be fatal, especially against Sikh horsemen whose expertise was much greater than the average British trooper:

> It frequently happened during this campaign that some dragoons in a charge lost all control over their horses, whilst the Sikh horsemen were turning their spirited steeds in all directions. Picture to yourself a British, or Anglo-Indian trooper, dashing onwards with a most uncontrollable horse, and a Goorchurra, or Sikh horseman, often allowing his enemy to pass, turning quickly round to deal him an ugly wound on the back of the head.[42]

In such circumstances, the panic demonstrated by the men of Pope's cavalry brigade at Chillianwallah becomes more understandable, feeling themselves outclassed in both horsemanship and weaponry.

The defining weapon of the lancer was of course the lance. This consisted of a nine foot long pole of ash (damaged lances were replaced in India by bamboo), tipped with a steel fluted blade; the butt also terminated in a steel point.[43] The lance carried a forked pennon in red and white (the Polish national colours). Lieutenant Charles Abbot Delmar of the Ninth, eager to see action for the first time, had great faith in this weapon:

> Our Regt. has a good chance [of seeing action] as it is the only Lancer Regt. now in India. I imagine we shall work them with our *Lances down at full charge* – a charge at full speed in line, I think, would astonish them a little ... [44]

Nevertheless, much controversy surrounded the effectiveness of the lance throughout its deployment with the British army (which did not end until the 1930s). It had a long reach (useful for pursuing fleeing infantry), and was formidable in a charge, although many argued that the cavalryman's main offensive weapon was the speed and weight of his horse, and what weapon he carried was of little importance.[45] If a lance hit home, its victim was likely to be fatally wounded, but unless the lance was quickly withdrawn, it could easily become stuck, as Delmar noticed at Chillianwallah:

> ... our own men ran their lances so far thro' the Sikhs, that they could not pull them out again, & were oblig'd to leave them ... [46]

Once the charge was broken up, and the men became involved in individual combat, the lance could easily become a liability, despite training which included many manoeuvres such as 'Right rear parry and point' and 'Reverse lance and rear point,' designed to engage the enemy on foot or horse, from whichever quarter he attacked.[47] In such desperate

---

42 Thackwell, *Narrative*, p. 57.
43 C ffoulkes and E C Hopkinson, *Sword, Lance and Bayonet* (Cambridge, 1938) pp. 102-5. The Regimental Museum, Derby, contains two lances owned by Captain (formerly RSM) Robert Cooke, adjutant 1827-42.
44 NAM 8301-38 C A Delmar, Letter, 11 May 1848.
45 C B Mayne, 'The Lance as a Cavalry Weapon.' *JRUSI* 49 (1905) 118-140.
46 NAM 8301-38 Delmar, Letter, 21 January 1849.
47 Horse Guards, *Instructions for the Carbine Exercise; the Pistol Exercise; and the Lance Exercise* (London,

circumstances, the sword, or the pistol (if loaded) was much handier, especially against a skilled and brave enemy like the Sikhs:

> It may be doubted by many, that one Sikh foot soldier repulsed three lancers at Chillianwallah, but such has been stated to be a fact. He received the thrust of the lance on his shield, and rushing under it, cut at the lancer or shivered the lance into atoms with his *tulwar*.[48]

Each lancer carried a single smoothbore, muzzle-loading pistol, at first with a flintlock firing mechanism, replaced in 1845 by the more reliable percussion weapon.[49] These were inaccurate except at very close range, and were difficult to reload on horseback. Therefore the lancer's other main weapon was the sword. The Ninth were armed with the 1821-pattern light cavalry sword, first issued to them in 1831.[50] This replaced an older, heavily curved sabre, and was designed as a compromise to provide a weapon suitable for both cutting and thrusting.[51] Unfortunately, it did neither very well. It had a slightly curved 90cm long blade, and a guard consisting of three bars which gave protection to the hand against a cut, but not a thrust. The blade was quite weak, and was easily blunted by constant movement against its steel scabbard. Although the Ninth Lancers were described in 1847 as 'very fair swordsmen,' the men of the Fourteenth Light Dragoons, according to their commanding officer, seeking to excuse the debacle at Chillianwallah, 'were young and slight, and ... their swords were too heavy for them, moreover that their swords were not so sharp as those of the Sikhs, that they would not take the same edge.'[52] From all this it can be seen that the British cavalryman did not enjoy any particular advantage over his Sikh opponent in terms of equipment or weapons skill. Only superior discipline and leadership would tip the balance in his favour with a usually numerically superior enemy.

The regiment which Gilling finally joined at Cawnpore in April 1844 was by that time acclimatised and experienced. Half the regiment (four troops) had recently taken part in the short-lived campaign against the state of Gwalior, including the Battle of Punniar on 23 December 1843, where they had been under fire, but suffered no casualties. Some officers and men had also seen active service with other regiments. These include officers such as Lieutenant Philip Kemp and Captain J R H Rose, who had served in Afghanistan with light dragoon regiments.[53] Later, four officers, Captains E J Pratt and R A Yule, Lieutenant Trower and Veterinary Surgeon R J G Hurford, who had served in the first phase of the Afghan War in 1838-39 with the Sixteenth Lancers, transferred to the Ninth along with many men, when the Sixteenth returned to England in 1846. Such transfers by officers were commonplace. The main motive was financial: living in India was cheaper, and an

---

1844); Dighton, *The Lance Exercise*.
48 Thackwell, *Narrative*, pp. 236-7.
49 TNA WO 27/27.
50 Two paintings of the Ninth, executed in 1831, show a sergeant carrying the old 1796 pattern, and a corporal with the 1821 pattern: J Spencer-Smith, *Portraits for a King: The British Military Paintings of A-J Dubois Drahonet* (1791-1834) (London, 1990) pls 36 and 36A.
51 B Robson, *Swords of the British Army: the Regulation Patterns 1788 to 1914* (2nd edn, London, 1996) pp. 24-7.
52 BL Add. 49116 ff 160-2 papers relating to the suicide of Lieut Col J W King.
53 Kemp, with the 4th Light Dragoons, TNA WO 76/538 Officers' Services; Rose, with the 3rd Light Dragoons, H G Hart, *The New Annual Army List, and Militia List* (London, 1848) p. 135.

officer could exchange his place in the regiment going home with a richer officer in a regiment warned for overseas service who did not want to exchange hunting in the shires for the dusty plains of Bengal.[54] The wealthier officer would pay an unofficial fee for this exchange. However, many officers saw it as important to their professional development and ambitions to take part in active service, rather than to spend their time in what Yule called 'the scrag of mutton life in barracks at home.'[55] There was therefore a dichotomy between officers who served only at home, and those who deliberately sought service overseas. The officers in India were by no means the dim and eccentric amateurs that caricature made out British cavalry leaders to be after the disasters in the Crimea. Almost without exception, the officers of the Light Brigade at Balaclava, being drawn from the army at home, had seen no active service, and very few saw further war service after 1856,[56] whilst those with regiments in India often had much campaign experience.

For officers, the normal route into the army was to purchase a commission, aided by a letter of recommendation from a patron such as a senior officer or aristocratic neighbour. The lowest commissioned rank in the cavalry, a cornet, cost £840 (compared with £450 for an ensign in the infantry). The basic dress and undress uniforms for a lancer officer cost about £170. This did not include boots, linen, accoutrements, white clothing for India, or horses.[57] Commissions for more senior ranks were correspondingly higher: lieutenant £1190, captain £3225, major £4575, lieutenant colonel £6175.[58] Unofficial payments, which could almost double the above figures, were often made to persuade an officer to exchange regiments, or to retire, thus opening a rung on the promotional ladder. An officer therefore had a considerable sum invested in his commission, which he could recoup by selling it on retirement, as long as he was of no higher rank than colonel. If promoted to major general whilst still serving, he lost the whole value. This happened to James Hope Grant of the Ninth Lancers, who was unexpectedly promoted in February 1858 for distinguished service in the Mutiny, but thereby lost the price of his colonel's commission, valued, with its unofficial premium, at £12,000.[59]

Since a cornet's weekly pay was £2-16-0d, and even in India the mess fee alone was £1-18-6d, it can be seen that a cavalry officer had to have a private income to pursue a military career. This arrangement ensured that most officers came from comparatively wealthy backgrounds, and in fact most were drawn from the landed gentry or the professional classes. This suited the view of the Duke of Wellington and other figures of the military establishment, that the army was best served by officers 'who have some connection with the interests and fortunes of the country, besides the commission which they hold from his Majesty.'[60] Contrary to popular belief, cavalry officers, at least those serving with regiments overseas, were not normally aristocrats. In 1848 only one officer of the Ninth Lancers, Capt the Honourable Charles Powys, had any kind of title. This compares with the fashionable Tenth Hussars, serving at home with a much smaller establishment of officers, whose ranks

---

54 A P C Bruce, *The Purchase System in the British Army, 1660-1871* (London, 1980) pp. 82-3; Yule, Letter 4 November 1846, *JSAHR* 61 (1983) p. 135; J Anstruther Thomson was one officer of the 9th Lancers who preferred to exchange out of the regiment when it went to India: *Eighty Years' Reminiscences*.
55 Yule, Letter 10 February 1848, *JSAHR* 61 (1983) p. 138.
56 W M Lummis and K G Wynn, *Honour the Light Brigade* (London, 1973); Hart, *Army Lists*.
57 Price guide for young officers, Horse Guards Circular 7 July 1829, printed in *USJ* 1829 (2) p. 250.
58 *The Naval and Military Almanack* (London, 1841) p. 65.
59 Knollys, *Life of Grant*, 2-5, 160.
60 Quoted in Bruce, *The Purchase System*, p. 65.

included two lords, a baronet and an honourable.[61] Most officers were educated either by private tutors or at public schools.[62] A few had attended an institution of higher education. The splendidly-named Captain William Wellington Waterloo Humbley held an MA from Trinity College, Cambridge, and Captain Yule had attended the Royal Military College, Sandhurst in 1842-3, an indication that he took his profession seriously.[63] Such officers sometimes became authors: Humbley published a two-volume journal of his service with the Ninth Lancers in the Sutlej campaign, and Captain H A Ouvry wrote his memoirs of service with the Third Light Dragoons and Ninth Lancers in India after his retirement. The most prolific author was Captain Yule, who published a treatise on the co-operation between cavalry and horse artillery in 1856, as well as several literary works.[64]

Standing a little apart from these wealthy upper class officers were those who had worked their way up from the ranks. Such men were always in a minority, but formed an important element in the administration and command of the regiment. The normal route to a commission for such men was through promotion to senior non-commissioned rank such as regimental sergeant major, paymaster sergeant or quartermaster sergeant. From there they could hope to be promoted without purchase to cornet, with an additional staff appointment such as adjutant, quartermaster, paymaster or riding master. The adjutant of the Ninth when Gilling enlisted was William Hamilton. He had enlisted in 1833, and was promoted to regimental sergeant major only five years later, an exceptionally rapid rise which suggests a man of notable abilities. He was commissioned in 1842, and reached the rank of captain in 1857, but died a year later. Described as 'a zealous and meritorious young officer,' he served at Punniar, in both the Anglo-Sikh Wars, and throughout the Indian Mutiny.[65] The regimental sergeant major in the 1840s was Robert Mills, who had enlisted in 1829. He was commissioned cornet in 1850, and retired on half-pay as a captain in 1859.[66] Another man of obvious ability who rose rapidly through the ranks was Richard Freer Thonger. Born in Boston, Lincolnshire, he enlisted in 1841, and was already a corporal when Gilling joined the Ninth in India. When Gilling, still a private, bought himself out in 1850, Thonger, the career soldier, was a troop sergeant major, and he became regimental sergeant major the following year. Commissioned cornet in 1857, he was appointed adjutant the next year, and retired as a captain in 1865. After leaving the army he became land agent to the Duke of Manchester.[67] It was therefore possible for an intelligent, diligent working-class man to rise to the status of a gentleman through a career in the army.

Yule, it must be said, was not impressed with his new regiment:

> The Regiment is a fine one to look at but wants the discipline system and style of the 16th. Our present Major Grant is a very good man but not a great soldier.[68]

---

61 Hart, *Army List*, (1848) pp. 135-6.
62 C B Otley, 'The social origins of British Army officers.' *Sociological Review* 18 (1970) 213-39; Spiers, *Army and Society*, p. 8.
63 W W W Humbley, *Journal of a Cavalry Officer, including the Memorable Sikh Campaign of 1845-1846* (London, 1854) title-page; Yule, *JSAHR* 61 (1983) p. 130.
64 *Notes on the employment of cavalry and horse artillery, with instructions for the evolutions of a brigade* (Calcutta, 1856); poems and a translation of Schiller's Maid of Orleans: *JSAHR* 64 (1986) p. 154.
65 TNA WO 76/538; WO 27/353.
66 TNA WO 76/538.
67 TNA WO 76/538; Census 1881.
68 Yule, Letter 8 May 1848, *JSAHR* 61 (1983) p. 139.

28 THE LIFE OF A LANCER IN THE WARS OF THE PUNJAUB

Ninth Lancers in heavy marching order c.1840. A print by Hayes and Lynch. Although this scene is set in Britain, the uniform worn on campaign in Bengal was almost identical, with the addition of white cap covers, and probably plain horse blankets replacing the elaborate embroidered shabraques. (Anne S K Brown Military Collection, Brown University Library)

These opinions (he also thought the officers 'the greatest snobs I see any where') form an interesting but not wholly incompatible comparison with Major Grant's own view of the regiment at about the same time:

> The men were a fine, tall set of fellows, well-behaved and well disposed, but they needed ruling with a tight hand. A dreadful apathy and listlessness creep over both officers and men in these regions, and nothing short of a red-hot poker will rouse them. The men were recruits, and only half-drilled; but drill, it was supposed, would be detrimental to them during the hot weather. To me the exact converse appeared more likely ... to shake the listlessness out of them does them all the good in the world.[69]

That Grant succeeded in his aims is shown by the comments of the inspecting officer at Wuzeerabad in April 1849, after the rigours of the Punjab campaign and before the Ninth could be expected to have settled down in its new and imperfect quarters:

> This Regiment is in a very efficient state – the Men healthy and the Horses in fair marching condition. The greatest attention appears to have been paid to its discipline and interior economy by the former commanding officer Major H Grant CB, and is

---

69 Knollys, *Life of Grant*, pp. 52-3.

now being given to it by Lt Col Fullerton.⁷⁰

Grant's remark that the men were 'recruits' is interesting, but should not be taken too literally. When a man enlisted in a regiment serving overseas he might spend anything up to a year or more at the home depot (in the case of light cavalry regiments this was at Maidstone), undergoing training. However, in order to catch the 'trooping season,' timed so that men would arrive in India during the 'cool' season, preferably in November or December, and thereby have time to acclimatise, a draft might be made up from men who had only recently been enlisted. This was the case with Gilling and his draft: having arrived at Maidstone in July 1843, he embarked for India on 4 September,⁷¹ before he had had time for more than foot drill and perhaps some basic weapons training. It is unlikely that he had even sat on a horse before he reached the regiment, at a time when it was reckoned to take three or even four years to produce a fully-trained lancer.⁷² It was up to the adjutant and regimental sergeant major to make such men into efficient soldiers after they had arrived at Cawnpore.

Gilling's comrades were from diverse backgrounds, although all could be described as 'working class,' in contrast to the gentry from which their officers were drawn. Cavalry regiments at this time had no fixed depot home or county affiliations. Men were raised by sending recruiting parties to wherever the commanding officer thought they would find suitable material. This usually meant that the recruiters were based in large towns, despite the fact that most officers would have preferred men from agricultural backgrounds, whom they thought were hardier and more amenable to discipline.⁷³ The majority of men in the Ninth were English,⁷⁴ with most of the rest being Irish, with a few Scots (Welshmen were included under the 'English' category). The Englishmen came from counties all over the country, but with a slight concentration in the Home Counties and the south-east generally, reflecting the major recruiting area of London. Men were not always recruited near their place of birth. Industrial cities in the early Victorian period achieved their phenomenal growth not only by natural increase of existing populations, but especially by immigration of men from country areas and smaller towns, looking for work. Gilling himself, as he states, deliberately travelled from his home town to London in order to enlist.

Men had to state their trade on enlistment (although not whether they were actually employed at the time), and this can tell us a little more about their background. The most frequent occupation given was 'labourer', with 31%.⁷⁵ This was a lower rate than that for the comparable civilian population as a whole,⁷⁶ and certainly lower than for infantry regiments, with over half their men ex-labourers.⁷⁷ Over-represented in the ranks of the

---

70 TNA WO 27/387.
71 TNA WO 12/891.
72 R Elias, 'Lancers and Lances.' *JRUSI* 33 (1889) p. 766.
73 Spiers, *Army and Society*, p. 48; H Strachan, *Wellington's Legacy: The Reform of the British Army 1830-54* (Manchester, 1984) p. 53; H Marshall, *Hints to Young Medical Officers of the army on the examination of recruits* (London, 1828) p. 69.
74 73% in 1844, rising to 81% in 1850: TNA WO 27.
75 Based on a sample of 380 men serving in the 9th Lancers in India in the 1840s. Trades are taken mainly from TNA WO 25 Casualty Returns and WO 12 Muster Rolls.
76 About 37%: J Burnett, *Useful Toil: Autobiographies of working people from the 1820s to the 1920s* (London, 1974) p. 27.
77 J H Rumsby, *The Sixteenth Lancers 1822-1846: the Experience of Regimental Soldiering in India* (Unpublished PhD Thesis, University of Leeds, 2004), pp. 67-75.

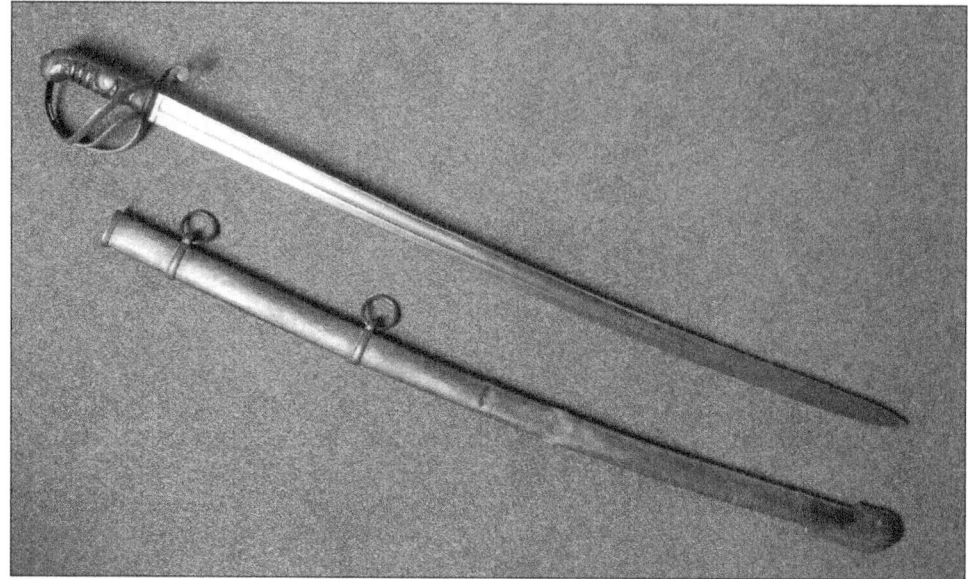

Light Cavalry sword, other ranks' pattern. This sword was approved in 1821, but the Ninth Lancers did not receive theirs until 1831. The blade was not really curved enough to be a good cutting weapon, but was not strong enough for thrusting. This specimen, like many surviving examples, demonstrates the weak scabbard, vulnerable to denting and rusting. (Private collection)

Ninth, compared to their civilian counter-parts, were men of the skilled 'artisan' classes: men who worked with their hands and minds at jobs requiring training, practice and the acquisition of special skills and dexterity, or in other trades requiring numeracy and literacy, such as shop-work and clerical jobs. There was a very wide range of these trades represented in the Ninth. As well as such industries as textiles (weavers, lace-makers, spinners etc.), metal-working (smiths and farriers), skilled hand-crafts (tailors, shoe-makers, clock-makers, cabinet-makers and joiners), there were at least three french-polishers, a pipe-maker, three druggists, butchers, and one hair-dresser: James Gilling. This profile, which is confirmed by studies of other cavalry regiments, suggests strongly that recruiters were deliberately targeting the 'aristocracy' of the working classes: intelligent, probably literate, skilled with their hands, capable of independent thought and action. These were precisely the qualities needed for soldiers required to work in small groups on outpost duty, on whose judgement and initiative the safety of the army might depend or, as George Farmer put it, with many years of experience behind his opinion, ' ... in the cavalry at least, your imaginative people make the best recruits.'[78] The regiment would have need of all these skills when they faced the Sikhs in 1846.

The Sikhs[79]

The origins of the Sikh state lie with the foundation of the Sikh religion by Baba Nanak

---

78 Farmer, *The Light Dragoon*, I p. 84.
79 Patwant Singh, *The Sikhs* (London, 1999); G Bruce, *Six Battles for India: The Anglo-Sikh Wars 1845-6, 1848-9* (London, 1969) pp. 17-62; H C B Cook, *The Sikh Wars: The British Army in the Punjab 1845-1849*

(1469-1539), later referred to as the 'First Guru.' Developed as a synthesis of Islam and Hinduism, whilst developing its own ethos of monotheism, and the equality of all people before God, Sikhism laid emphasis on social equality, good conduct and tolerance. Sikhs (the word means disciples) believed in the unity of God and the brotherhood of man, and their religion was open to all men and women, irrespective of race or caste.

The First Guru was born near Lahore, and the new religion was centred in the Punjab. The Punjab, 'land of the five rivers,' is named after the Rivers Jhelum, Chenab, Ravi, Beas and Sutlej, which all rise in the Himalayas and flow south-west over mostly flat plains, eventually uniting with the River Indus. The soil of the region is fertile, and where sufficiently close to the rivers to receive water, provides rich agricultural land, supporting numerous villages as well as large cities such as Lahore and Multan. The Punjab is also strategically placed across the trade routes between northern India and Afghanistan, and beyond to Persia. This position also however means that the Punjab has been repeatedly crossed and recrossed in the course of its history by armies intent on pillage or conquest.

The Punjab was part of the Muslim Moghul Empire. Sikhism was at first tolerated by the emperors, but from the seventeenth century faced increasing persecution. The fanatical emperor Jahangir put the Fourth Guru, Arjun, to death in 1606, and the Ninth Guru, Tegh Bahadur, was executed by the emperor Aurangzeb in 1675. Under this persecution Sikhism assumed a more militaristic nature. The Tenth and final Guru, Gobind Rai, reformed and codified Sikhism, instituting a new religious and military community known as the Khalsa, as well as introducing features by which Sikhs are still immediately recognisable today. These include the use by all men of the name Singh (lion) and by all women of the name Kaur (princess), and the adoption by men of the 'five Ks' symbolic of the tenets of the religion: the uncut hair and beard (*Kesh*), a comb (*Kanga*), knee-length shorts (*Kaach*), a steel bangle on the right wrist (*Kara*) and a sword (*Kirpaan*).[80] This element of militarism enabled the Sikhs to maintain their religion and distinctiveness through repeated attacks and persecution over the next 175 years, although no such thing as a 'Sikh state' existed at this period. From the 1730s the Moghul empire began to fall apart under repeated attacks from Persia, Afghanistan and the Mahrattas. It was in this vacuum that there arose the short-lived Sikh kingdom as the creation of one man, Ranjit Singh, the 'Lion of the Punjab.' Ranjit Singh (1780-1839) was the son of one of the independent landowners in the Punjab. Brave and cunning in equal measure, he soon began to unite large tracts of the region under his control by a judicious mixture of military force and marriage alliances. The turning point was his capture of Lahore from the occupying Afghans in 1799. As his kingdom expanded, he came into dispute with another expanding power, Britain, over control of the Malwa, the lands between the Rivers Sutlej and Jumna. Recognising the power of the British, he chose to cede suzerainty of these territories to Britain by the Sutlej Treaty of April 1809.[81] This declaration of 'perpetual friendship' between the British government in India and the state of Lahore became a cornerstone of Ranjit Singh's policy, enabling him to turn in other directions to expand his kingdom. He seized Attock, an Afghan possession which guarded a major trade and invasion route into India, in 1814. This was followed by the annexation of Peshawar and Multan in 1818, and the conquest of Kashmir in 1819. The

---

(London, 1975) pp. 11-23; J D Cunningham, *A History of the Sikhs* ed H L O Garrett (Lahore, 1915).
80   Amandeep Singh Madra and Parmjit Singh, *Warrior Saints: Three Centuries of the Sikh Military Tradition* (London, 1999).
81   The text of this treaty is given in Cunningham, *History of the Sikhs*, p. 352.

32 THE LIFE OF A LANCER IN THE WARS OF THE PUNJAUB

Seat of the Anglo-Sikh Wars

treaty of 1809 also suited Britain, providing a friendly (albeit increasingly powerful) buffer state on the north-west border of British India. Ranjit Singh's achievement in uniting the Punjab into one kingdom is all the more remarkable when it is remembered that the Sikhs themselves always remained a minority. It is estimated that Sikhs constituted only about 7% of the population, with 42% Hindu and over 50% Muslim.[82] Both by necessity and inclination, Ranjit Singh included men of other faiths and races in all aspects of government, civil administration and the army, as well as attracting artists of many styles and faiths to his court.[83]

Worn out by years of campaigning, as well as excesses in other areas, Ranjit Singh suffered strokes in 1835 and 1837, and a more serious one in December 1838, during a visit from Lord Auckland, the Governor-General of British India. He died on 27 June 1839. As so often when one man builds up a strong state by the force of his own personality, it began to fall apart on his death. His eldest son, Kharak Singh, succeeded him, but he was a much weaker character than his father – Isabella Fane, in Auckland's entourage, called him 'a booby and lout.'[84] Kharak Singh died in November 1840, possibly poisoned. Now began a long, confused and bloody struggle for power. Kharak Singh's son and successor died accidentally (or was assassinated) the day after his father. Next Shere Singh seized power, after the murder of Kharak Singh's widow. Shere Singh's rise to power had been aided by the army, who thereby, as the most powerful single force in the country, became cast in the king-maker's role.[85] Shere Singh in his turn was assassinated, with his son, in September 1843, but his rival Dhyan Singh (a Rajput, not a Sikh) was also murdered. The army rallied behind Ranjit Singh's youngest son, Duleep Singh, a young boy under the control of his mother Rani Jindan. After several more killings, Lal Singh (reputedly Rani Jindan's lover) became prime minister, and Tej Singh the commander-in-chief of the army. Both men appear to have been afraid of the army to which they owed their position, and were probably in touch with the British in an attempt to ally themselves with the major power on their doorstep. Their actions during the First Anglo-Sikh War certainly seem to justify this suspicion. Standing on the sidelines, waiting to see which of the several factions would prevail, was Gulab Singh, brother of Dhyan Singh, who had his power-base in Kashmir, and was also in secret contact with the British. The British, naturally, were not indifferent to what was happening on their borders. Deprived of their strong ally, Ranjit Singh, they followed a policy of playing off the candidates for the succession against each other. This was of course difficult when the succession was changing hands so quickly. Another problem was that, despite Tej Singh's title, there was no single leader of the army, which had reverted to the old Sikh republican custom of *punchayats*, or councils of representatives.

In anticipation of hostile action against its territories in the Malwa, the British government from at least April 1844 started to move troops and supplies up towards the River Sutlej. Not surprisingly interpreting this as a threat of invasion, the Sikh army under Tej Singh crossed the Sutlej on 12 December 1845, thus precipitating the First Anglo-Sikh War. In the words of one Sikh historian,

> Heedless of the menacing forces against them, Ranjit Singh's successors destroyed the

---

82 Patwant Singh, *The Sikhs*, p. 139.
83 S Stronge (ed), *The Arts of the Sikh Kingdoms* (London, 1999).
84 I Fane, *Miss Fane in India* ed J Pemble (Gloucester, 1985) p. 194.
85 Patwant Singh, *The Sikhs*, p. 147.

promise of the Sikh State through self-destructive moves and betrayals. In the end they not only tarnished a noble heritage, but destroyed themselves as well.[86]

The Sikh Army

The Sikh state may have been fatally weakened by the struggle for succession, and the leaders of its army were deep in intrigue with its enemies, but the men of the army still constituted the most formidable opponent that Anglo-Indian forces ever faced in India. Diplomatic ties between the British and Ranjit Singh in the 1820s and 30s enabled each side to assess the other's military capabilities. The British were accustomed to their armies being much superior in everything but numbers to the forces of other Indian states, but what they saw of Ranjit's army in the 1830s gave them much food for thought. During the state visit of Lord Auckland in 1838, Auckland's sister Emily Eden described the effect on British officers who had a chance to inspect the Sikh forces:

> All the gentlemen went at daybreak yesterday to Runjeet's review, and came back rather discomfited. He had nearly as many troops out as Sir G R had; they were quite as well disciplined, rather better dressed, repeated the same military movements and several others much more complicated, and, in short, nobody knows what to say about it, so they say nothing, except that they are sure the Sikhs would run away in a real fight. It is a sad blow to our vanities.[87]

The quality of the Sikh forces should have come as no surprise. They had behind them many successful campaigns, and as far back as the early 1820s Ranjit Singh had set about creating, from his brave but unruly soldiers, a balanced, disciplined force of cavalry, infantry and artillery, equipped, uniformed and trained on European lines. He imported over forty military advisors, French, Italian, German, British and other nationalities, chief amongst whom were the generals Allard and Ventura, French veterans of Napoleon's wars, and the Italian Avitabile. Traditionally, Sikhs had fought on horseback, but Ranjit Singh, influenced by his European advisors and perhaps by the example of the East India Company's regiments, developed a formidable force of infantry. The core of this was the *Aieen* battalions. An officer of the Sixteenth Lancers, present at a parade of 40,000 of Ranjit's troops in 1838, particularly noticed these battalions:

> A broad street now appeared formed of the Regular Infantry drawn up three deep à la Française on one side and two deep on the other; these troops wore scarlet cloth jackets, generally faced with yellow, red turbans and white trowsers: their arms the musket and bayonet, the belts, black leather. I have never seen so tall a body of men collected together, or so steady, standing under arms.[88]

As well as being trained in European drill, the *Aieen* corps was armed not with the Indian matchlock musket, but with European firearms. Some were of French manufacture,

---

86 Patwant Singh, *The Sikhs*, p. 140.
87 E Eden, *Up the Country: Letters written to her Sister from the Upper Provinces of India* ed E Thompson (Oxford, 1930) p. 209.
88 Lowe, *Diary of an Officer*, p. 290.

but others were 'Brown Bess' muskets purchased from the East India Company.[89] After the Battle of Aliwal, a sergeant of the Sixteenth Lancers noticed that the muskets of the Sikhs whom they had charged had Birmingham manufacturers' markings on them.[90] Not for the last time, British troops had faced an enemy armed with British-made weapons. The *Aieen* battalions, well-armed and disciplined, were the backbone of the Sikh infantry, but the majority of foot soldiers were irregulars, armed with matchlocks and swords. The most formidable of these were the religiously-inspired *Akalis*. The Sikh troops to which the Ninth Lancers mostly found themselves opposed were the cavalry, many of whom were in fact Afghans. This was the weakest arm of the Sikh army, and varied widely in effectiveness. They were personally brave, and skilled horsemen, as Lieutenant Delmar observed:

> ... their cavalry seem well mounted – each man appears arm'd with a matchlock, a spear, & a sword – they are wonderful horsemen – many of them dismounted the other morning when the 14th charged them [at Ramnuggar] & fir'd at our men as they pass'd them.[91]

The irregular *Goorchurra* horsemen would rarely stand against a disciplined charge by British cavalry, as the Ninth discovered at the Battle of Gujerat, but they were adept at exploiting any weakness or hesitation displayed by a foe, as their overthrow of Pope's brigade at Chillianwallah demonstrated. Gilling's experiences show that they were also cunning and merciless at cutting out and ambushing small groups of soldiers on outposts and picketing duties.

The Sikh army was especially renowned for its artillery. Ranjit Singh had begun to build up huge stocks of guns from about 1805. He set up several foundries and repair shops, notably at Lahore and Multan.[92] His Sikh, Hindu and Muslim technicians studied the best examples from France and the East India Company, copying them in large numbers. He was particularly proud of his horse artillery. Most guns were of light calibre (six and nine-pounders) although some of those mounted in fortifications were much heavier. At the commencement of the First Anglo-Sikh War, it is estimated that the Sikh field army had over 250 guns, with probably as many more held in fortresses such as Multan. Despite the capture of 256 guns during that war, they could muster over one hundred more at the start of the second war. Some of these guns, complete with carriages and ammunition and the loan of instructors in their use, had been presented to Ranjit as diplomatic gifts by the East India Company, and were used against the British at Chillianwallah: cannon-balls fired at that battle were found to bear the Company's distinctive mark.[93] The artillerymen, many of whom were Muslims, were élite troops, and often fought to the death rather than give up their guns.

Despite its training, discipline and equipment, the Sikh army did have weaknesses. Its standard tactics on the battlefield were where possible to produce formidable entrenchments,

---

89 J M B Neill, *Recollections of Four Years' Service in the East with H.M. Fortieth Regiment* (London, 1845) p. 295; D F Harding, *Smallarms of the East India Company 1600-1856 Vol IV: The Users and their Smallarms* (London, 1999) p. 586.
90 QRLA, Thomas, Diary 1845-6, p. 6.
91 NAM 8301-38 Delmar, Letter 28 November 1848.
92 N Carleton, *Lion's Teeth: The Artillery of Maharaja Ranjit Singh* www.sikhspectrum.com/112005/artillery_maharaja_ranjit_singh.htm (19 Jan 2006).
93 Thackwell, *Narrative*, p. 115.

anchored by fortified villages, with the guns ranged at intervals along the front. The infantry stood behind the guns, and the cavalry clustered on the flanks. This worked well up to a point, forcing the British into costly frontal assaults that were not always successful. However, when this hard 'crust' had once been pierced, the command of the infantry was not sufficiently flexible to allow them to manoeuvre to retrieve the situation, and the guns could not be quickly withdrawn, especially if their gunners had fought to the death. Once driven out of their trenches, the Sikh formations usually disintegrated and retreat became rout, with just individual *Aieen* battalions rallying against their pursuers, until shot to pieces by horse artillery or charged by cavalry. As Major Grant of the Ninth remarked

> ... though these natives fight well behind intrenchments, and stand to their guns like men, they are no match for our disciplined troops in the open, and they are quite unable to withstand the resolute charges of our infantry and cavalry.[94]

The Sikh army was not helped by the divided leadership which prevailed in most of the battles, where it was suspected that some of their generals were actually in favour of a British victory, to weaken the power of the *Khalsa*. The ordinary Sikh soldier was a formidable foe, and the most serious threat to Britain's empire in India. The Sikh expected no quarter, and gave none. His skill at arms, bravery and refusal to admit defeat were recognised by the British who lost no time in recruiting Sikhs in disproportionately large numbers into the Indian army after 1850. Subsequently, Sikhs served with distinction in scores of minor campaigns on the borders of India and in Africa, as well as in two world wars. This martial spirit impressed many contemporary writers, who paid tribute to their enemy's courage. Typical is the description of one wounded but undefeated Sikh, left on the field of Chillianwallah:

> He was clothed in the infantry uniform, red jacket with white stripes across the breast, and blue trowsers. He sported the usual quantity of black beard, whiskers, and moustaches. A cannon ball had shattered his thigh bone, and he could not stir. On my first approaching him, he was stuffing *bang* into his mouth as fast as possible. The outside pockets of his jacket were filled with this intoxicating drug. He was seeking relief from the excruciating agony of his wound. On my arriving close to him he made a desperate effort to collect his almost dormant energies and, worked up into a convulsive paroxysm, grasped at a *tulwar* lying within reach of his arm. His strength, however, failed him.[95]

Gilling's memoirs

In his preface James Gilling claims 'I have no pretensions to classical knowledge or an erudite style.' This can be taken as conventional modesty, since he has pretensions to both. His talk of chimeras, Esculapians, Vulcan and Greek names for Indian rivers show that he must have had access to some works on the subject, if only to Classical dictionaries or encyclopaedias. Similarly he makes reference to literary works such as Chaucer's tales, the Arabian Nights, Don Quixote and Dr Syntax, as well as to various historical and travel works. His use of technical military terms such as *epaulments* and *fausse-braie* shows he had

---

94 Knollys, *Life of Grant*, p. 79.
95 Thackwell, *Narrative*, p. 182.

referred to at least one text on fortification. This range of reading shows that, contrary to the popular image of the Victorian soldier, Gilling was both literate, and had access to a variety of books during his service. As has been said, recruiters for the cavalry targeted especially the skilled 'artisan' sections of the working classes, many working in jobs which required some literacy.[96] The result was that cavalry soldiers displayed higher literacy rates than the infantry, and indeed higher than the comparable civilian population. Gilling's father was a publican, an occupation requiring literacy and was likely to be prosperous enough to allow his son to be educated. Gilling's own writing testifies to his literacy. British soldiers in India certainly had access to libraries,[97] and an inspection report for the Ninth Lancers in 1848 records that nearly 70% of the men were subscribers to the library.[98]

Gilling had read widely enough to attempt a 'literary' style which can be long-winded and even tedious at times. His prefacing each chapter with a piece of verse is a typical device of the time. He is perhaps at his best when describing anecdotes of his own and his comrades' experiences in battle. One can imagine him noting down these stories after an evening spent around a camp-fire. But his literary set-pieces do sometimes contain some fine descriptive writing. His account of the advance of the army onto the plain outside Lahore after the Battle of Sobraon sees Gilling at his 'purple prose' best:

> All at once the whole line emerged from the jungle on to the open plain, and advancing for about 500 yards halted; aides-de-camps were seen galloping along the line, and the next minute the whole, like the simultaneous working of a machine, 'deployed into line,' extending nearly three miles along the plain; and now the grandeur of 45,000 men was fully developed. In this order the line advanced over the plain directly towards the Sikh capital. The sun was shining in all its splendour on the furbished arms, which flashing and glistening over the dark ranks, produced a scene truly grand and imposing, and one calculated to raise, even in our hearts, feelings of pride and enthusiasm.

Similarly Gilling conjures up a memorable vision of his sense of loneliness and vulnerability on a solitary night patrol near the Sikh lines in the period of tense inaction between the combat at Ramnuggar and the crossing of the Chenab.

One may ask if Gilling relied on his memory when writing of his experiences. There were no 'security' restrictions on soldiers writing diaries at this period, such as were imposed in twentieth century wars. Despite assertions to the contrary,[99] it was surprisingly common for soldiers in the ranks to write diaries or notebooks of their experiences. For example, at least eight journals are known to have been written by ordinary soldiers of the Sixteenth Lancers in India in the 1840s, and even infantry regiments such as the 32nd Light Infantry had their diarists.[100] Gilling mentions having a notebook to hand whilst

---

96   Rumsby, *The Sixteenth Lancers*, pp. 75-80.
97   See Note 3 on pp 149-150.
98   TNA WO 27/376.
99   For example, Michael Brander, who claimed that the journal of Charles Godward was a unique survival of a private soldier's journal in India of that period: M Brander, *The Sword and the Pen* (London, 1989) p. 88.
100 Three have been published for this regiment: H Metcalfe, *The Chronicle of Private Metcalfe* ed F Tuker (London, 1953), J Ryder, *Four Years' Service in India* (1844-48) ed J Thompson (Burton 1853, 2nd edn 1854) and R Waterfield, *Memoirs of Private Waterfield* ed A Swinson and D Scott (London, 1968). Another typical published example is William Taylor's *Scenes and Adventures in Affghanistan*, (London,

writing, and this may have contained many types of material – a day-to-day narrative, anecdotes of incidents narrated by friends, copies of daily orders and official despatches (which circulated freely in camp, judging by the frequency with which they are quoted in journals), and extracts from regimental records such as muster rolls. Evidence for all these sources exist in *The Life of a Lancer*. His precise account of numbers and fates of his draft to India, for example, suggest he had a list of their names copied from the muster roll, which he kept and annotated through to the end of his service. Sergeant Pearman of the Third Light Dragoons maintained a similar practice, incorporating the list of his draft into the memoirs he wrote long after leaving the army.[101]

Of course, the use of these contemporary sources, and Gilling's writing so soon after the events he describes, does not ensure that he gives us an entirely accurate and comprehensive account of life in the British army and its campaigns in India in the 1840s. His view is very much his own, the 'life of a lancer' as his title emphasises, with his own opinions and feelings given equal weight with the narrative of great events as he saw them. It is this indeed that gives *The Life of a Lancer* its particular value.

When not using great words like 'olfactory,' 'refulgent' or 'gastronomic avocations,' which were not, one imagines, commonly heard around the horse-lines, Gilling demonstrates the talent of British soldiers before and since for picking up 'native' words and using them in his narrative. This habit was demonstrated to a new recruit to the Fourteenth Hussars (formerly Light Dragoons), Edwin Mole, in the 1860s:

> There were fifteen men in my mess, fourteen of whom wore three or four medals. They were good-hearted fellows in the main, though a little short-tempered; and all bore signs of their long residence in India ... They used many queer Hindustan names and terms, which it took me some time to get the hang of. For instance, they never spoke of knives, or salt, or bread, but always 'Give me a *Churrie*!' 'Pass the *neemuck*!' or 'Sling over some *rootee*!'[102]

The result of this activity has of course been the enrichment of the English language by many words of Indian origin, such as dixie, pyjamas and dinghy, to cite just three that Gilling uses.[103] Soldiers in India, before the great mutiny of the Bengal native army in India led to increased segregation between Britons and Indians, often came in contact with native Indians, in bazaars, on sight-seeing and hunting trips, as well as in day-to-day converse with servants. Many British other ranks, therefore, (possibly proportionately more than their officers) became fluent enough in the local languages to enable them to carry on often quite complicated conversations on history and religion.[104] It is natural therefore that Indian words should be used by Gilling as part of his narrative, and a glossary of them (as well as some technical military terms) is provided.

1842), published seven years after the events he describes.
101 Pearman ed Steedman, *The Radical Soldier's Tale*, p. 247.
102 E Mole, *A King's Hussar, being the Military Memoirs for Twenty-five Years of a Troop-Sergeant-Major of the 14th (King's) Hussars* ed H Compton (London, 1897) pp. 29-30. These men would have been veterans of the campaigns of the Sutlej, Punjab, Persia and the Indian Mutiny.
103 For other examples, see D Crystal, *The Cambridge Encyclopedia of the English Language* (Cambridge, 1995) pp. 126, 360.
104 See Godward's sight-seeing trips in Brander, *The Sword and the Pen*.

A note on the text

Gilling's military memoirs must have been subject to a very small print-run, and is now extremely rare. Apparently no copies survive in any public collection, including the British Library, the Bodleian Library, and the regimental archive. A copy was purchased in 1968 by the public library at Worksop (Gilling's home town), from a descendant of the author. This copy cannot now be traced. Fortunately a photocopy was made from this copy by the National Army Museum, along with some notes on Gilling's life, which were presumably supplied by the descendant. The present text has been taken from the NAM photocopy, which has a few minor gaps, each of a small number of words, due to misalignment during the original copying. These gaps are indicated by [gap in text].

The original editing was somewhat haphazard, possibly because Gilling had left for America whilst the text was being prepared for publication. For example, there was little attempt to rectify inconsistency in spelling, resulting in such place-names as Ramnuggar being spelt in three different ways, and Ferozeshah as Feroozeshah and Ferozesha. There were some obvious misreadings by the typesetter, such as Soodiana for Loodiana, and at one point *Goorchuma* for *Goorchurra*. The date of the Battle of Sobraon was printed as August instead of February. These inconsistencies have been removed. Names have been made consistent within modern accepted forms (although these too can vary). Some old spellings have been modernised, such as 'Jackalls' changed to 'jackals' and 'serjeant' to 'sergeant.' In a very few places, punctuation has been slightly amended, or words added in square brackets, to make the meaning clearer. Chapter titles have been added. No other attempts have been made to alter, rearrange or abridge the text in any way. Apart from the above-named instances, and the addition of explanatory notes, the text remains exactly as Gilling's printers reproduced it.

Preface to the original edition

For since the world with writing is possest;
I'll scribble on in spite; and do my best
To make as much waste paper as the rest.

It has been asserted, and the assertion is in no wise an idle one, that the vicissitudes of a soldier's life, especially a campaigner, would, if faithfully narrated, be both instructive and amusing, and having myself experienced many of the incidents common to such a life, and trod the hard and rugged path of war, I lay down my trusty sword with an endeavour to wield the pen, seeking to narrate in a plain and unvarnished style some of the circumstances and incidents connected with the late warfare in the Punjaub.

To carry out this object then, I propose to write an autobiography, commencing with my enlistment, and to carry the reader step by step, and link by link, through the hardships and chequered scenes of my military career, interspersing the same with sketches, anecdotes, incidents, characters, &c., with an occasional peep into the Indian Barrack Room, and here and there a stray shot at the military authorities.

In writing this autobiography, I trust the reader will exonerate me from all egotistical motives, and as I have no pretensions to classical knowledge or an erudite style, I trust they will be lenient in their criticisms. With Chaucer I would say:

But, Sirs, because I am a borel man,
At my beginning first I you beseeche
Have me excused of my rude speeche;
I learned never rhetorike certain
Thing that I spake, it mote be bare and plain.

JAMES GILLING

1

Enlistment

A fountain of ambition and bright hope.
It was on a fine day in June 1843 that I left my paternal home, my youthful and ardent mind full of utopian ideas and wild chimeras; while bright visions of 'honour and glory,' the pride, pomp, and circumstances of war, seemed to paint the army in such glowing colours that I resolved on embracing the military profession.

Being desirous of going to India, having heard much of its riches and luxuries, I determined to join a corps serving out there, hence I proceeded at once to London, where I felt convinced I could obtain the necessary information as to the regiment I should join.

The morning after my arrival in the great town, I sallied forth to the Horse Guards, where I met with an old acquaintance, then in the *Blues*[1], and on duty: we entered the canteen together where was a recruiting corporal, with whom I soon came to an understanding, and with the usual ceremony, I enlisted in the 9th, or Queen's Royal Lancers[2], serving in Bengal.

The shilling, which was the price of my liberty, and perhaps of my life, was immediately transferred over to old Boniface of the canteen for another pot, by way of ratification of the contract just made.

The next morning I, with several other fry caught in the same net, went through the disagreeable and indelicate ordeal of bodily inspection, examination, and lastly attestation.

I confess I was somewhat abashed and had a sort of repulsive feeling when ordered to strip, and in nature's garb alone, perform various motions, such as genuflection, leaping, springing, and other gymnastic exercises in the presence of several doctors and other officers of the recruiting service. After having performed this physical sort of pantomime to the full satisfaction of the Esculapians[3], who doubtless thought me fit food for powder, I was duly attested and sworn to serve Her most gracious Majesty Queen Victoria, to the utmost of my abilities; which, being interpreted, means to kill, destroy, and otherwise disable, as far as lay in my power, all who might hereafter be considered her enemies. Thus I obtained a situation *under* government, which though perhaps not so lucrative as that of a Governor General, promised at least to be a permanent one; indeed so lasting, that I might like many others, spend the whole of my existence in it, with the additional satisfaction of dying in the midst of 'honour and glory.'

After having thus passed this ordeal, I received ten shillings as part payment of my bounty money,[4] and was at the same time invested with due authority to quarter myself on mine host of the H—— H——-, a public house in Westminster, the landlord of which was in no way scrupulous about *fleecing* the inexperienced recruits who were so unfortunate as to be billeted on him.

However I believe the old peccant does not always have it his own way, for sometimes it is 'diamond cut diamond.' I was told that he had been done rather *brown* a short time prior to this by a young fellow named Brown, from the country, who, when the long list of 'dittos' was produced, declared in his simple manner that he had never eat or drank any 'dittos,' neither could all the logic or explanation the landlord could muster, convince him to the contrary; and he firmly persisted in refusing to pay more than half the charges against him, saying he 'was no Frenchman and didn't eat ditties.'

I visited my friend of the Blues before I quitted London, and there I found that every thing denoted comfort and plenty; a state of things very gratifying to my feelings, as in it I fancied I could read my own future comfort in the same profession, my ignorance of the army not leading me to think that regiments of the line differed in any way from the household troops; however I was soon undeceived.

Early on the Tuesday morning subsequent to my enlistment, about thirty of us were mustered and marched down to London Bridge, where we took steamer for Gravesend, and from thence we marched on foot to Maidstone, the cavalry depôt, where we arrived about twilight.

The treatment a recruit meets with on his first launching himself on the tempest-tossed waves of military life, at Maidstone especially, is neither gratifying nor calculated to inspire him with any flattering ideas of the life he has chosen. Indeed it often annihilates the ardent predilection a young aspirant possesses on enlistment, and, the tide of his military aspirations being thus turned, he becomes disgusted with the army, ere he literally knows what it is; hence the frequent desertions from that depôt. Immediately on arriving in the depot you are sent to the hospital, and there remain for the space of eight or ten days in close confinement, little better than a prisoner; that too which renders it more so, is the meagre and prison-like diet. In the morning for breakfast you have a basin of 'skilly' - a mixture simply of oatmeal and water, with a small bit of bread just sufficient to bait a rat trap; then that which should be dinner is only just sufficient to tantalize the stomach: in short, the whole is but sick allowance, that is, 'half diet.' To hearty, healthy, and growing lads it is almost starvation. Then again there are the incessant drills, parades, guards, and fatigues;* of the last of which there is more than enough. If there is anything calculated to engender in the breast of a recruit a prejudice against the service it is this most unwarrantable employment; for the fatigues we performed, lessened not our military duties one jot. These were picking up the garrison yard, rolling the same, and picking grass, &c.; every moment thus occupied being properly required to clean our 'traps.'

---

* Fatigues are employments which are neither part nor parcel of military duties. [Gilling's note.]

2

Voyage to India

Adieu! my native land, adieu!
The vessel spreads her swelling sails:
Perhaps, I never more may view
Your fertile fields, your flowery dales.

If there be a scene pathetically touching and truly affecting – next to that of seeing the remains of a parent, brother, sister, or dear friend deposited in the cold and silent tomb – that of leave taking of friends and kindred who are on the point of sailing to a far, far country, is the one. Many a one as they pronounce the sad 'farewell' feels a conviction that it is for ever in this terrestrial world. And as the tall vessel gradually recedes from the shore, and becomes dimmer in the haze, until she finally disappears from the tear-dimmed eyes of those assembled to see their departing friends, they feel, if a parent, brother, or sister, that a link of the family chain is severed, perhaps never more to be reunited; and, if a lover, the dear object of her fond hopes and dreams seems cruelly torn from her, and she is left often broken-hearted, like a blighted flower, to droop and die.

> Out of the *thousands* who annually leave their Friends, their homes, and native land
> For 'India's parched and burning strand.'

how few return! Many a fine and gallant youth, in the pride of health and strength, light hearted and happy in the day dreams of youth, leaves his home and all that is dear to him, to find, alas! a premature grave, or to fatten with his flesh the pariahs and jackals, and whiten with his bones the plains of India. That this is a true picture, alas! too true; how many a sorrowful and bereaved parent can bear the sad testimony.

Our embarkation at Gravesend was marked by some of those adieu's I have just described[1]. Here might be seen a fond mother embracing her son, the big tears coursing each other down her cheeks, while she invoked the protection and blessing of God on him; there a fond sister locked in the embrace of her brother and the companion of her youth, now a soldier, about to be severed from her for years, perhaps for ever; and last a little remote perhaps from the rest, might be seen lovers in silent grief, embracing each other while they bid a final adieu. The ship in which we soon found ourselves was a fine vessel; indeed her name (the *Queen*), would imply that she was no commoner. As her sails were unfurled and swelled in the breeze, she glided majestically through the water and bore us away from our friends.

I know not whether the Board of Ordnance, when they issued out our hammocks, intended to try practically what our heads were made of, or whether it was acting on the principle of the old saying, that 'use is second nature,' – they thought to render our craniums, by hard knocking, impervious to the cannon and musketry to which they were going to be exposed. But this much I do know; that no sooner had we swung ourselves in these novel sleeping apartments than we descended with violence to the deck, owing to the strings slipping through the eyelet holes. Many an unlucky wight came bump on the deck, followed by a loud and boisterous laugh at his expense. One in particular, set the whole of us laughing, as immediately after his head had bumped on the deck, he raised his hand and scratching the injured part; at the same time leering round at us in the most comical manner, he exclaimed, 'Blood an' 'ouns, talk about hardships, but this is the *hardest* ship ever I was in.'

To an Englishman going to India, the long voyage he has to make is an excellent preparative. The temporary absence of ordinary scenes and employments produces a state of mind peculiarly fitted to receive new and vivid impressions. The vast space of waters which separates the two countries, is like a blank page in his existence. There is no gradual transition by which, as in Europe, the scenery and population of one country blend almost imperceptibly with those of another. From the moment you lose sight of the land you have left, all is a blank, until you step on an opposite shore, and are launched at once into the bustle and excitement of other scenes, as it were of another world. As I saw the last blue line of my native land fade away like a cloud in the horizon, it seemed as if I had closed one volume of the world and its concerns, and had time for meditation ere I opened another. That land, too, now vanishing from my view, which contained all that was dear to me in life, what vicissitudes might occur in it! – what changes might take place in me, before I should visit it again! Who can tell when he sets forth to wander, where he may be driven by the uncertain currents of existence! or when he may return, or whether it may ever be his lot to revisit the scenes of his childhood! All that I had clung to for support and protection, all that I had ever loved, and all that had ever loved me; in a word all that I cared for, and all that cared for me, seemed to sink from my sight with the lessening cliffs of my native land. The past, as if in mockery of my woe, freshened up in colours brighter than reality, while the future appeared to my view as the dreary waste of waters before me.

Our ship contained about three hundred passengers of various grades, classes and denominations. The cabin passengers were about fifty, among whom were a number of young cadets[2] just launched on the voyage of life; as a contrast to which were half a dozen old Indians, returning with jaundiced countenances, patched up livers, and somewhat repaired constitutions to drag out a few more years in a withering climate, *still hoping*, and hoping on still, for that promotion and rank which few reach until they have become old, withered, and superannuated. Last not least were a number of young ladies, just in the prime of blooming youth and beauty; who, having received their education in England, were now returning to their relatives in India. The remainder being soldiers and sailors, I need not describe every character. Suffice it to say that amongst a people of such multifarious tastes, and dispositions, there was no lack of amusements. Nine years – but a particle in the infinite sands of time, have passed away since my voyage to India, and when I bring before my mind's eye the little groups who used to assemble on deck, to tell the tale, to pass the joke, or to sing the jocund song, I see the faces of many whose names have long since ceased to be born on the rolls of their regiments. (Out of the one hundred who left England with me for my regiment in 1843, only thirty-five remained when I left in 1850.)[3] Some have died a soldier's natural death in the field of battle; some have fallen victims to the climate, and some few, like myself, have preferred struggling for a living in a more genial land with half a liver, to ease with scarce a liver at all.

During a calm in the tropics the sailors amused themselves by catching sharks, which

Punjab and Indian Mutiny medals of 1303 Private Thomas Derome. Derome, a tailor by trade, enlisted in the Ninth Lancers on 15 June 1843. He was shipped to India in the same draft as James Gilling. He served in India for over fifteen years, being finally discharged in 1860 as a consequence of a fractured wrist. He was also entitled to the Sutlej Medal for Sobraon. (By courtesy of the 9th/12th Lancers Museum, Derby)

Medals of Samuel Higginson. No 1076 Private Higginson was born in Brighton, Sussex, and served in the Sixth Dragoon Guards before transferring to the Ninth. His medals are (left to right): Punniar Star, Sutlej (for Sobraon), Punjab, Indian Mutiny, and Long Service and Good Conduct Medal. He was discharged in 1864 after nearly 28 years' service. (By courtesy of the 9th/12th Lancers Museum)

inhabit the seas in those parts and will sometimes follow a ship for weeks together, in the hope of coming in for a share of the offal and other refuse which is cast from the ship. I have heard many marvellous stories told of their voracious swallow of indigestibles, or of any substance that falls in their way, some of which are hardly credible. However, on opening one that we caught, we discovered the pillow of a hammock, which had fallen overboard three days before. It was whole and uninjured, and when dried was restored to its original use.

In the south seas somewhere off the Cape of Good Hope, we suffered a most terrific hurricane, but having fortunately plenty of sea room we managed to ride safely through the storm. Nevertheless, during the prevalence of the gale there were many anxious thoughts sent back to that home, those friends, and that English fire-side, we had so recently left, as the angry elements were seen lashing the surging ocean into foaming mountains and deep chasms and gulphs, and while the awful fact was before us, that but a plank stood between us and eternity. As night approached, our fears were in no wise lessened or soothed; for with the darkness the storm increased, and the sea was lashed into tremendous confusion. There was a fearful sullen sound of rushing waves, and broken surges. Deep called unto deep. At times the black volumes overhead seemed rent asunder, by flashes of lightning that quivered along the foaming billows, and made the succeeding darkness doubly terrible. The thunders bellowed over the wide waste of waters, and were echoed and prolonged by the mountainous waves. As I saw the ship staggering and plunging amongst these roaring caverns, it seemed miraculous how she gained her balance, or preserved her buoyancy. Her yards would dip into the water, her bow was almost buried beneath the waves. Sometimes an impending wave seemed ready to overwhelm her, and nothing but a dextrous move of the helm preserved her from the shock. Altogether the time, the circumstances, the apparent danger, and the confused noise of the storm, rendered it a scene of awful and mighty grandeur. When I returned to my hammock the awful scene still followed me. The whistling of the wind through the rigging sounded like funeral wailings. The creaking of the masts; the straining and groaning of bulk-heads, as the ship laboured in the weltering sea, were frightful. As I heard the waves rushing along the sides of the ship, and roaring in my very ear, it seemed as if death was raging around the floating prison, seeking for his prey; and that the mere starting of a nail, the yawning of a seam might give him entrance. The long wished for morning at last broke forth, but with it came no cessation of the fearful tempest, and the sea presented a scene awfully terrific.

For three successive days and two nights, raged this fearful war of the elements. Amidst this scene so appalling, and so pregnant with danger, the brave sailors, as if aware of the many lives depending on their exertions, performed their duties with exemplary coolness and promptitude. To them and to the captain's judicious management is greatly attributable the ultimate safety of the ship. Yet even with all this good management and human skill, the merciful finger of an all-wise Providence was discernible. To Him at whose command the winds are hushed and the waves subside, the supplications of his ministers (there were three missionaries aboard)[4] were sent from that vessel, and even amidst the howling and roaring of the tempest they were heard, and we were spared from the dangers of shipwreck.

'After a storm comes a calm,' but the calm which followed was if anything the greater evil of the two. For the sea which was like a boiling cauldron, still continued to surge and roll with a heavy swell; and our ship, for want of wind to steady or propel her onward, reeled and tumbled about like one drunk. However as some alloy we were highly amused with innumerable aquatic birds of various hues and sizes, from the large Albatross to the little 'Mother Carey's Chickens,'[5] which hovered about the ship, and by way of variety, the whales, of which there were numbers here, as if delighted at the cessation of the storm, were gambolling about and spirting out their jets, which in the sun's rays seemed like so many miniature rainbows.

About a week after the storm, we passed alongside of an American whaler, a handsome built little barque, 'lying to,' having a fine whale lashed alongside, which the sailors were then busy in cutting up preparatory to being rendered down for oil. All around the vessel the sea was dotted, and in some places, literally covered with numberless sea-birds, attracted to the spot by the particles of blubber which floated from the whale during the process of dissection, and seemed to dispute with the sailors the right to the prey.

On board with us was a woman, the wife of a soldier of the 3rd Dragoons[6], who from the moment she entered the ship seemed to sicken and droop. Most probably she had long been marked as a victim by consumption. Probably she might have hoped that a sea voyage would perhaps restore her. If so, alas, she soon had to feel the fallacy of those hopes; for in little more than ten weeks after she had left her native shore, she had sunk quietly, and peaceably in the arms of death. If there be more than ordinary solemnity in a military funeral, a burial at sea is, of all others, the most mournful. On land while the body of the deceased is consigned to its early bed, and the coffin echoes to the sound of 'dust to dust,' the flight of the soul to the regions of immortality is for the moment lost sight of, in the narrow limits of the grave. The scene is mournful, truly, for our thoughts are all on mortality. But at sea, when at the words 'We commit his or her body to the deep,' the corpse glides into the ocean, it seems as if it as well as the soul, were launched into eternity; and nothing occurs to disconnect the mind from the awful contemplation of immortality. On this occasion, as is invariably the case on board ship, all hands were assembled on deck to witness the mournful ceremony; and as the corpse, which was stretched on a grating and covered by the Union flag, was borne upon deck and placed in the embrasure of the gangway, preparatory to its being plunged into the deep, one common feeling of awe and solemnity seemed to pervade the whole. That beautiful service for the dead was read in a most solemn and impressive tone by a missionary, and when he came to the words 'We commit her body to the deep' the corpse, which had two heavy shot attached to its feet, glided from the grating and plunged with a heavy splashing sound into the briny abyss, there to await the final day of resurrection, when 'the graves shall open and the sea give up her dead.'

During the progress of the voyage, the following incident occurred, illustrative of the manner in which young soldiers fraternize together to resist any species of tyranny which may be inflicted on a brother comrade.

Amongst the men of the 3rd Dragoons, was one named Kelly, a remarkably clean and good soldier, and beloved by all his comrades on board. For a trivial 'soldier's crime' – I know not what – he was put in irons in the forecastle. This was no sooner known to all hands than, without considering the merits or demerits of Kelly's crime, or caring for the consequences of our insubordination, we resolved at all risks to release him from a punishment we deemed not only unjust, but extremely degrading in the eyes of the sailors. Soldiers seldom project a scheme, however difficult, but they find means to execute it. Having procured some implements from the sailors, who heartily joined with us, we knocked off Kelly's manacles with a scientific dexterity that would have done credit to a Newgate jailor, or even old Vulcan himself. And to prevent the possibility of their subsequent use for so degrading a purpose, we cast them into the sea, wishing that the old martinet who had ordered their use was sent along with them. An investigation was made in the matter to discover the delinquents, but of course no one knew anything about it.

Some time after this, a sad accident occurred, by which we lost one of our comrades. The captain of the ship, wishing to cut a good figure at Calcutta, would have the hull of the ship painted, and one of our men, by name Baker, was employed for this purpose. One day, just as we had grouped ourselves in messes for dinner, we were aroused by shouts of 'a man overboard.' Every one sprang up in a moment, consternation and curiosity depicted in each countenance, some rushing to one side of the ship and some to the other. In the mean time one of the sailors had magnanimously risked his own life by leaping into the sea after him. When I reached the stern, I saw at a distance of about a quarter of a mile, a small speck on the water like a log of wood, now rising on the top of a wave and now disappearing for a moment in the hollows between them. This was the sailor, whose efforts were unavailing, for poor Baker, being no swimmer, had sunk, alas, to rise no more. And now our whole anxiety was for the sailor who, though a good swimmer, might become exhausted: for though the ship had been put about as speedily as possible, and a boat lowered, it would be some minutes ere the latter could reach him. Fortunately however he preserved his buoyancy until the boat took him up, and he was hailed by all as a gallant fellow. It appeared that Baker was endeavouring to get on deck, when by some means he unfortunately lost his hold and fell into the sea.[7]

Baker's sudden disappearance from us, cast a general gloom throughout the ship; for, being a jovial and vivacious companion, his place was sadly missed in our evening groups. Indeed, on board ship, where society is so limited, and where the same individuals are perpetually brought together, ties are engendered which every day become stronger, and when one of these links of friendship is suddenly broken, it is felt as one link less in the chain or group of friends around you. The noble-minded sailor did not go unrewarded for his praiseworthy conduct; for Cornet King[8], of my regiment, generously presented him with five sovereigns, and every one of the soldiers gave him a shilling each; besides a handsome sum subscribed amongst the passengers.

We arrived within sight of the Sundarbunds[9], about four o'clock p.m., of the 6th of January 1844; and those who have been pent up for months in a crowded vessel, can well understand the feelings of joy with which we hailed the prospect of our approaching deliverance.

Some few there were, however, who looked upon our release with very different feelings. This was particularly applicable to the passengers; amongst whom friendships and attachments had been formed and cemented during the progress of the voyage, that were destined to be interrupted or broken up by this event; and those who had abandoned themselves to the delightful intercourse which so soon springs up between kindred feelings and tastes, could not help manifesting their regret at its speedy termination. There were others too who felt a sad consciousness that they were approaching the European's grave, and painful memories crowded upon and depressed them; their pale and dejected countenances reflecting but too faithfully the character of their thoughts, and forming a sad contrast with the joyous faces around them.

The delightful, though rather monotonous appearance of the coast, so different in its character from anything we had before seen, and the singular costume of the natives, who came swarming round the ship in their boats, or *dinghees*, offering various wares for sale, as well as the novel nature of the commodities themselves, had all a new interest for us.

We anchored that night, for the first time since leaving England, near the mouth of the Hooghly, and early the next morning were taken in tow by a steamer up the river. At night we again dropped anchor in the middle of the river at a little distance from a rude hamlet. Here on the banks of the river we witnessed a most revolting sight, a woman and child left on its slimy banks by their relatives, to be taken down the stream by the receding tide. The child was dead and partly devoured by the *pariahs*, (domestic dogs of India,) though the woman had in vain used all her remaining strength to drive them away with a stick she still held in her hand, but she was unable to use it with effect, owing to her excessive weakness. A number of birds called Adjutants[10], vultures, crows, &c., were waiting quietly at a distance until the dogs had satisfied themselves on the child. Some philanthropic ladies on board were anxious that they should be removed, and the mother have medical aid administered, but were told that it could not be allowed, as they were left there in consequence of an incurable disease, in order that the 'holy water of the Ganges' might waft their souls to the realms of everlasting bliss.

All who read of the customs and religion of the Hindoos, are aware that the Ganges is considered most sacred by them, and as such is worshipped as all efficacious in cleansing them from sin while living, and when dead, if committed to the holy stream, it insures them a safe transit to the Harem of everlasting bliss: therefore all Hindoos who die within twenty or thirty miles of the Ganges, are conveyed to the sacred stream and cast therein. If a Hindoo is afflicted with a dangerous disease which is thought by his friends incurable, he is conveyed to its banks, and after various incantations, &c., from the Padre, is left there to await approaching death, which is certain with the rise of the tide. Should they escape from this immolation, they are forever afterwards outcasts from their relatives, and as they have forfeited all claims to paradise, are considered by all as polluted and unclean.

In our way to Calcutta, we passed several Hindoo dead bodies, tied on small rafts, on which were often perched various voracious birds, eating leisurely as the stream carried them along; occasionally they were disturbed by an alligator, putting in a claim for a share of the spoil, by pulling the raft and what remained of the body suddenly under water, where he tore away his share, and then allowed the carcase again to float for the birds.

At four o'clock p.m. on the 7th of January, just one hundred and fifteen days from leaving Gravesend, we dropped anchor opposite Fort William, Calcutta.[11]

3

First experiences of India

Then on! then on! where duty leads,
My course be onward still,
O'er broad Hindostan's sultry meads,
O'er bleak Almorah's hills.

On the morning of the 9th, we were transferred from the *Queen* to a steamer to proceed up the river to Chinsurah, a cantonment about thirty miles above Calcutta. The morning was delightful, and the picturesque appearance of the country on each side of the river rendered our passage extremely interesting. About ten o'clock we passed Barrackpore, a cantonment of native troops. The Governor-General has a very pretty residence here, in a small park, on the banks of the Hooghly, offering as beautiful a display of turf, tree, and flowery shrub, as any scene in the world can produce.

To Chinsurah, the river continues of nearly the same width as at Calcutta; its banks are covered with fruit trees and villages, with many very handsome *pagodas*. These latter, when they adjoin the river, have generally a noble flight of steps the whole breadth of the portico, leading from the water to the entrance. We arrived at Chinsurah a little before sunset, and immediately disembarked and proceeded to the barracks, a short distance from the river.

The first night I passed in India I was almost devoured by mosquitoes, for nothing is so delicious to these insects as newly imported European blood. This tormenting insect, happily known only by report in England, is justly an object of dread to all new comers. They swarm in every building in India, and especially Barracks. Their bite is painful and excessively irritating, and if the person suffering from it scratches the part affected it is sure to rise into a small scalding blister.

The Barrack at Chinsurah is, I think, the finest and best in India. It has a first and second floor, is spacious, open, and well-ventilated, with a verandah on each side, forming a sort of arcade, enclosed by palisading. The verandah of the second or upper storey forms a sort of platform, from which you have a beautiful view of the surrounding country and the river. Our mess-tables were placed here, and I have often, when at meals, been amused at the astonishing boldness of the crows and hawks. They would settle on the palisades, and when everyone was busily engaged in eating, they would suddenly hop on the table and help themselves to a piece of meat and immediately make their exit. The hawks in India are certainly the most bold and impudent thieves I ever met with. They frequently dart down upon the cook's basket and spoil a dinner, to the vexation of the mess to whom it belongs, and the merriment of their more fortunate comrades. Every night the jackals, in large troops, serenaded us with a most charming concert; for they came to our very bed sides, howling, screaming, and caterwauling, as if all the inhabitants of the lower regions were let loose upon us. Nearly a mile from the Barracks, on a beautiful grassy plain, stands a neat little Protestant Church, from which a direct road, shaded with evergreens, leads to the Barracks. About two miles east of Chinsurah, stands Chandernagore, or French Town; one of the remnants of their former possessions in India, two others of which they still retain. Toddy, from the Palm and Toddy trees, is plentiful and cheap here. It is a pleasant and refreshing beverage, and the natives have little difficulty in procuring it here where the trees are very numerous. They make an incision in the body of the tree about two feet from the top, underneath which is slung a *chatty* (an earthenware vessel) to receive the liquid or sap which issues from it. For the first three months in the year each tree will average about two quarts per day. The liquid in itself, though of a slightly stimulating quality, is wholesome, yet when mixed with country liquor it is extremely intoxicating. The last-named drink is too plentiful here, and, though the natives are strictly prohibited from selling it to European soldiers, they generally manage, through their own tact and strategy, to serve them with quantities of it with impunity. The *Chokedars*, or native policemen, too often connive with them; indeed I never knew but one instance where a native grog dealer was fined for illicitly selling to the soldiers, such adepts are they at stratagem and finesse.

4

Calcutta

The double peal of the drum was there,
And the startling sound of the trumpet's blare,
And the gong that seemed with its thunders dread
To stun the living and wake the dead.

While at Chinsurah I witnessed the celebration of a Mussulman festival, called the *Mohorum*[1], which continues throughout seven days, during which time great processions are perpetually parading through the streets. Nothing can exceed the wildness and the discord and din which characterises these parades.

The van is taken by a party of fanatics bearing numerous flags, staves, tridents, and superstitious devices. Next come a dozen Mussulmans, half maddened with opium or *chang* (a decoction of hemp seed,) and dressed and painted in a fantastic style, armed with wooden swords and shields, and performing a lot of antics, accompanied by wild gestures and strange mutterings, while the beating of the tom toms (Indian drums) and gongs, the clattering of cymbals and the sounding of trumpets produced the most discordant and wild din that ever assailed the human ear. Numerous *tazzees* (a fabrication of paper, tinsel, &c., representing Hindoo temples,)[2] precede and follow this strange mob, some borne on elephants' backs, and the more cumbrous ones placed on a sort of caravan, drawn by the multitude. Keeping time by a *Fakir*, or priest, who goes in front of the whole, the multitude simultaneously exclaim, 'Hussain, Hassain,' alternately rising and dropping the voice from 'Hussain' to 'Hassain,' accompanied by beating the right and then the left breast. The origin of the *Mohorum* I never could correctly learn. I have heard several different versions of the story from the natives, but so contradictory that they were not worth credence. I believe two-thirds of the natives know no more of the origin of their *burra din's* (great days, and they have many) than the clay and wooden idols they worship.

Early in February, we had to change quarters to Dum Dum; accordingly we were conveyed by steamer about thirty miles down the Hooghly, where we disembarked at a large *ghaut*, or landing-place.

On our way down we witnessed the Hindoo ceremony of burying, or rather in this instance casting into the sacred stream, the *tazzees*, banners, &c., which had formed so imposing a spectacle in their late processions. I will here remark that in all towns within fifteen or twenty miles of the Hoogly, these trophies are brought from hence to the sacred stream; but in the interior of the country they are buried in a consecrated spot near to the town, with much ceremony and superstitious nonsense.

In this case they were mostly borne on elephants, which were made to walk up to the middle in the water. As these huge animals thus stood with the numerous fairy-like fabrics, thousands of spectators and Hindoo devotees, dressed in various colours and costumes, many in silken and tinselled attire, formed a striking and imposing scene. Numbers of Priests presided over the ceremony, and as each fairy-like fabric was released from its support and fell with a splash into the water, the multitudes on shore rent the air with shouts, calling on their gods, and accompanied by the beating of tom toms, and blowing of horns and trumpets.

The first object which met our eyes on landing was a Hindoo boy about 14 years of age, lying dead on the slimy bank. He had probably lain there some hours, for the pariahs had already devoured a great portion of his flesh. We could not interfere to have it removed, although we had to pass and repass it as we conveyed our luggage to the shore. It was astonishing with what apathy and indifference the natives passed close by this disgusting object, to fill their vessels with the water tainted by such bodies.

The baggage being got ashore, the detachment immediately marched on to Dum Dum; but no carriage having been procured for the baggage, I, with eleven others, and an officer, were left here to guard it. Having neither tent nor bedding with us, this was rather an unpleasant duty; however we managed to rough it through the night, as it was not excessively cold, though extremely damp and unwholesome from the dews and noxious vapours which arose from the banks of the river[3]. During the night we had numerous visits from those nocturnal prowlers the jackals, which as usual serenaded us before they left us. We had become pretty well acquainted with them by this time, so that they caused us little fear, but great annoyance. Indeed like most other animals they will generally shun man, though they frequent his haunts in search of prey; and I never heard of any one being bitten by them, only of course in self-defence.

The next morning we made our breakfast from the milk of cocoa nuts and plantains, a truly novel and somewhat delicious repast but for the disgusting sights and effluvia which assailed our optic and olfactory nerves, for we were lying on the bank of a tributary stream to the Hooghly, and the tide now receding brought with it numerous bodies in various states of decomposition, some of which would become entangled amongst the boats which lay moored there, when the *dandees,* or boatmen, would with the greatest apathy and unconcern imaginable simply shove them away with an oar, just as a boatman in England would a lot of weed which obstructed his boat. *Hackeries,* rude and awkward carts, were at length procured, and about ten o'clock we marched for Dum Dum where we arrived about 2 p.m. Dum Dum is a remarkably good and pleasant station. The Barracks form three sides of a square, but a small interval being preserved between the angles, they constitute three separate and distinct buildings, each Barrack having two stories, and being altogether compact and convenient. These and the Barrack at Chinsurah, are I believe the only Barracks in India having two stories. Why Barracks are not built so in the upper provinces I cannot imagine; for one would naturally suppose that in a low flat country such as India is – where through the greater part of the year, the refulgent rays of a vertical sun heat the ground until it becomes almost as hot as burning lava, and in turn emits its heat to the atmosphere, rendering the lower current of air almost insupportable – that the higher a room is from the ground the cooler and more airy it would be, and in consequence the more conducive to health. In support of this opinion we have only to look at the houses of the richer classes in India, which have invariably three or four stories or floors, with windows on every side to admit of a free current of air. If it is economy which induces the government to immure their soldiers in such miserable cow-shed-like Barracks as they do, it must be a greatly mistaken idea, and they come far short of realizing their object, seeing that the mortality of the troops is greatly increased thereby, many proofs of which I could adduce, but such matter is not essential to my story.

Dum Dum is pleasantly situated on a small grassy plain. It is appropriated exclusively to the company's troops, and is made a recruiting depôt for new comers, from whence they are drafted to their respective troops or companies in various parts of the country.

We were visited here by some of the 'tars' of the *Queen*; amongst them the sailor who had made so noble an effort to save poor Baker. In true Jack Tar style he was accompanied by his 'moll,' a native girl rigged out in a style half English, half Asiatic, and bespangled all over with trinkets, petty jewellery, and bangles. Jack was one of those free-hearted fellows that always spend their money as soon as they get it, and I believe that most of what he received as a reward for his brave conduct was spent amongst his companions.

Early in February, we, with 100 men of the 50th Foot[4], were removed to Fort William, preparatory to proceeding up the country. On arrival, we were crammed into one of the dungeon-like rooms of the Fort, called 'Bomb-proof Barracks,' which being low, and in close proximity to the moat which surrounds the fort, are extremely unhealthy. The fort has nothing imposing in its external appearance, being rather low. However it is deemed very formidable, and if well manned would be able to resist a long and vigorous siege. There are three gateways, all circuitous and intricate, with flanking towers for cannonading the gateways and drawbridges. Seven years' provisions for 1,200 troops are always kept in the fort. A place so low and enclosed as this is, is ill-adapted for Europeans. Yet it invariably happens that regiments just arrived from the cool and refreshing gales of their own native country, are doomed to pass their fiery ordeal in this oven-like fort. That this is a dangerous mode of acclimatizing new comers, none can for a moment doubt; and that it is a serious sacrifice of human life – not to say of consequent loss to government – the quarterly returns of the mortality of each regiment but too truly testify. That it is necessary even in times of profound peace, to have a due proportion of European soldiers in a place of so much importance as Fort William, every one must admit; but, *as it is a necessary evil* which must be practised so long as the British have an eye to the safety of their empire in India, why should not those regiments whose allotted time in India was within one year of being completed, be moved down and quartered in the fort previous to embarkation for England? Hardly a year passes but a regiment leaves the country, so that generally *one* corps need remain but *one* season, and to them many advantages would be derived therefrom, seeing that they could there facilitate the necessary preparations for the approaching voyage. This method is sometimes adopted, but not so generally as is practicable. In 1849, the 75th[5] lost more than 100 men in about four months; they arrived in the country at the commencement of the hot season. When we were there the weather was becoming extremely hot, and in the fort oppressive and almost insupportable. That which rendered our situation worse, was an order strictly prohibiting us from leaving the fort. This order originated partly from fear of some of our men taking 'French leave,' as some have done, and partly from the misconduct of some men of the –th Foot, lying there at that time, who had so impudently broken the 8th Commandment, as to stop and rob an officer of their own regiment in broad daylight.

Unfortunately we were not invulnerable to the injurious effect of this incarceration; for that fearful disease the cholera, broke out among us, and soon made sad havoc in our ranks[6]. So fearfully prevalent did it become, that it was no singular thing for a man awaking in the morning to find that some half dozen of those who had retired to rest the previous night in health and strength, had been carried away to the Hospital during the night, some of whom, on enquiry, were already dead, or in the last stage of that fearful disease. In twenty-four hours after our arrival here, I was called on to follow to their graves some of my fellow comrades. On arriving at the Hospital, which is about a mile from the fort, a sad and mournful scene presented itself. The ward I entered was crowded with sick, and in the verandahs were lying those attacked with cholera. Some were writhing in the most intense agony, others in a state of insensibility and sullen apathy, their leaden and sunken eyes, with the varying dark hue of their flesh, but too palpably shewing that death was fast overtaking them. On entering the dead-house, five of my comrades, who but the day before were all life and animation, now lay side by side, their once familiar faces having in a few short hours become, through their intense sufferings, distorted and sunken so as hardly to be recognized. Then as we marched at a slow and measured pace – unaccompanied by fife or drum – to the repository of the dead, it seemed as if we were truly in the dark valley and shadow of death; for the native coffin-bearers, dressed in black, in unison with their whole appearance, seemed like the minions of Death transporting his victims to his greedy consort the grave. One poor fellow, Serjeant Willoughby[7], a man beloved by all his comrades, who was present on this sad occasion, was attacked with the disease the same night, died early the following morning, and was laid alongside of his comrades, whom he himself had followed in health, but twenty-four hours before. To us new comers who were unused to such sad and melancholy scenes, this was extremely dispiriting, and a general gloom seemed to pervade the fort. However, thank God, the authorities, after we had paid dearly for our quarters, at length awoke from their lethargy, and we were suddenly ordered to leave the fort, and proceed on board steamers. Accordingly, on the 24th March, we were released, and on the river inhaled, if not a salubrious, at least a refreshing air. It is worthy of remark that from the moment we left the fort, the cholera disappeared from us entirely.

The cold season was now far advanced; and as we were to proceed in fast-sailing flats, the danger of sickness was obviated. These are flat-bottomed iron vessels, which are well adapted to the shallow rivers of India, as they will sail in eight inches of water, and are towed by steam tugs. Having to pass through the Sundarbunds, the rivers of which are salt, from the many branches which communicate with the sea, we took in seven days supply of fresh water from the Hooghly.

We left Calcutta the morning after embarking, and the same night anchored in one of the many rivers which intersect the Sundarbunds, a practice which was followed throughout the voyage, as it was unsafe to travel by night, owing to the many sandbanks in the river. During the height of the tides, the greater part of the Sundarbunds, being low and flat, is covered with water. This vast aquatic forest was nowhere inhabited by human beings, but numerous water fowl, and forest birds of various species and plumage, seemed to delight in these wild haunts. Numerous animals also were denizens of the woods, whose howls and shrieks at night were far from harmonious. About the tenth day of our inland voyage, we were visited by a river storm, which endangered the safety of our vessels, and had well nigh cost us serious if not fatal injuries. It came on about 2 p.m., very suddenly, without any previous indication; consequently we were taken quite aback. However, no sooner did we feel it than all hands lent their aid to contribute to our safety. Anchors were cast, but the river having a sandy bottom, they obtained no permanent hold, and we for some time drifted down with the stream and wind, and eventually towards a high bank, which, from the action of the waves beating on the sub-soil, was perpetually falling in large masses, and threatening to overwhelm and sink us beneath them. However, we fortunately managed, by dint of much exertion, to avoid the impending danger. But while we providentially escaped, our attention was drawn to the opposite side of the river by shouts of 'Allah, Allah, Kudah,'

&c., seemingly approaching us. On looking in the direction from whence they proceeded, I saw a large Mirzapore cotton boat carried past the head of the creek with the rapidity of lightning. Its deck and roof were covered with the crew, and a few native passengers, who shrieked to us piteously for help as they flew past us. In a few minutes she gave a fearful reel, and at once the whole disappeared from our view, excepting the top of the mast, which was still seen hurrying on with the torrent, with a few helpless creatures clinging to the ropes, in all the agony and struggling terror of death. The buoyancy of the cargo, or probably the *choppah* of the boat, prevented it sinking altogether for a brief and awful moment. I felt a wish to aid, but it was unavailing, for the mast suddenly went down, and I could plainly perceive one poor wretch struggling on the bosom of the merciless waters; till he also, after a strong and despairing struggle, sunk within the waves, and disappeared. How the mind shrinks back into itself, and quails in horror, at witnessing, so nigh, the sudden, unprepared, consignment to eternity of a whole band of fellow-creatures.

These hurricanes, or typhoons, are of frequent occurrence along the Ganges, for about two hundred miles from the Sundarbunds, and at some seasons are most violent. They are justly dreaded by the native boatmen. Her Majesty's 62nd Foot,[8] while proceeding in a fleet of boats to Dinapore, in 1842, were surprised by one of them; when, unfortunately, two boats, with their crews, the regimental colours, and other property, were wrecked, and all but five men lost. No words can be too condemnatory of the injudicious practice of sending troops up the river in small boats; for, besides being overcrowded and pent up in small narrow spaces, the voyage is both long and tedious; while the men are exposed to a burning sun during the day, and dews and noxious vapours at night. My regiment, most unfortunately, paid dearly for this injudicious mode of travel to the upper provinces. In their passage up the river, in 1842, the cholera broke out amongst them, and in one short month they lost upwards of 150 men, women and children. From Monghye – where the disease showed its first symptoms – to Allahabad, sad momentos of the fearful mortality which fell to their lot may yet be traced. Many a *tope* and tree mark out the expatriated soldier's last retreat[9].

The river now began to assume a different aspect from what we had hitherto seen, and numerous huge alligators were basking in the sun at the water's edge. It abounds with fish, whilst wild geese, ducks, and snipes frequent the banks, offering plenty of amusement for the sportsmen. The natives have a very novel and shrewd method of catching them. They take a large *chatty*, knock a few holes through, and walking into the river with it over the head, float quietly down the stream. The birds, which are generally attracted to anything floating on the surface of the water, flock round it, when its occupant quietly draws them under the surface one after another until he has secured a handful, when he swims to shore, bags them, and again returns to his aquatic sport.

5

Upriver to Cawnpore

Our task is done, on Gunga's breast,
The sun is sinking into rest,
And, moored beneath the tamarind bough,
Our bark has found its harbour now.

Monghye, as one approaches it, presents an imposing appearance; and the *ghaut* offered a scene of bustle and vivacity which I by no means expected. There were so many *pulwars* and *budgerows*, that we had considerable difficulty to find a mooring for our own vessels; and as we approached the shore we were beset with a crowd of beggars, some wading up to their knees in their endeavours to be the first supplicants for our charity; and numerous artisans soon thronged our deck, displaying their various wares. This place is remarkable for its manufacture of guns, swords, pistols, &c., generally of a very neat description, but not always to be depended on. Having taken in a supply of wood and coals for the steamers, we again raised anchor, and about one o'clock were gliding up the stream. As we quitted Monghye, the Coruckpoor hills on the left hand continued to offer a very beautiful succession of prospects. A chain of marshy islets extended across the river, by the aid of which a large herd of buffaloes were crossing with their keepers. It was very novel and curious to see them swimming across this broad and deep stream. With their noses just raised out of the water, they swam almost as fast as a man would, and managed to keep well together, like a drove of cattle in a narrow lane, their drivers clinging to the tails of first one and then another, and beating the beasts with a bamboo stick.

The atmosphere this day had been extremely hot, and about two o'clock the hot wind began to blow with great fury. On each side of the river extended a vast tract of white sand, in which were particles like small scales of silver, producing in the glaring sunshine a most painful sensation to the eyes; the wind streaming over the surface of this was increased to an intense heat, causing a dry and prickly sensation in the skin. This was the setting in of the periodical hot winds, which we had to endure during the remainder of our passage, generally accompanied with clouds of dust and hot sand, which sometimes half suffocated us. We shortly afterwards passed Dinapore, and Gazeepore, two military stations, the latter of which is rendered interesting to an Englishman from the monument to Lord Cornwallis[1], who died here on his way up the country. It is a very conspicuous object from the river. It has a white dome, and is surrounded with beautiful evergreens, which gives it a striking appearance. Two days further sail brought us to the famed and holy city of Benares[2]. The sun had set as we approached it; the evening was serene, though hot, and night was just throwing her grey mantle around us. Through the grey twilight we could distinguish numerous mosques, domes, and tall minarets; while the distant hum of myriads of animated beings, intermingled with the sound of gongs, tom toms, and rams horns, and the Muzzein's call to prayer, were wafted on the water to us. These, together with the flickering of thousands of lights on the mirror-like stream, impressed upon my mind

Cawnpore. For many cavalry soldiers arriving by *budgerow*, this was the first glimpse of their home for the next year. The exotic nature of their surroundings in Bengal – people, houses, transport and wildlife – was a continuing source of fascination for many soldiers, who often compared the sights to scenes they had read of in the Bible. (Author's collection)

that we were in the vicinity of a vast city more purely Asiatic than any I had hitherto see; carrying me back to the tales I used to read in the 'Arabian Nights Entertainments.'

We anchored opposite a noble *ghaut,* and the next morning developed to us a truly magnificent and picturesque scene. The city is situated on a rising ground, and a sloping high bank leading from the river is beautifully studded everywhere with magnificent mosques and palaces. These are rendered extremely imposing by their tall and glittering minarets, domes and spires. The picturesque beauty of the scene was completed by numerous large and beautiful *ghauts* running down to the water's edge, with pretty little bathing-houses connected, which were now thronged by the natives of both sexes, performing their morning ablutions, and muttering certain incantations. This pleasing illusion, however, vanishes away on entering the city. Like all other Asiatic cities, the streets are narrow and filthy, and here thousands of sacred monkeys roam and hop about from house to house unmolested, while the mosques and streets are literally choked up with fakirs, beggars, and decrepid pilgrims, who come from all parts of India to die in the 'Sacred City.'

We next passed Chunar. Here a fortress stands high and very conspicuous; the rock on which it is placed is perfectly insulated, and either naturally or by art, bordered on every side by awful precipices, flanked wherever it has been possible to obtain a salient angle, with towers, bartizans, and bastions of various forms and sizes. There are a good many cannon mounted, and a noble bomb-proof magazine for powder. This fort has become very interesting in history; from containing as state prisoners, first, the celebrated Maharata chieftain Tuinbuckjee, long the inveterate enemy of the British power, and the fomenter of all the troubles in Berar, Mulwah, and the Deccan. And, latterly, of the consort of the famed

Runjeet Sing – the intriguing and licentious Ranee Chunder of Lahore, who was placed under British restraint in 1848, for her designs to subvert the British power in the Punjaub[3].

In the latter part of 1849, she effected her escape in a manner both artful and interesting in its details. Eastern princesses never expose their features to vulgar gaze; they would deem it the very height of indecency to permit any but their lords, and their maids, to view their faces, a custom, the breach of which would not only degrade them in the eyes of the higher classes of Asiatics, but would call down the fierce vengeance of an exasperated and jealous husband. For the same reason, when travelling they are not only closely veiled, but entirely concealed in a *palanquin,* or covered *howdah,* well enveloped in drapery. Such a sense have the Asiatics of this species of etiquette that the utmost deference is always paid to these conveyances on their route.

The European officer who accompanied the Ranee to the fort of Chunar, and who afterwards had charge of so fair and illustrious prisoner in the fort, did not violate so sacred a custom, and, although he had been necessarily within a few yards of her for months, had never seen anything more than her fair hand from the folds of the drapery of the *palanquin*. Hence it was that neither the officer nor any of the guard under him knew the form or features of their prisoner. The artful Ranee, availing herself of this advantage, one morning dressed herself in her waiting-maid's attire, while the maid assuming the Ranee's, took her place. In this guise the Ranee, with a small basket on her arm, as if going to the bazaar, as was the daily custom of the maid, quitted her room and passed the sentries, and soon was placed in a *palanquin* in waiting for her, by some of her partisans who were cognizant of the scheme. Before this mistake was discovered, the Ranee was far on her way to Nepaul, an independent state, where she safely arrived.

We reached Allahabad on 17th April, and anchored in the Jumna opposite the west side of the fort, where we remained until the following evening. During the day we were highly amused by a number of young urchins of both sexes, some totally naked, swimming, diving, and performing various antics in the water for our diversion, for which we threw them a few *pice*. At sunset we disembarked, and immediately proceeded to camp about two miles from the river.

Allahabad is an ancient Hindoo city, and, owing to its situation at the confluence of the Jumna and Ganges, is a place of resort for pilgrims from all parts of India. The sacred water is conveyed by Hindoos to some of the most distant parts of the country, where it is purchased at a high price by rich Brahmins and Rajahs, and is deemed most invaluable from its sanctifying qualities. From Allahabad to Cawnpore – ten days march – we had to 'pad the hoof.' We always marched in the night, so that we could get our canvas up before sunrise. The nights were hot and oppressive, and the hot winds blew with all their withering influence throughout the day, and were very trying to us who were just arrived from England, and the hospital *Dhoolies* were soon filled with sick. One morning it fell to my lot to be on baggage guard, when I was almost scorched and dried up like a herring. Of all animals in creation the draught buffalo is the most stubborn, and this day we could not get them to move out of their usual crawling pace, though every means to give them an impetus was resorted to. Hence it was near noon when we arrived in camp; and having been exposed to the sun's fierce rays for so many hours, I was almost consumed with fever, which, however, abated at sunset, but the skin peeled off my face just as it does off a new potato.

When we were within two marches of Cawnpore, we had a specimen of Indian 'devils,' or dust storm. It had been an extremely hot and sultry day – such a day as no one can

Barracks canteen, c. 1850. This scene is probably in England, but canteens in India were similar, with food on offer as well as local liquor and, for those who could afford it, imported English beer. (Author's collection)

conceive but those who have been in a tropical climate – when, about three o'clock p.m., the western horizon presented a dark and livid appearance, and the grumbling of distant thunder portended a storm. The darkness arose higher and began to expand itself over the western hemisphere; the lightnings became more vivid and quicker in succession, followed by peal after peal of thunder. Suddenly a dense mass of a brownish hue seemed to stretch from north to south, the very heavens and earth seeming to unite together. Onwards it came, sweeping over the plain like a mountain torrent, and in a moment we were enveloped in darkness, so intense that it could literally be *felt*. Never having heard of anything of this description, we were awe stricken; some prostrated themselves on the ground awaiting the result, while others strove to prevent their goods from being carried away by the storm. In its fury, tents, bedding, and everything not heavy enough to preserve its gravity, were tossed about at its mercy, and few tents remained standing when it had passed over us. Happily it was of short duration, and was succeeded by a heavy shower of rain which cooled the air.

We arrived at Cawnpore on the 27th April. Here my regiment was stationed, and we were distributed into different troops, and I became a G Trooper[4].

6

Life in the Regiment

Who can say, however fair his view,
Through what sad scene his path may lie?
Who can give to others' woes his sigh,
Secure his own will never need it too?

Arrived at my regiment, the first months of my novitiate passed in the usual routine of facing, fronting, marching, halting, wheeling, forming, quick, slow, and double quick, with a variety of other innocent and diverting recreations, more pleasing in the detail than the performance. To this succeeded a truly delightful course of 'equestrian studies,' unusually denominated 'rough riding,' which is, riding without stirrups, no easy matter for a recruit; agreeably diversified with the broad sword and lance exercise, forming altogether a most charming and engaging variety, heightened by the excessive heat of the season[1]. During my equestrian probation I experienced many ups and downs, at the expense of wounds, bruises, and aching bones, for it was my lot to have a horse appointed to me that was fonder of the stables than the menage, and knowing, from my inexperienced hands and legs when mounted on him, that he had got a 'joskin' on his back, he frequently galloped away with me towards the stables. 'Use,' they say, 'is second nature,' and I soon got so used to falling that I thought it little more than diversion; however I was determined to get the master of my runaway little steed, for, but for this fault, he was a fine little fellow. So, after about two month's practice, having become a pretty good rider, I resolved on my plan; and one morning, at the word 'trot,' I permitted him to gallop away as he had done before, but instead of allowing him to go towards the lines, I directed him across the open plain, where I should have, what sailors term, 'plenty of sea room.' I permitted him to gallop for his own diversion until he began to slacken his pace, and now thinks I for my turn, so bending him to the left I formed a circle, and spurred him round and round until he was fairly exhausted and he gave in. This had the desired effect, for he never ran away with me afterwards; but a recruit took him one morning, about two years afterwards, when I was sick, and he served him as he had done with me before.

Cawnpore is justly deemed the hottest station in India – so fearfully hot that it has given rise to the following profane question among soldiers when suffering from it: - 'If God made hell, why did he make Cawnpore?' meaning thereby that Cawnpore was as hot as that awful place, and, I suppose they thought that one place was sufficient. From the latter end of March, until late in June, the hot winds blow in all their fury, commencing with the rising sun and increasing throughout the day, and subsiding with the setting sun.

Tattees, wicker frames with *Cuscus* grass drawn through them, are placed in the doorways at the windward side, and when a strong wind is blowing, if they are kept well wet, they produce a current of air five or six degrees cooler than the prevailing wind outside. But, tempered though it is by these artificial means, it is still excessively hot, and that, combined with myriads of obnoxious insects, renders it impossible to obtain a moment's peace, unless in a state of unconscious drunkenness.

The wind dying away at night leaves the air oppressively hot and suffocating; while, to add to this, you have prickly heat tickling and smarting all over your body, with thousands of bugs, mosquitoes, sand flies, and even centipedes, which fall from the thatched roofs, and form a combination of evils rendering life almost insupportable. To obviate these evils in some degree, many will resort to lying outside in the open air, often in a state of nudity. Indeed, during the hot nights, few men lie in the barracks, and the ground outside resembles a battle field strewed with the dead. Some will even have a skin of water thrown over them, and lie throughout the night in the pool; while others lie immersed in the horses' drinking troughs; in short every means which could neutralize the heat. None but those who have experienced such nights, can form any idea of the miserable manner in which they are dragged through. Many a long and painful night the soldier suffers in India, without having one hour's sound repose; and when at gunfire in the morning he rises, he is parched, feverish, and spiritless, and has hardly animation enough left to crawl over to his stables; and it is no uncommon thing at this season to see men fall down in the ranks, as if dead, from sheer weakness.

One evening, about two months after joining the regiment, myself and a chum were sitting on a step of our barrack, when we were suddenly startled by the report of a pistol, which sounded as from the rear. Hastening over to the spot, an awful spectacle presented itself to us. In one corner of the building, with his head leaning against the wall, and a pistol firmly grasped in his right hand, lay a poor fellow of the name of Sloane. He was quite dead, having placed the pistol in his mouth and discharged its contents into his head; his face was frightfully torn and disfigured.

Sloane was a remarkably clean and good soldier, and on this day he had mounted orderly duty; a parade on which a man must, in the 9th Lancers, appear exceedingly bright, and perfect in all his accoutrements. On this occasion Sloane had been at more than ordinary pains in burnishing, polishing, &c., and when he was mounted he appeared faultless. But the Argus eyes of his inspectors detected *one fault*. He was minus one button from the cuff of his jacket, and for this trivial fault he was ordered to 'Turn out again." Sloane was one of those soldiers who pride themselves in the appellation of being a clean and smart soldier; this was the first time he had ever been ordered to "Turn out again,' which he felt a disgrace, and it touched his pride to the quick. When he returned to his barrack room he broke out in the most violent fit of passion, cursing the adjutant, saying, that 'He had ordered him to turn out again, but he'd never go.' How truly this promise was kept the reader has seen. It subsequently appeared that he had loaded his pistol with two buttons from the cuff of his jacket; thus, taking his life with the unconscious cause of his trouble[2].

This season was very trying; fever, bowel complaints, and apoplexy made sad havoc amongst us; and in less than six months from our arrival at the regiment, upwards of twenty of those who joined had died. In the rainy season (from June to September), I was attacked with fever and ague, which made me an inmate of the hospital for two months. During that time I witnessed the last death-struggle of many a fine fellow. One I remember died in a most horrible state; he was brought to the hospital about ten o'clock in the morning, suffering with the cholera, but that dire disease was partially cured in a few hours, only to be followed, however, by one as terrible in its effects – Asiatic apoplexy. As his sufferings increased, his curses, prayers, and imprecations, were truly awful. He died about three o'clock in the morning, cursing God with his last breath, for so punishing him. How one shudders at the bare recital of a fellow creature being summoned before the Great Judge, with blasphemy on his lips; how much more awful was it to me, who heard it on a bed of sickness. Even now, while writing, the awful curses seem to ring in my ears.

While the regiment was in Cawnpore, the men drank excessively; indeed, I dare assert that no other regiment in India consumed so much 'blue ruin' as the 9th Lancers did at this time. Some of the causes which tend to this general evil in India are obvious to any reflecting person. A soldier comes to India full of vivacity and youthful spirit, and perhaps big with expectation of seeing plenty of 'life.' No sooner, however, does the interest and excitement, incident to his passage out, and his march up the country, subside, than he begins to look round for the pleasures and amusements he has been accustomed to, but in vain. He has probably been used to change and social company, but here his life is one of indolence and monotony.

In the hot season he is pent up in an oven-like barrack or shed, grilling and boiling from seven o'clock in the morning until six in the evening. It is true there are libraries to every regiment in India[3], but all are not readers, and even to the lover of literature, reading becomes irksome from the perpetual annoyance of flies and dust. In the evening, he goes to the stables, and when that duty is performed he returns to his cheerless domicile. The attractions of the country are no inducement for him to take a recreative walk, and if they were so, he has neither the strength nor the spirit to do so. If he is a man of reflection, he looks back with regret on the easy happy hours he has spent in days gone by, and longs again to make one of the circle he has left. And if he tries to look through futurity, all seems dour and uncertain. He knows he has to drag through perhaps twenty hot and withering seasons, ere he dare *hope* to return to his native land, and the chances of climate and war are so much against him, that his *hope* becomes very vague indeed; and should he be so fortunate as to escape the thousand and one dangers, and finally return to the home of his youth, he returns but a shadow of his former self, to find friends changed and gone, and the home he left perhaps in the possession of strangers.

Thus reflecting, home seems lost to him for ever, and seeing his comrades going to the canteen, he follows the stream, and in his libations seeks to drown all thought and reflection, and thus lays the foundation of habitual drunkenness, and too often it is the first step of many to a premature grave. I remember in the hot season of 1845, one of our men, with two artillery men, were drinking together down the bazaars, where they got a liquor termed 'fire ball.' Having become thoroughly drunk, they left the place and staggered about the roads until they became totally 'upset' from the heat of the sun, and they foolishly laid down on the side of the road to sleep. Two of them slept their last; they were brought to the lines in the afternoon, scorched, blistered, and dead; and the third, though he reached his barracks about noon, was attacked with a severe fever, which had well nigh carried him to his grave also. That habits inimical to the health and morals of the British soldier prevail to a more alarming extent in India than in any other of our military stations, whether at home or abroad, is a fact that will not admit of dispute, although there are many opinions as to the causes to which it is to be attributed[4]. Equal, if not superior, in physical organization to the troops of almost every other country, it has often been demanded why the soldiery of Great Britain stand so much lower in the social scale. The answer is a simple one – because the whole scope and tendency of military legislation is calculated to degrade the soldier in his own estimation, and to leave his moral feelings no room for play. He is regarded as a mere animal, endowed only with brute instincts, and the consciousness of

"Our Moonshee." A satirical depiction of British life in India, from George Atkinson's *Curry and Rice (on Forty Plates)* published in 1853. The *moonshee* was a language teacher, but the officer seems more interested in the bottle being opened by one of his other servants. Note the *punkah* overhead to provide a cooling draught. (Author's collection)

this humiliating fact lowers many a highly-gifted and sensitive mind to the common level. Once a man's moral responsibility is destroyed, it cannot be expected that he will become either a good soldier, or a useful citizen. The motives that incite other men to exertion, and the feelings of self-respect which prevents them from yielding to temptation, are wanting in his case. Penal regulations and restrictions greet the unfortunate tyro on every side, and the few indulgences that his hard lot admits of, are watched and curtailed at the pleasure or caprice of his superiors. Is it to be wondered at then, that he should feel a sort of savage gratification at breaking through restraints which those in authority do not impose on their own conduct, and which savour of unnecessary despotism. Hatred of oppression seems a principle implanted in our nature, and to this impulse, rather than to any real passion for the vice prohibited, may be traced much of military crime.

Amongst the great variety of characters that a regiment includes, there are always some to be found of a stamp superior to the rest – some who have, perhaps, been forced into their present circumstances by the pressure of unavoidable misfortunes, the faults of others, or indiscretions of their own. Many I have known whose high talents and gentlemanly manners have not prevented them from falling into the depths of infamy and vice, whose consciousness of their own abilities has only added a double bitterness to their already humiliated condition, and whose superior acquirements, when joined to low and depraved habits, have only rendered them more odious and contemptible to their comrades. Amongst such a medley, a man may obtain companions enough, but the contented and cheerful spirits that make up the pleasant circle of an English fire side, form no feature of Indian life.

"Our Theatricals". Another of Atkinson's well-observed scenes of garrison life; all the parts are played by men. The Sixteenth Lancers had a particularly renowned theatre troupe. (Author's collection)

No sooner had the penetrating Sir Charles Napier[5] arrived in India, than he became sensibly awake to the degrading evil in question, and he at once took immediate steps to suppress it. An order was promulgated limiting each soldier 'to two drams per diem, to be issued one dram at noon and the other at night;' thus striking at the very base of intoxication by depriving the toper of his morning libations. I need not say that it has rendered Sir Charles extremely odious amongst the old topers, his very name sounding like a death knell to their only pleasures and indulgences. It yet remains to be seen how far the end in view may be obtained.

In December, 1844, two men of my troop disappeared in a somewhat mysterious manner. At first it was supposed that, as they had gone out in the country for a day's shooting and had not returned, they had been murdered by the natives; but circumstances were subsequently elicited which left no doubt but they had deserted. It was discovered that they had for some time been in the habit of attending a native writer, who initiated them into the Persian and Hindoo languages, and also a geographical knowledge of the country, with a route overland to Europe. To enable themselves to get clear from the cantonments, they had obtained leave for the day, for the ostensible purpose of shooting, but in reality for *racing*, for they were last seen going at a rapid pace on an elephant in a northerly direction, towards the Punjaub[6]. Theirs was a bold and dangerous enterprize, in the face of the thousand unseen dangers and difficulties which India presents. Strange to say no correct account had been obtained, at the time I left the regiment, as to their fate. It was rumoured that they had taken service at Lahore, and some of our men went so far as to say that they saw them leading the Sikh cavalry at Chillianwallah, but in the absence of better proof this was doubtful.

Another man deserted, and succeeded in getting home, in the following artful and daring manner. He told his comrades that he would go and bathe in the Ganges, and left the barracks before breakfast one Sunday morning. In the course of the forenoon his clothes were brought in to the regiment by some natives, and it was of course concluded that he was drowned. However in about twelve months afterwards, his 'chum' was surprised with a letter from his defunct comrade, who had safely arrived in England[7].

About this time, strong rumours of war became rife amongst us, and from the aspect of affairs at Lahore it seemed no idle hypothesis. Visions of honour and glory, change and excitement, prize-money and medals, silver bungalows, &c., began to float across each man's mind, and many a young aspirant already fancied his breast decorated. Few but rejoiced in the prospect of a relief from the dull monotony of barrack-room life, to the change and excitement of a campaign. At this time we had nearly one half of the regiment in hospital; but for those who were able, 'marching order' was the order of the day, and we were soon in all the stir and bustle consequent on preparations for a campaign.

7

The Sutlej Campaign

And there was mounting in hot haste: the steed,
The mustering squadron, and the clattering car,
Went pouring forward with impetuous speed,
And swiftly forming in the ranks of war.

We quitted Cawnpore, for ever, on the 16th October 1845, en route to Meerut, where we arrived about the middle of November. We proceeded at once to encamp on the plain to the northward of the station. The 16th Lancers[1] were cantoned here, and immediately we arrived on the ground, a number of cheerful faces awaited us, and, having provided an excellent breakfast for us, a deputation from each troop invited the troops of the same name to join them at breakfast. But, as if to insult the 16th, our commanding officer[2], in a despotic manner, would not permit 'one of the 9th Lancers to quit his camp.' This order, so unnecessarily tyrannous, had quite an opposite effect; for the men, with few exceptions, broke through all restraint and went and had breakfast with the 16th Lancers. This brought on a deal of trouble in our regiment, for all who absented themselves were punished on their return; but the old martinet who exercised such unwarrantable severity, has long ceased to tyrannize over his fellow-beings.

We had remained in camp here about a week, when, from the reports coming from Lahore, it was evident that a collision betwixt the British and Sikh troops was fast hastening to a crisis. The turbulent Sikh soldiery, long familiar with rapine and bloodshed, and lately victorious against all the petty states around them, became unruly and desirous of war. Numerous, well equipped, elated by a long tide of victories, and stimulated by the love of plunder, they might well long to measure their strength with British troops, against whom they had long covertly retained both jealousy and hatred.

That our authorities had long anticipated such a result, may be inferred from the unusually large quantities of provisions and military stores which had been quietly accumulating during the last two or three years, and from the general movement of regiments towards the frontier.

Up to December, however, all was uncertainty, but early in that month the news ran across Hindostan that the Sikhs had actually crossed the Sutlej, and threatened the destruction of our frontier fort Ferozepore. Lord Gough[3] was, I believe, at Umballa (about 15 days' march from Ferozepore) when this important news reached him. He at once concentrated as many battalions as could be got together in reasonable time, and with about 18,000 men, and a great disproportion of artillery, he advanced towards Ferozepore. After long and forced marches he came up with the Sikhs on the 18th. They were encamped in a strong position of breastworks, abattis, entrenchments, &c., near to a village called Ferozeshah. Our army had taken up ground for encampment near a village called Mudki, about four miles from Ferozeshah. The Sikhs, determined not to allow our troops breathing time, came out of their entrenchments in force and attacked our troops, even while they were pitching camp. The battle commenced about four o'clock, and continued with the greatest fury until dark, when our troops, worn out, their ranks terribly thinned, and the artillery without ammunition, bivouacked on the field, awaiting the morning for a renewal of the fight.[4] The enemy kept up a continuous fire on them during the night, but on the morrow they retired into their entrenchments. Lord Gough was reinforced on the 19th and 20th, and on the 21st he renewed the fight, this time being the assailant. Night again put an end to the strife, and again our troops bivouacked on the plain, but this time out of reach of cannon. Another battalion arrived during the night, and on the morning of the 22nd, the British, now about 22,000 strong, made a vigorous attack; the Sikhs gave way, became panic stricken, and fled, leaving a portion of their camp and military stores, and 62 guns to the captors.[5]

To return. My regiment, with two *sepoy* corps and a heavy battery, marched from Meerut immediately on the receipt of general orders. Our first march was to Sirdhana, a town rendered interesting both on account of the Begum Sumroo, who once resided there, and for a beautiful little Catholic Chapel which she erected. There are yet several good and neat Bungalows in Sirdhana, once the residence of the Begum's officers and other followers. To the south-west of the town is a large burial ground, whose storied obelisks, tombs, &c., shew that Italians, French, and English (indeed where will you not find John Bull's offspring), were once her votaries. She has long since gone to rest; her remains lie in the chapel, but she still lives in British Indian history. She is represented as a woman of extraordinary abilities, duplicity, and finesse; and a perfect Amazonian; for when the British army were marching to Bhurtpore, in 1825, she offered to join her troops, led by herself, with the British. She had four husbands during her lifetime, all of them foreigners, from the last of whom she took the name of Sumroo. The manner in which she got rid of her second husband is worthy of notice, as manifesting her character, and shewing that a change of religion from Hindooism to Catholicism had effected no change in her Asiatic nature. Having set her desires on a young and handsome Italian, she informed her husband that she had been told of a conspiracy against her life, and that nothing but flight could save her; accordingly they quitted the palace at night in separate *palanquins*. It appears he was passionately fond of the Begum, and swore to save her, or perish in the attempt. They had not proceeded far, however, when his ears were arrested by the shrieks and screams of his consort; and running from his *palanquin* to her rescue, three men rushed at him with swords, and he fell a victim to her diabolical treachery.

On the 17th, we encamped on the plains of Kurnaul, formerly a British cantonment, but since abandoned from its being extremely unhealthy. On the 21st our march lay through a low and monotonous jungle, but about ten o'clock, this was relieved by a number of glittering domes, and minarets, peeping over the tops of the trees in the distance, and we passed through the streets of the town of Peshwa, and encamped on the northern side of it. This place was filled with Brahmins and Hindoo devotees, and numbers of sacred monkeys frisk and play about the tops of the religious edifices. During the day I witnessed a painful scene, and one which I believe is of frequent occurrence at this place, as it is a general resort for pilgrims to do penance under the superintendence of the Brahminical priests, who reside here in great numbers. Suspended by the heels from the arm of a tree was an Hindoo, while beneath him a slow fire was burning, about two yards from which was a heap of small shells. He was made to oscillate to and fro, like a pendulum, over this slow fire, and to pick up these shells one by one and drop them into a vessel placed about two yards on the other side of the fire. His shaven head occasionally brushing the hot embers as he oscillated over them. How long he would be able to bear such punishment I know not, but most probably he had to complete the removal of the shells before he had appeased his god. During this cruel operation, three Fakirs sat looking on and smoking their *hookahs* with the greatest indifference.

Towards evening we heard a distant rolling of musketry and cannon, and many were the conjectures as to where they proceeded from. It subsequently transpired that this was the exact time that the action of Ferozeshah commenced, and the sound was conveyed over a distance of about 80 miles.

On the 23rd, our march lay over a large tract of loose sand, in which two heavy guns sunk up to the axles, and we had great difficulty in extracting them. This evening, about seven o'clock, the camp was thrown into some excitement by the report of firearms; the cause, however, was soon ascertained, for it was discovered that a man named Driscol, had shot himself. He was discovered by the side of his tent, quite dead, with his discharged pistol firmly grasped in his hand. Driscol had been drinking throughout the day, and had disposed of some of his clothing to supply him with drink. No other reason for this rash act can be assigned, than that he feared the punishment consequent on the detection of the crime of making away with his 'regimental necessaries.'[6] On the 30th, at the second halt, a despatch met us, and immediately there were whisperings that we were approximating towards an enemy. The advance guard was now augmented, and in battle order we resumed our march. We had proceeded about four miles, when we approached a village and a well constructed mud fort. We drew up under it and prepared for cannonading, when it was ascertained that no enemy was in it, so we immediately took possession. It appeared that about 500 Sikhs had been thrown into this fort to cut off our supplies as they were draughted up to the army; however on our approach they wisely beat a retreat.

On the 5th of January, 1846, we marched to Mudki, and encamped near the village of that name. Everything here presented an awful aspect of havoc and devastation. The evils of relentless war were depicted in the whole scene around us. The village was partially destroyed, and deserted by all except a few old and decrepid men and women, and troops of *pariah* dogs, which had become bloated and fattened on the bodies of the dead on the field. Immediately in front of our camp was a thick cluster of fresh mounds and hillocks, the wholesale graves of the fallen in battle. The field of Mudki was studded with scattered jungle, which had served the enemy the double purpose of concealing them and breaking our ranks. Numbers of dried, blackened, and shrivelled bodies, both of men and cattle, lay strewed over the plain. The field of Ferozeshah is about three miles from the village of Mudki, and from the latter place they were strewed all the way; but on reaching the entrenchments which had surrounded the Sikh camp, a more melancholy spectacle presented itself, and told of the fierce struggle that had been made. In many places the trenches were literally filled with arms, legs, and bodies; side by side, and pile on pile, Briton and Sikh were mingled together; their arms, which had been raised in battle against each other, were now powerless and shrivelled. Numbers of broken gun-carriages, limbers, military belts, dress caps, epaulettes, broken swords, and firelocks, were strewed confusedly over the field, while whole strings of gun traces, with horses, lay just as they fell.

At four o'clock a.m., on the 6th, we marched to join Sir Hugh's force, and arrived at the commander-in-chief's camp about three o'clock, where we were met, cheered and animated by the gallant fellows we had come to join.

Anxious to hear how the freaks of war had dealt with some of my old comrades and friends of the 50th, and 3rd Light Dragoons, I hastened to their camps, but out of thirty-five shipmates of the 3rd Dragoons, but twelve were left; and out of five *townees* of the 50th, who I often used to meet in Cawnpore, and talk of home, friends, and bygone days, only one was left[7].

On the 12th, the whole army was put in motion, and advanced in a parallel with the Sutlej, but about three miles from the stream. Having marched about twelve miles, the camp was pitched in battle order, opposite to, and fronting the village of Sobraon, forming one continuous line of about four miles, and presenting an imposing and formidable appearance.

On the 13th, just as we were about to dine, we were interrupted by an aide-de-camp galloping furiously along the line. In a moment, 'turn out' resounded on every side, the camp was in a strange state of excitement, and, in less time than it takes me to write this, long lines of infantry, and squadrons of cavalry were drawn up in front of their several camps. Presently each battalion joined its brigade, and the whole forming a compact line, flanked by cavalry, advanced to the front, throwing out skirmishers. For some time, the cause of this sudden movement was unexplained; however, we were not left long to conjecture, for having advanced about two miles, we could perceive the enemy crossing a ford from this to the other side of the river. Their presence on this side seemed to threaten an attack on our camp, hence this sudden move. As we debouched over a rising ground, the whole of the Sikh camp suddenly developed itself to us on the opposite side of the river. Myriads of tents of various shapes and colours extended along the sandy bed of the river, almost as far as the eye could reach from right to left; while, drawn up in front to defend this fairy-like city were the turbaned and long-bearded Sikhs, the whole presenting a strikingly picturesque scene. As we approached the river the enemy opened a desultory fire on us, and as we still neared them, gun after gun belched forth its angry missiles, until the whole opposite bank seemed one continuous line of smoke and fire. For some time our batteries made no reply, but at length, the Sikhs having developed their batteries, a few guns opened, which, pitching some shot and shell with precision into their ranks, showed them that British powder and shot were not to be so foolishly expended as theirs.

In this manner, night closed around us, and we returned to camp and to our dinners, which we had left in the camp kettles, having done nothing further than finding out the position and batteries of the enemy. The next day we were again diverting ourselves in the same manner with similar results. From this day, until the 19th, nothing important occurred, but on that day some battalions of the enemy crossed the river and attacked our pickets; my regiment galloped out to their support, and the long bearded visitors beat a retreat.

On the 20th, the 16th Lancers, the Body Guard[8], and four battalions of infantry were detached to reinforce a division which was marching up to join us, having the siege train and some stores with them, the Commander-in-Chief having received information of a strong division of the enemy being on the march to our right for the purpose of intercepting and capturing these most important and valuable materials.

The readers of these interesting times will remember that this little band encountered about 20,000 Sikhs, near to a village called Budiwal; and, being but few in numbers, they retreated towards Loodiana, a British fort. The hardships and sufferings of this unfortunate detachment were very great; they lost a great proportion of their baggage, and many of them their bedding and all belonging to them; but the most painful of their misfortunes was the cruel and inhuman butchery of the sick and wounded, who, being abandoned by the timid *dhooly* bearers, were left to the vengeance of the vindictive Sikhs. After a long and painful march, they formed a junction with the division I have spoken of, and under their able and gallant leader, Sir Harry Smith, they returned with renewed vigour to chastise their recent spoilers. Full of conceit and pride at having thus gained some advantages over a handful of British soldiers, the Sikhs, in fancied security, were encamped on a level plain at Aliwal. A battle ensued, in which the true character of British valour and discipline were shown, and the lance – a weapon which before had not been so well tested by British troops – was established as the finest weapon ever used in British cavalry[9]. The brilliant and overwhelming charge of the 16th Lancers – which absolutely swept down squares of Sikh infantry – is well known. The enemy were driven from every position, and finally took to flight across the river, abandoning many guns and other munitions of war.[10]

To return to the main army opposite Sobraon. My regiment changed position to the extreme right for outpost duty, the river here being fordable. Opposite to us the enemy had posted a picket of about 5,000 men, thus we were confronting each other. In the midst of the cluster of tents opposite us, was one more conspicuous than the rest, from being of a brilliant crimson. This was the field tent of Lalla Sing, since so notorious in Sikh history from his connexion and secret intriguing with the Ranee Chunder, the dowager queen of Runjeet Sing.

On the 21st of January, my troop was on outpost duty, and as soon as darkness set in, a party of twenty men was sent to the river to sink some boats which the enemy had used to come over in and annoy our pickets at night. The work of destruction was silently and effectually executed without any opposition.

On the 23rd, we were again suddenly turned out, about dinner time; we all wondered 'what was up,' and the only elucidation we could receive was from dense clouds of dust and the manoeuvring of the Sikh troops opposite.

On the 24th, my squadron was appointed for reconnoitring, and accordingly we advanced in front of the British line until we approached the river, where we had a fine view of the Sikh camp, which seemed to have been thrown back considerably since the long ball affairs of the 13th and 14th insts. Having approached the verge of the river we dismounted, whilst our officer took observations with a telescope. While all eyes were stretched towards that camp which was destined to fall into our hands, a troop of *Goorchuras* suddenly emerged from some brushwood, but a short distance from us, and commenced firing away at us most unmercifully. In a moment we were mounted and advanced in a line to chastise them, but after firing a volley almost harmlessly at us they fled. Advancing a little further, a scene presented itself resembling a newly turned up ant hill. Some thousands of Sikhs and Coolies were busy throwing up breastworks, epaulments, fascines, &c., on this side of the river, and the cavalry, who had been so liberal with their bullets, just before, were there to protect them. This position was destined to become the scene of that fearful and bloody struggle, the Battle of Sobraon, which paved us a way to Lahore.

Our chief doubtless thought that it would be easier to strike a decisive blow on this side the river than to force a passage across into the Punjaub, hence the enemy were permitted undisturbed to complete their field works. However, jealous of their propensity to encroach, a redoubt and an intrenched outpost were constructed intermediate of the two camps, which, with their menacing and formidable appearance, seemed to say, 'Thus far shalt thou go, and no farther.'

The Sikhs, however, to show their dislike to them kept up a perpetual fire, sometimes perforating the tents like riddles, and rendering them anything but comfortable quarters. This species of annoyance was a source of continued trouble to the cavalry; 'turn out' being perpetually ringing in our ears, disturbing us both of our meals and our rest, and was rendered the more vexing from their result; for our long bearded neighbours invariably scampered off on our approach.

It would be tedious to the reader were I to carry him along with us in our operations, and detail all our turns out, alarms, skirmishes, &c., during a month's proximity to our active enemy. Suffice it to say that we were by no means idle, and of course the ordinary share of hardships and privations fell to our lot. There is, nevertheless, as Capt. Franklin justly observed in his travels[11], nothing that leaves so slight an impression on the memory as bodily pain. It is well it is so; for were it otherwise, life, in some circumstances, would be scarcely endurable. This applies more particularly to campaigning; for no sooner do you find yourself again in comfortable quarters than all your hardships and privations are forgotten, or at least so buried in the memory as not to be easily raked up.

8

The Battle of Sobraon

By heaven it is a glorious sight to see,
For those who have no friend, no brother there.
Siege of Corinth.

Now comes the 'tug of war.' The British army was now concentrated, and numbered 45,000 of all arms; the enemy were computed at 65,000.

All necessary dispositions being made, the 10th February was appointed for a great battle. Accordingly at 9 o'clock in the evening of the 9th, orders were issued to each battalion to fall in the next morning in front of the camp, without sound of trumpet or drum, each battalion to proceed as silently as possible to the ground assigned to it, and there await further orders.

The eve of battle! What solemn recollections do the words awake, while memory wafts me back to that most eventful scene, as I once beheld it on a distant land. Again I fancy I see my messmates looking to their arms, or formed in a group round the dim light of the tent fire, discussing the all important subject, and offering their different opinions as to the intended plan of attack, the positions assigned to different corps, and wondering what work was laid out for themselves. Few, however, seemed to give a serious thought that ere tomorrow's sun had set they might be numbered with the slain, or if such there were, they kept it a secret in their own breasts. Instances of secret forebodings of death, however, evince themselves in individuals, either in silent sadness, or that which is seldom indeed – as it would be deemed tantamount to cowardice – open confession. It is really astonishing with what indifference the approaching contest is beheld by the generality of those who are to take an active part therein; it would seem, at the moment, as though it were nothing more than one of those every day events of common place routine; a march, parade, resting in camp, a field day, or battle, it is all alike to soldiers; I mean those who are regularly and *bona fide* soldiers – who, without spending a moment's thought upon the subject, evidently betray much more anxiety as to when, or where, the commissary is to shew his face, or as to the quantity or quality of the grog.

At 3 o'clock on the eventful 10th, we were noiselessly aroused from our sleep, and ordered at once to tie up our beds, dress, and saddle. At half-past 3 our daily bread and a dram of grog were served to us. At 4 each battalion was drawn up in front of the camp, their dark outline topped with forests of glittering arms, presenting a striking scene in the moonlight. The morning was clear and light from the moon, then but a day on the wane, and the air was sharp and frosty. Nothing could be heard save the 'right, centre, left,' and so on, in an under tone, of our ranks. The ranks of my regiment being formed, we were put in motion, and marched along the front of the camp towards the right, then, in column of troops, we wheeled half left, and moved off in an oblique direction towards the river. We soon came up with a division of infantry, formed a junction with them, and again moved on until we came within a short distance of the river; the whole then formed line to the left, and in this order we awaited the break of day to develop the enemy's position. The whole of the army, in brigades, had acted in a similar manner, and long before day-break every corps and battery had taken up its position, and this was executed so noiselessly, that not a single shot was fired from the Sikh outposts. While we were thus anxiously awaiting day-break, I will attempt briefly to describe the nature and locality of the scene of the approaching struggle. The bed of the river, to the extent of three or four hundred yards from the stream, was at this time dry and sandy, then a perpendicular bank abruptly rose to an undulating plain, intersected with both dry and wet *nullahs*, and covered – except here and there where the peasant has cultivated small patches – with long elephant grass and stunted underwood. The Sikhs were entrenched in a position forming a crescent, with the extreme points resting on the river, the whole covering an area of about four English miles. To attack this position, the British troops were so disposed as to form a large semi-circle with the points at about 1,500 yards distance.

As the first grey tints of the morning tinged the East with a golden hue, a light vapoury mist rose from the river, and, spreading itself like a thin cloud over the plain, rendered distant objects invisible. However, a slight breeze from the East soon sprung up, the mist rolled away from before us, and the Sikh camp was all at once developed to us, its many coloured tents presenting a magnificent appearance in the morning sun. The next moment a flash issued from our centre, the welkin rang with a thundering report, and a 24 pounder was performing a *reveille* in the Sikh camp. It was evident that until this moment they were not acquainted with our proximity, for a most confused din of trumpets, gongs, and tom toms, all at once issued from their camp, and full five minutes elapsed ere they returned a shot; but soon a terrible fire of shot, shell, and rockets was opened on both sides. I now quote some passages from the Commander-in-Chief's despatches,

> But it was half-past six before the whole of our artillery fire was developed. It was most spirited and well-directed. I cannot speak in terms too high of the judicious disposition of the guns, their admirable practice, or the activity with which the cannonade was sustained. But, notwithstanding the formidable calibre of our cannon, mortars, and howitzers, and the admirable way in which they were served, and aided by a rocket battery, it would have been visionary to expect they could, within any reasonable time, silence the fire of seventy pieces behind well constructed batteries of earth, planks, and fascines, or dislodge troops covered by redoubts or epaulments, or within a treble line of trenches. The effect of the cannonade was, as has been since proved by an inspection of the camp, most severely felt by the enemy; but it soon became evident that the issue of this struggle must be brought to the arbitrament of musketry and bayonets. The Infantry, except the reserve, were then ordered to advance, covered by artillery, which kept taking up successive positions as the Infantry advanced, and firing over their heads into the Sikh entrenchments.

> As these attacks of the centre and right commenced, the fire of our heavy guns had first to be directed to the right, and then gradually to cease; but at one time the thunder of full 120 pieces of ordnance reverberated in this mighty combat though the valley of the Sutlej; and as it was soon seen that the weight of the whole force within the Sikh camp was likely to be thrown upon the two brigades which had passed its trenches, it became necessary to convert into close and serious attacks the demonstrations with skirmishers and artillery of

the centre and right. The Sikhs, even when at particular points their trenches were mastered with the bayonet, strove to regain them by the fiercest conflict, sword in hand. But it was not until the full weight of three divisions of infantry, with every field gun which could be sent to their aid, had been cast into the scale, that victory finally declared for the British. The fire of the Sikhs first slackened and ceased, and the victors then pressing them on every side, precipitated them in masses into the Sutlej, which a sudden rise of seven inches had rendered hardly fordable. In their efforts to reach the right bank through the deepened water, they suffered from our horse artillery a dreadful carnage. Hundreds fell under this cannonade; hundreds upon hundreds were drowned in attempting this perilous passage.

> *Deep groaned the water with the dying sound!*
> *Repeated wounds the red'ning river dyed,*
> *And the warm purple circled on the tide.*

Their awful slaughter, confusion, and dismay, were such as would have excited compassion in the hearts of their generous conquerors, if the Kalsa troops had not, in the earlier part of the action, sullied their gallantry by slaughtering and barbarously mangling every wounded soldier, whom, in the vicissitudes of attack, the fortunes of war had left at their mercy. I must pause in this narrative especially to notice the determined hardihood and bravery with which our two battalions of Goorkhas[1] met the Sikhs wherever they were opposed to them. Soldiers of small stature, but indomitable spirit, they vied in ardent courage in the charge with the grenadiers[2] of our own nation, and, armed with the short weapon of their own mountains, were a terror to the Sikhs throughout this great combat.

I now return to my own narrative, and to the proceedings of the right flank. During the heavy cannonading above described, a light field battery was moved up to the verge of the bank before described, to silence, if possible, several two and three gun batteries, which the Sikhs had posted on the opposite side of the river to enfilade the right flank of our army. A portion of my regiment was detached to cover the guns, and after about an hour's admirable firing, the Sikh batteries were effectually silenced. The whole of the right division then moved up to the front. About 10 o'clock the reserve infantry on the right, consisting of the 50th Foot, the Goorkhas, and a *sepoy* corps, were ordered to move up to the support of the two brigades which had passed the trenches, which they did in beautiful style, like men used to such work. With the coolness and precision of a parade they advanced to the onslaught, and wavered not when the sweeping grape and musketry mowed down their ranks in sections. Poor fellows, we cheered them as they passed us, and many responded to that cheer whose voices were soon to be hushed in death.

Owing to the impracticability of cavalry against the Sikh field works, we were not required to charge, but to move up in support of the infantry. As we did so, the whole of the enemy's fire on that part we menaced was hurled upon us, and the shots flew over the heads of the infantry into our ranks, this enabling them to reach the trenches ere the fire was directed at them. The shots came fizzing and whizzing about our ears most unpleasantly, and rattled amongst the lances and horses' legs, and in less than five minutes upwards of twenty horses were disabled. To render it difficult for the Sikhs to get our range, we kept changing ground alternately to the right and left. By this means we fortunately lost but two men, a trumpeter, and a trooper named Day, who wore a star for the battle of Punieu [sic – Punniar] in 1843; a nine-pounder hit the very spot where he wore it and drove it clean through his shoulder[3]. His death, of course, was instantaneous. As the infantry forced themselves into the trenches, the 'long balls' decreased; at the same time we moved up to their support at a trot, and as we approached the trenches the last expiring shot the Sikhs fired on this side the river fell scattering – for it was grape – at our horses' feet. The day was lost to them, and British troops were now in possession of their camp and guns.

This battle, which has been justly termed a second Waterloo, is beyond the powers of description. It was a mighty combat between two gigantic armies, each making a desperate struggle for supremacy. For three hours the battle raged in all its terrific fury; full 120 guns were thundering and reverberating through the valley at one time, and near upon 100,000 small arms and musketry were blazing out their rolling vollies; while shot, shell, and rockets were whistling and hissing like so many furies in a tempest. Sixty-seven pieces of cannon, upwards of 200 camel swivels,[4] numerous standards and vast munitions of war, captured by our troops, were the pledges and trophies of this victory. The loss of the enemy was immense. An estimate must be formed with a due allowance for the spirit of exaggeration which pervades all Asiatics, where their interests lead them to magnify numbers; but observations made on the river banks and in the enemy's camp, together with the reports brought in, convinced us that the Kalsa casualties were between twelve and fourteen thousand men, killed, wounded in action, and drowned in the passage of the river.

That this great victory was not achieved without great loss in our ranks, is proved by the returns of killed and wounded, which amounted to 2,383. The 50th and 31st[5] Foot and the Sepoys brigaded with them, were the greatest sufferers in this, as they had been in the three previous actions with the Sikhs. These brave and gallant corps, to whom too much praise cannot be given, nobly sustained the honour of British arms. From their first collision with the Sikhs at Mudki, they fought like the most tried veterans; but, alas, their intrepidity cost them dearly, for they were all but exterminated. It is worthy of remark that these two corps were on the point of being sent home when the war broke out and detained them; hence a general opinion prevailed that it was on this account they were pushed into every action; an opinion founded on the fact that the Indian government could better afford to lose them than soldiers who would have to serve many years in India. It may have been an erroneous supposition, but such was the general impression[6]. Certain it is, however, that but few survived the campaign to return to their native land; the battle field, or the grave yard of Ferozepore, was the last home of two thirds of these devoted corps. The 'fighting 50th' came out of the trenches of Sobraon but a wasted remnant; their bronzed and sunburnt cheeks besmeared with dust and sweat, and their mouths black with biting cartridges.

I will now relate, briefly, a few instances connected with this great fight which came under my own particular notice. A man of my troop, named Nugent, having had his horse shot from under him just at the time the 50th were passing us, he fell in with them, and with that brave little band entered the trenches, and with his lance disturbed many of the Sikh gunners, who got under the gun carriages to avoid the bayonets. He had two narrow escapes of his life, for just as he mounted the breastworks a cannon shot caught the front corner of his lance cap, and he fell back into the trench; he however soon recovered himself, and entering the trenches, a musket shot hit and penetrated through his pouch, but was fortunately turned off by the brass tip of his belt, which by a lucky accident, had slipped down into the pouch – one of the many instances of the bullet or sword being averted in the battle-field. Though he entered the trench dismounted, he came out mounted on a Sikh horse, and did not go unrewarded, for in two days afterwards he was made full Corporal, and when I left the Regiment he was Sergeant[7].

Just as the 31st had crossed the trenches and mounted the breastworks, a loaded mine exploded under their feet, and annihilated a whole sub-division. It was a fearful sight to witness. All at once a dense volume of smoke and dust was thrown with violence in the air, and a report followed rendering all other noises as nothing, and the ground shook for miles around, while muskets, disjointed arms, legs, and bodies, were seen mingling in the black volume, and again descending to the ground. Most melancholy indeed was the spectacle this spot presented when the din and excitement of battle was over. There lay the blackened and dismembered corpse of many a brave fellow.

As we advanced towards the trenches, numbers of poor wounded fellows, both Native and European, were struggling to get to the rear out of reach of the shot which still fell amongst them. Many crept under the bank I have before mentioned, where the river had left pools of water. Numbers, with their life's blood oozing from their undressed wounds, had crawled to the water's edge to cool their painful thirst. It was gratifying, amidst such a scene, to witness the brotherly kindness of the English and Native soldiers one to the other.

The *dhoolies* not being sufficient to carry away the wounded as soon as desirable, a party of my Regiment was appointed to go to the trenches and bring in such of the wounded as could be conveyed on horse back. I was one amongst the rest for this melancholy duty. One thing I noticed worthy of remark was, that nearly all who had been killed by musketry had fallen forward on their faces, especially those who had died instantaneously from a shot in the head or heart, although the shot had penetrated at their front. On the contrary, those who had fallen from cannon, mostly lay on their backs. We found several poor fellows almost expiring from loss of blood, among whom I was sorely grieved to find poor Firth of the 50th, the only surviving acquaintance of mine in that corps, and one who was a native of a village called Clayworth, not many miles distant from my native place; hence our intimacy. He had received a musket shot in the right thigh, from which the blood still oozed. Fortunately I had still a small draught of water left in my bottle, which he greedily drank, and was revived. He touchingly desired me, in the event of his death, to communicate the same to his mother, at the mention of whose name he seemed in much trouble. I procured him a *dhooly* and he was taken to the field hospital. I never saw him more. Some months afterwards, however, when we were in quarters, I received a letter from him; he had fortunately recovered from his wound, and was made full Corporal for his gallantry in the field. From that time I lost sight of him[8]. The 50th was broken up in 1847 and returned to England; and since my return I learn that he was one of the few of that corps who arrived in England, but being worn out, (though only 27 years of age) and unfit for further service, he was discharged, and was *handsomely remunerated* for spending the prime of his youth in hard service, by a pension of *sixpence per day for two years*. Such is the mean and paltry reward of a *just* and *generous* government towards its soldiers who waste their youth and strength in its service, while one individual – whose services to England I however fairly appreciate – has had hundreds of thousands of pounds lavished on him[9]. Such extravagant reward on the one hand, and such shamefully mean provision for the worn out soldier on the other, recoils with shame on our government. Poor Firth, who had served eight years, and fought in four actions, in two of which he had received wounds, died before the two years had expired[10].

It was about 3 o'clock in the afternoon when our victorious army returned to camp. Many places in the tent were vacant, and the beds and the few necessaries of those who had

Captured Sikh guns after the Sutlej campaign, 1847. The vast number and great size of the Sikh artillery pieces exceeded anything the British forces had ever faced before in their Indian campaigns. (Author's collection)

fallen, served the more strongly to remind the survivors of their lost comrades. But, though each soldier had his own share of sorrow, yet it was manifested by no strong ebullition of feeling. A few remarks would be made, such as 'poor Jack,' or 'poor Bill,' or 'He was not a bad hearted fellow,' and so on. On the morning of the 11th an order came rather suddenly for us to march; accordingly we struck tents, and in double quick were on the march. The suddenness of this general move set us all on the *qui vive*, and we wondered what next; however after marching all day along the left bank of the Sutlej, we halted about sunset, and pitched camp on a sandy plain. At 2 o'clock the next morning we were again on the move in the same direction as yesterday. At daybreak we halted and the lines were taken up for our camp. While we stood to our horses an incident occurred, which, under ordinary circumstances, would hardly excite a remark, but here it brought a world of associations to my mind. An English lady, the consort of one of the officers, appeared on the scene, from Ferozepore. It seemed as if an angel had suddenly appeared amongst us, for nearly all eyes were attracted to the strange and unexpected apparition, in a scene so stern and rugged as this. Her soft and delicate features presented a strange contrast to the bronzed cheeks and warlike bearing of the thousands around her.

This little incident also reminds me of the praiseworthy and magnanimous conduct of some ladies towards the sick and wounded at Ferozepore. This place, from being the nearest British cantonment to the scene of operations, was made a general depot for the sick and wounded of four battles, and so numerous were the poor sufferers, that it was necessary to pitch tents in the hospital yard for their accommodation. With nothing but their campaigning beds to lay on, and very indifferent attendance, the poor fellows were in much misery and suffering. But a few "good Samaritans" did much to alleviate them. Throwing aside all aristocratic pride and prudery, and actuated only by philanthropy, they visited the abodes of the suffering and dying soldiers, passing from ward to ward and from tent to tent, cleansing and binding their wounds, administering to their wants, and by their encouraging language cheering the drooping spirits of the languishing and faint.

To return. At daybreak on the 15th, the cavalry crossed the Sutlej, (ancient 'Hyphasis,') by means of a pontoon bridge; the infantry and heavy ordnance followed during that and the following day. The Sutlej differs in no respect from the Ganges, and has a rapid current. It plays some strange freaks, and has, by its deviating course, more than once caused nations to war with each other, and deluged plains with blood. It not unfrequently happens that the corn sown or cotton planted on one side of the river, ripens on the other, the stream having during the floods from the periodical rains, made a detour either to the right or to the left. This, of course, led to disputes, strife, and war – the sower putting forward his legitimate claims, while his opponent claimed it as being now a part and portion of his territory; in such times of anarchy, turbulence, and unscrupulous tyranny, as may be supposed, might invariably was right. The scene and country in which we now found ourselves was very pleasing to the eye. Green corn fields now in ear, and waving in the breeze and sunshine, spread themselves before us; the vast level tract interspersed everywhere with trees rich in foliage, and dotted here and there with little hamlets. We had already imbibed strange Utopian notions as to the splendours and riches of the Punjaub, and the first appearance of the country encouraged this impression. However, a few days after this, these illusions all vanished. This part of the country, owing to its proximity to the river, was in the highest state of cultivation, and at this season of the year presented its brightest aspect. The Punjaub, on the whole, when we entered it, was not so well cultivated as Bengal; thousands upon thousands of acres of good land, which required little more than irrigation to make them produce abundantly, were left waste. The Punjaubees, however, have a better and more facile method of irrigating the soil than the Bengalese. It was somewhat surprising to see with what indifference the natives viewed us as we marched by the villages. The reason of this is explained from the fact that this part of the country bordered the British territories, and the natives had constant intercourse with British subjects, from whom, most probably, they learned that the British army did not oppress conquered countries as Asiatic armies generally do. They seemed to know that their lives and property would be respected, hence that general indifference I have just spoken of. That their confidence was not misplaced, I am happy to have it to say; for I believe not one single act of plunder was known on our route to Lahore.

While we are on the route to the Sikh capital, I will give the reader some idea of the prevailing opinions in our ranks respecting the future conduct of the Sikhs. Knowing their obstinate and indomitable spirit, it was generally supposed, even after the battle of Sobraon, that they would make another stand against us. Before we crossed the river, the general opinion was that they would oppose our passage, but that being now accomplished, we believed that all their energies and force would be directed against us at, or near, the city of Lahore.

These suppositions were strengthened by rumours amongst the natives, some of them of the most extravagant absurdity, such as that 15,000 Sikhs were encamped around Lahore; that a great battle must be fought on the plains ere we dare hope to see the city; that the guns of the citadel were of such immense calibre, that were we to approach within sight, we should be blown across the Styx, and that for five miles around the city the ground was everywhere charged with loaded mines which would send all the *Feringhees* to the bottomless pit. This sort of Asiatic bombast would not do for us, so onward we pushed, though not without due caution. Scouting parties spread like bees over the country, eyeing every village, *tope*, or brake, least it might conceal an ambushed enemy.

About 3 o'clock in the afternoon we entered the town of Kussoor. A small fortress, which stood on the south side of the town, was immediately possessed by a dismounted troop of my Regiment; some guns and munitions of war were seized, and the garrison surrendered without firing a shot. The infantry coming up soon after, the place was formally invested by two companies of *Sepoys*; this done the cavalry then marched through the town to the north, or Lahore side, on to a large plain, and took up ground for encampment. It was near sunset when we arrived on this ground, and as we had been mounted ever since 4 o'clock in the morning, and had had nothing to eat all day, many anxious eyes were turned in the direction we had come; the infantry were debouching in successive columns, but no beds, no tents, and worse than all, no commissariat, consequently no bread, no grog, made their welcome appearance, while hunger seemed strongly indexed in every man's long visage, and our horses reminded us more forcibly of the gnawing demon by their 'Rosinante-like'[11] appearance and snappishness one with another. Wrapping our cloaks round us, and slipping the hand through the bridle, we took up our lodging on the cold ground. The night was cold, long, and wearisome; the horses, many of them, got away from their owners and were galloping about and fighting one with another, endangering the lives of those who still lay on the ground. However it wore away, and with the morrow came a bright sunshine, and that which was far better, our tents, baggage and commissariat. From daybreak until mid-day the camp equipage, &c., were perpetually pouring on the plain, like the pouring of many streams into the sea, and the camp again assumed that well regulated and compact appearance our British Indian army is so superb in. Of course the commissariat made everything smooth and easy by supplying our rations. Indeed nothing is so soon forgotten as bodily pain or hardships; the soldier who today is enjoying ease and plenty forgets the hunger and hardships of yesterday.

During the day myself and some comrades resolved on visiting the town of Kussoor, being curious to know something of the people we had conquered. It is needless to say that the bazaars and streets differ in no way in the Punjaub from those of lower India, although from report we had expected to find them magnificent. The natives here, however, are much finer and nobler looking than the Bengalese; dressed in long flowing robes, with beards reaching down to the stomach, and their heads mounted by a massive scarlet turban, they presented quite a picturesque appearance. In keeping with the warlike state of the Punjaub, many artisans were employed in making swords, shields, fire-arms, &c. This trade was destined in a few more years to receive its death blow, for on the annexation of the Punjaub every individual was dispossessed of them, and none permitted to carry them but by special authority. The women, too, are here of higher stature and better proportioned than those of lower India; are generally good looking, and some are really pretty. As we passed through some of the better streets, numerous piercing black eyes kept peering from the doorways and balconies, with expressions of curiosity and surprise, at seeing the white faced *Feringhees*, who had doubtless been their constant theme for some months past, from the important part they had taken in these eventful times. As for some of the grey headed old gentlemen, why they were obliged to put on their specs to look at us, and even then, so strange was it to see *Feringhees* walking their streets, that they seemed half inclined – like the Africans with Mungo Park – to feel and examine us ere they could be convinced of so strange a phenomenon.

The following very graphic and interesting description of Kussoor I have extracted from *Adventures in the Punjaub*.

> Kussoor, this city of the dead, this mighty mass of ruin, and its territories, has many interesting, and even romantic recollections attached to it. The present town occupies the enceint of one of the twelve Pathan forts of modern days, while the remains of the ancient city lie in massive ruins for miles to the north and east. As the traveller approaches Kussoor from the *Kadin* (banks) of the Sutlej, his eye is attracted in the far distance by the high Kemker bank of what must have been the old bed of the Beas river, rising two hundred feet above the plains, sprinkled with date trees, and the highest cliff capped by a Fakheer's *takra*, (pillow, or resting place) close to the ruins of an ancient tower; the last remnant of the castles of the old Rajpoot lords, when Kussoor was a Hindoo principality, and when, as history, or rather local legends say, a king of Delhi came, wooed and won the daughter of the prince, and by degrees converted his bride, her father, and subjects, to the tenets of Mahomed. It was not always thus persuasively that Islam gained her converts. The legend is probably correct, for all along this border, and indeed from the Jumna to the Attok, are tribes after tribes of converted Hindoos, still bearing their old Pathan designations, and retaining many of their old prejudices and customs. The Rajpoot dynasty fell under an inroad of the Affghans, and their descendants, the Pathan chiefs, were driven out by the Sikhs. The many forts, still in repair, with the many others of Pathan times, now crumbling to the dust, tell of the troubles and insecurity of the day, and the desolation of the country for miles around, tell the same tale, as does Sirhind and old Lahore.

I now return to camp. About 2 o'clock P.M. today, a number of poor fellows, who had been kept prisoners in the Sikh camp, came in. They were mostly men that had been taken at the retreat of Budiwal, and having been missing so long, their appearance amongst us today, seemed as though they had arisen from the dead, and most heartily were they welcomed to their own camp. They came mounted on an elephant, and dressed in Asiatic costume, for they had been stripped of their clothes as their captors' perquisites. The poor fellows in describing their misfortunes, said they had been much insulted and abused by the common soldiery in the Sikh camp, until Tej Sing, one of their generals, took them under his charge, and did much to ameliorate their condition. This was the first happy evidence we had of the honourable humanity of our enemy to prisoners of war, and in justice to them be it said, it was not the last; many a one now living owes his life to this noble feeling of the Sikh soldiers. It is true we shewed them the first example by humanely treating their wounded who fell into our hands, and sending them back to their own camp to tell of the goodness of the *Feringhees*. Such acts as these may have awakened the better feelings of the higher grades of our foe; whatever were the motives for these commendable acts in warfare, whether of policy or humanity, it is a trait which will ever redound to their honour.

On the 15th it was announced that Goolab Sing would come into the British camp on a diplomatic mission. Accordingly my troop augmented the out-lying picket to one squadron, so as to form an escort. At 11 o'clock we advanced about a mile to the front, and on a rising ground awaited his arrival. About 12, a cloud of dust arose over the tops of the trees to our front, and soon after a cavalcade, with some companies of infantry, emerged from the jungle; we approached to meet them, and when about ten yards distance, we 'formed line to the front.' They did the same with as great celerity and precision as ourselves, and, for the first time, Sikh and British ranks were harmlessly confronting each other at ten paces distance. The illustrious *Sirdar,* Goolab, was sitting with several officials in an *howdah,* on a richly comparisoned elephant, himself in a rich and imposing Asiatic costume. His escort consisted of two companies of foot, and about twenty horsemen. The infantry were a fine specimen of the *Khalsas,* with whom we had had four such fierce contests. They wore splendid dresses, their large turbans and *pajams* were of the purest white, with a coatee of brilliant scarlet, after the fashion of our infantry, and they were armed exactly the same, but their belts were of scarlet silk and gold lace. As to their officers, their dresses were rich and gorgeous in the extreme. After a few ceremonies Goolab Sing proceeded, under a small escort, to the British camp, his soldiers remaining outside our pickets. Goolab Sing was at this time a fine, hale, good looking man, and about 50 years of age. There is much that is interesting in his history and the power that he now possesses. He was of good birth, but his family suffered from the predatory incursions of the Affghans, and sank into poverty and obscurity. Young Goolab, as soon as he was able to wield a sword or lance, became a *sumen* (mounted swordsman) and joining Runjeet Sing's army in the perpetual strife with the Affghans, soon distinguished himself by his talents and personal bravery, by which he was brought to the notice of the Runjeet, who took him into favour, promoted him, and by degrees he rose to be prime minister. Soon after being established in his patron's favour, he introduced his brother, Dyem Sing, into court, and he in turn brought in his brother, Narain Sing, who all in turn rose to office and influence in the state. Goolab, by a great share of tact and finesse, managed to obtain the government of Cashmere, when that province was conquered from the Affghans, where he still remains. Dyem Sing too obtained a *Jagheer* (estate) in the hilly districts, but being a great favourite at court, left its administration to a Frenchman, who brought it into a highly flourishing state; he died from a fall from his horse shortly after Runjeet's death in 1841. Narain Sing was a thorough voluptuary, and by his excesses brought himself to a premature grave.

Few politicians could have acted with more success than did Goolab Sing during the whole of the struggles between the two belligerent powers. With an army of 15,000 men he stood aloof from either party, but all the time watching, ready to take advantage of any favourable circumstance, or to espouse the cause of the stronger side. When called upon by the Sikh chiefs to bring his army into the field against the *Feringhees,* his answer was that 'he must remain at home to protect his own states from predatory tribes,' and thus he managed to satisfy the jealousies of both parties. Having thus forborne to raise arms against the British, he was selected by the Durbar of Lahore as the fittest person to negotiate with them. His ambition was flattered on this occasion, both on account of the confidence placed in him and the great importance of the mission; he most probably hoped, too, to secure the favour and alliance of so potent a power. How he succeeded in both points history will record. Successful he was, and when I left India he was still Governor of Cashmere, and one of the most powerful princes in India.

The soldiers who formed Goolab's escort were bivouacked a little in advance of our pickets. They were doubtless the very *élite* of his army, for a finer lot of fellows I never saw. Tall, athletic, and well proportioned, their demi-asiatic costume, long, flowing jet black beards and moustaches, instead of giving them a ferocious or forbidding aspect, seemed to produce in them the fac-simile of real warriors. For 'bone, thew, and sinew,' few races are on a par with the Sikhs; many of their regiments were equal in size and stature to our Grenadier Guards. The Sikh tenets forbid them from shaving or cutting their hair, hence their beards reach down to the waist, and the hair when loose will flow down still lower. They take great pride, however, in cultivating and keeping it clean.

Early on the morning of the 18th we again struck camp and marched on towards Lahore. We encamped that night in a jungle near to a small village, the name I do not know, but the spot I shall ever remember, for it has some painful recollections connected with it. Only one well was to be found in the locality, the water of which was soon exhausted, consequently both men and cattle suffered much for want of that most necessary element. In the afternoon the rage for water was so strong that the well was actually stormed, and fought for by different parties in the vain hope of procuring a draught of water. My own thirst that day was painfully intense, rendered so by the duty I was on. At 2 o'clock two squadrons of ours moved off to the Governor General's camp, there to await the arrival of the young Duleep Sing, then a boy of ten years of age, and heir apparent to the throne, accompanied by Goolab Sing. With two squadrons of the Third [Light] Dragoons we were drawn up in two lines, forming a street to the Governor General's camp; here, like statues, we sat all the afternoon under a blazing sun. While in this state a native *qui hie* (servant) came out of an officer's tent with water in a *chillum chee* (washing basin); half a dozen men at once rushed on him, and taking the dirty water from him drank it up, so painful was their thirst. The royal Duleep and his cortege arrived about 4 o'clock, a royal salute was fired, and after a brief interview with Sir H. Hardinge,[12] returned about sunset. We returned to camp, but not to obtain relief from our thirst; the night wore through painfully slow to us; however, at the first peep of dawn, we quitted this arid spot, and having marched about 6 miles we fortunately discovered a large pool of muddy water, into which our horses rushed madly and drank deeply of the refreshing water, as did we ourselves.

At daybreak on the 19th we were making our last march for Lahore. About 10 o'clock we emerged from the jungle into an extensive open plain; about two miles direct to our front was a long range of gun sheds, and a little beyond them the Sikh barracks, with a goodly number of noble-looking bungalows sprinkled amongst them, the residences of the officers; and looming out in the far distance stood out in bold relief, a vast number of tall spires, minarets, mosques, and domes. This was the famed city of Lahore, the fortified capital of the powerful Sikhs, and the El-dorado of our Utopian ideas. We now stood on that very ground where Asiatic rumour had condemned us all to be blown to atoms. My regiment being an advanced guard, we were on the camp ground before the main body of the troops, and for the first time I had a full and advantageous view of our magnificent army. Each battalion marched that morning in column, so as to deploy into line if required, while guns were interspersed at regular intervals, the whole line flanked by cavalry. This order is called 'battle array.' All at once the whole line emerged from the jungle on to the open plain, and advancing for about 500 yards halted; aides-de-camp were seen galloping along the line, and the next minute the whole, like the simultaneous working of a machine, deployed into line, extending nearly three miles along the plain; and now the grandeur of a splendid army of 45,000 men was fully developed. In this order the line advanced over the plain directly towards the Sikh capital. The sun was shining in all its splendour on the furbished arms, which flashing and glistening over the dark ranks, produced a scene truly grand and imposing, and one calculated to raise, even in our hearts, feelings of pride and enthusiasm. Presently each battalion filed off to the ground taken up for their respective camps. Then came shoals of camels, elephants, &c., with camp equipage, and thousands of followers in their varied costumes and characters, flowing in with the general stream, spreading themselves like locusts on the plain. The army now having changed from compact ranks and columns to irregular and distinctive individuals, the scene is one of lively bustle and animation; presently up go bazaar flags, like so many Union Jacks in a fleet; tent after tent points itself towards the sky, fires are made and camp kettles set to work. In short a strange metamorphosis has come over the plain during the past half hour. From the silence and solitude of a desert, it is changed, as if by magic, into a vast and animated city, containing full 120,000 human beings of various nations and colours. Here we remained in *statu quo* for a month, during which time negotiations were being made, the full particulars of which it is not in my province to relate. However, the conditions were briefly as follows: - Every gun which had been pointed at the British was to be surrendered to them – that tract which formed the country between the Sutlej and Ravee was to be annexed to the British, and last, not least, some *lacs* of rupees were to be paid over to 'John Company' to defray the expenses of the war[13]. Up to within a few days prior to the army being broken up, we were strictly prohibited from going into the city, probably from an apprehension of our being murdered by the vindictive Sikhs. Being, however, extremely desirous to see a city which for some months past had been our constant theme, and one whose splendours and magnificence, according to Asiatic report, were not excelled, I was determined at least to *see it,* even though it were at a distance. About a mile from our camp were sprinkled the well built officers' bungalows I have before described, and I resolved to make one of these my Nebo[14].

Selecting the highest amongst them I was soon on the top of its flat roof, from which I had a fine birds-eye view of the interesting scene around me. There, about three miles to the north, to our view, stood out in bold relief against the horizon, the large and magnificent city, the capital and seat of the Sings, long the most potent princes in India; her snow-white minarets lifting up their proud heads to the sky, and her gilded and vari-coloured domes presenting a thousand different hues in the sunshine. Between me and the city was a continued heap of ruins, the remains of old Lahore, and the site of the Sikh capital prior to Runjeet Sing building the present fortified city. Like the ruins of Kussoor, the remains of old tombs, mausoleums, and mosques, were thickly strewn over the ruined heaps. On each side were three or four very large brick mounds; here and there a patch of green corn seemed to relieve the rugged and unpleasing scene of ruin, while the shady retreat of the *fakirs*, in the midst of which stood the white temples, presented a pleasing contrast to the desolation around them. Turning myself about, another city, but of a more temporary fabric, presented itself: the vast and well regulated camp of the conquerors of the mighty hosts whose capital I had just been viewing. It was truly a pride stirring sight thus to see the camp firmly established in the very heart of that nation who, a few months before, boasted that they would 'drive the *Feringhees* out of India.'

During our stay here constant interviews were interchanged between our diplomatists and the Lahore durbar in the process of the treaty. It was evident from the orders and counter-orders issued to us at different times, that they had a difficult and rather complex part to play, both from the quibbles of an Asiatic court, well schooled in tact and deceit, and the contumacy of some of the Sirdars or lords of the Punjaub. Some of the more obdurate and haughty, seeing that their power and influence were to receive a death stroke, began to clamour again for war, but these were overruled by others who pointed out to them the stubborn fact that an army which had already conquered them in four battles was close to their capital prepared to use coercive measures if necessary. Arguments so forcible as 45,000 bayonets and 120 pieces of cannon were not to be resisted – hence these haughty Sings began to sing small, and eventually signed the treaty. By way of ratifying the same an instalment was paid, for which generosity the Sikhs were favoured with the honour – I will not say the pleasure – of reviewing that army which had conquered them and humbled their pride.

On the 19th of March the camp was thrown into discomfort by a severe storm of hail, rain, and thunder. Some tents were blown down, and the unlucky wights in them left exposed to the pelting of the pitiless storm, with the additional discomfort of seeing their beds and chattels floating about in the mud and dirt. My troop was for outlying picket, and just as we had got our tents and bedding packed on the elephants, the storm burst over our heads in all its fury. However there was no help for it, so off we started for our post, and found ourselves in a woeful plight when we got there, every stitch belonging to us, tents and bedding, drenched through with wet, and the whole plain like a sea. But soldiers are not the men to look at the dark side of the picture, hence not a murmur was uttered, but the woeful plight each man was in served but to produce merriment to his neighbour. Fortunately the rain subsided about 11 o'clock, and a foraging party was made up for the purpose of procuring some fuel. A Sikh fort was less than a mile distant, we set off for it and succeeded in getting some dry spars, and in as short a time as it takes me to write it we made a good fire, which, together with an extra dram of grog, rendered us as merry as a pic-nic party (for we had now little fear of being molested by the enemy) and the woes of the past hour were forgotten.

At length, all preliminaries being adjusted, the vast and powerful machine, which had been united in all its particles, was now to be disunited; each wheel, axle, and lever, or each battalion, corps, and battery, which formed its component parts, were to be dissevered one from another, only to be re-united when *ambition* or *mammon* should call them forth.

On the 24th March my regiment, with bright anticipations of peace and quarters, quitted the plains of Lahore and marched towards Meerut. The Goorkhas marched along with us until we crossed the Sutlej, and I thus had an opportunity of becoming acquainted with some traits of their character. They are free from many of the religious prejudices of the Hindoos, and consequently are less scrupulous as to their articles of diet, and many of them will eat beef. They boast, to use their own metaphor, of being braver by six fingers than the Hindoo, but admit that we, the British, are the little finger braver than themselves. That they are a race of a brave and indomitable spirit our soldiers who fought side by side with them at Aliwal and Sobraon can testify, as well as the Chief's Despatches. It is related that at Aliwal one of these little fellows was seen, after having killed three or four Sikhs, covered with blood, and sharpening his knife[15] on a gun carriage wheel, at the same time in piteous tones calling his knife *crab*, (bad) and saying, *cutch com na curta*, (it would not do its work.) The third day's march from Lahore, being encamped near to a large village, out of curiosity I took a stroll thereto, and in one of the streets met with one of these little Goorkhas, who invited me to accompany him to a liquor shop. Entering a doorway we found ourselves in a little court yard, with small rooms on every side like a *seraie*. At the further end of the yard were a number of camp followers and three Sikh soldiers sitting on some *charpoys*, and indulging in their potations. The moment we approached them one of these Sikhs, a prodigious and ferocious looking fellow, arose from his seat and began to abuse my little companion with all the insulting epithets and invidious language he could muster. The little Goorkha, who understood every word, could no longer bear with such abuse, so snatching his knife from his belt he plunged it into the man's bowels and laid him weltering in blood at his feet. The Sikh's companions had hitherto taken no part in the fray, but on seeing their comrade on the ground, and one of their inveterate enemies standing over him, they in a moment sprang at him with their *tulwars*, but he wounded the first by rushing in at him, and evaded the other by springing through the entrance door. For my own part, not being juggler enough to swallow swords without injury to myself; being unarmed too, and having no particular desire to have my body perforated through and through with *tulwars* merely for the amusement of the Sikhs, I hardly stayed to see the end of the fray, but, like Hudibras,[16] took to my heels,

Not to shew how fights were won,
But to see how I could run.

I could hear some of them shouting behind me, and turning my head saw a whole mob close on the heels of my Goorkha companion, while *dhooi* (stop him) was shouted by a hundred voices, and some of the natives rushing from their houses seemed half inclined to stop me. Fear – for I admit that I was panic struck – seemed to lend me wings, notwithstanding which the enemy seemed to gain on me, but all at once the noise seemed to subside, and on turning my head I discovered that the infuriated mob had entered a new direction on the right, and but half a dozen kept up the chase after me. Fortunately I soon found myself outside the village and quickly reached the camp safe and sound. Talk of running a race; never did man run swifter than I did on that occasion. I knew that if caught summary vengeance would have been inflicted. How my nimble footed little companion fared I know not, but I have every reason to believe that he escaped his pursuers. The natives reported the affair to the Commander-in-Chief, and strict inquiries were made about the guilty party, but happily no one knew anything about him, and of course I did not.

The heat was now daily increasing, and ere we reached quarters it was insupportably hot in tents. We arrived in Meerut, our assigned quarters, on the 17th April, just six months from the time we quitted Cawnpore. In 1846 Meerut cantoned about 8,000 troops, but since the annexation of the Punjaub, owing to the many which that country has absorbed, there has seldom been more half that number at one time.

In the month of May I was attacked with a severe and dangerous fever, which for twelve days raged in all its burning fury, and so intense were my sufferings that I desired death as the only relief; but the *die* was not yet cast. Through the kind interposition of providence my young constitution triumphed over the dire disease, and my name was still borne on the roll of the living. In July we received our *battue*, 76 rupees[17]; a sum which produced a regular 'flare up' throughout the regiment and benefited few but the canteens and grog shops. Soldiers, like sailors, know but one use for money – drinking and spreeing, and no sooner do they receive it than they lavish it in dissipation. The commanding officer exempted the regiment from all parades for three days, and at the end of that time the elements favoured us with two days more, for it rained at the usual time for parades. Hence for five successive days dissipation and debauchery were universal throughout the regiment. Bottles of liquor were despatched as fast as the Sikhs were at Sobraon, and at the end of a week scarcely a *dunnree* or fraction of the £7 12s. was left. Two thirds of it had been

THE BATTLE OF SOBRAON 87

Sutlej Medal for Sobraon. This medal was awarded to Number 330 Private Cornelius McIneyrey. Although the rim of the medal gives his regiment as the 80th Foot, he earned the medal whilst serving with the Ninth Lancers, transferring to the 80th in July 1847. McIneyrey was born in Clonmel, Co Tipperary, Ireland, and was a labourer when he enlisted in 1829. He was discharged in 1851, whilst holding four good conduct badges. He was also entitled to the Punniar Star. (Private collection)

virtually returned to the government through the medium of the canteen. Such is the life of a soldier. The scenes exhibited in the barrack room during this spree are beyond description. It was one continued merriment, fun, and frolic. Here was a party half naked, owing to the extreme heat, trying a dance, and in their gyrations stumbling and reeling one against another, and every now and then setting up a whoop and halloo like so many Indians at a war dance. There, squatted on the floor like Hindoos, is a party paying their devotions to their gods – some half dozen bottles of grog – until they become *spiritualised*. And here and there is a half naked *devotee,* wallowing in a pool of water thrown over him by a comrade as a lark. To complete the scene, fancy broken bottles and plates, tin pots, bedding, clothing, accoutrements, &c., strewed in indiscriminate confusion about the room, while the whole is accompanied by a concert or rather discord of a hundred voices in various keys, some singing, some shouting, and other swearing; fancy all this and you have some idea of an Indian barrack room on such an occasion. As may be supposed these excesses were not indulged in altogether with impunity, for nine men of ours were carried to the Hospital having *delirium tremens,* five of whom never saw their barracks again. One poor fellow was drowned in a tank whilst intoxicated. Oh! drunkenness, drunkenness, the bane and destroyer of many a fine soldier; 'tis an evil which has long cried for suppression, and which the literary world has long descanted on, but little real good has yet been done. While I am on this painful subject I will deviate a little from my narrative to relate a few more instances of the evil results of intemperance which came under my own notice in the service.

In the cold season of 1847 an artilleryman was discovered dead in the interior of General Gillespie's tomb, which stands in the grave yard at Meerut, with a grog bottle and a pipe by his side, his clothes burnt to a cinder, and part of his body consumed away by fire. It was supposed either that his clothes caught fire from the lighted pipe, or that his body ignited by spontaneous combustion. The poor fellow had been absent four days. His was a strange choice for indulging in his libations, amidst the dead, and in the silent tomb. How degraded, how lost to all sense of self respect, must be the man who could thus select the precincts of the dead for his sottish indulgence[18]

In the hot season of 1848 a man of my regiment named Collins, was taken to the Conjee House[19], when drunk about 11 o'clock in the morning. He was locked up in his cell as usual, and no further trouble taken about him until the cook brought his dinner. The Sergeant of the guard on going with him to the cell, discovered Collins hanging by his braces from one of the bars of the inner window, quite dead[20].

About a month subsequent to this another prisoner, in a drunken state, attempted suicide in the same cell and by the same means, but the sentry discovered him in time to cut him down and save his life. In the same hot season a man belonging to the 32nd Foot,[21] having when intoxicated assaulted a sergeant of his company, was ordered to the guard room, and to evade the consequent punishment he leaped down a well, and was not extricated until life was extinct. A short time after a sergeant of the same regiment married the widow, but he on his wedding night, whilst in a state of inebriation, and it is supposed smarting from jealousy, in consequence of some undue familiarity of a fellow comrade with the bride, destroyed himself in the same manner as the last. Another of the 32nd was found dead in his bed from the excessive quantity of grog he had drunk the night before.

9

Military Executions

Justice is lame, as well as blind amongst us;
The laws corrupted to their ends that make them,
And made by Heav'n to be a monster's prey,
That every day starts up t'enslave us deeper.

I now come to the most painful part of my narrative, as it also was of my military career – the execution of three fellow soldiers, within the space of fourteen days. To elucidate the matter it is necessary to state that the crime for which they suffered had, since our return from the Sutlej, become a growing evil, and a flagrant act of insubordination. Many men of loose habits and discontented minds, becoming weary of the dull routine of barrack duties, and the restraints imposed upon their actions, conceived a preference for transportation to that of remaining soldiers in India. Actuated with this idea, they committed a crime, which invariably led to transportation, namely 'striking a superior officer.' Several men had already been sentenced to the penal settlements, and reports were almost daily coming in to the Commander-in-Chief of the growing evil, and he, seeing the necessity of resorting to prompt measures to suppress the offence, issued an order upon the subject, threatening what he would do if similar acts of insubordination should occur[1].

The order was read at the head of every regiment in the month of April, 1847, and it would seem that this had the desired effect for a few months subsequent, but at the end of that time the edict was treated lightly by those very men to whom it was applicable; for in September no less than three cases occurred in Meerut alone, followed by the extreme penalty of martial law. The first was a gunner of the East India Company's artillery, named Atkins[2]. He had been drinking for some days when *delirium tremens* came on, and he was sent into the hospital. The surgeon on visiting him, called him 'a scheming scoundrel,' and other epithets, when the poor fellow, becoming exasperated, gave the doctor a blow on the chest. The offence was complete; a General Court Martial was called, and the poor fellow was condemned to death.

At 5 o'clock on the morning of the 24th September, the whole of the troops in the station paraded to witness the execution. The spot selected was the infantry drill ground, a flat level plain on which were erected several butts – a sort of mound of earth or mud – used for musketry practice. The troops formed three sides of a square, while one of these butts occupied the centre of the fourth, a few yards in advance of which and conspicuous to the whole was a black coffin to receive the corpse of the doomed soldier. The morning was delightfully clear with cooling zephyrs streaming over the plain in soft and gentle currents, and all nature seemed to smile as if in mockery of the awful tragedy about to be enacted. For a brief space all was silent as the grave. The ranks, impressed with the solemnity of the awful occasion, were like immovable statues. Presently the culprit, accompanied by a clergyman, stepped into the open area of the square on the right flank, dressed in white civilian's clothes. With a firm and calm deportment he glanced round at the thousands of his comrades assembled to witness his execution. A military band (the 32nd Foot) then struck up that beautiful and impressive tune, the 'Dead March in Saul,' and the prisoner, falling in behind them, closely followed by eight men with muskets, his executioners, moved with slow and measured pace along the front of the ranks. How awe striking, how impressive, how heart thrilling, was this solemn procession. With firm and regular step, and calm deportment, conscious as he was of having committed no crime worthy of death, in the eyes of that God before whom he was so soon to appear, the poor victim marched along the front of the ranks; while the rolling of drums, and every step warned him of the diminishing distance between him and eternity. Having arrived at the extreme flank on the left the music ceased, and the procession wheeled to the right, and approached to within a few yards of the coffin. The prisoner was now halted and his sentence read to him. His discharge also was read and presented to him; this he calmly folded up and placed in his bosom, and then gazed around as if still hoping that even at the eleventh hour, he might receive a reprieve[3]. But his hopes were vain; the unjust, the severe, the cruel edict had gone forth, and was unrelentingly to be executed. Turning towards his coffin, he seemed for a moment unmanned. The provost proceeded to bandage his eyes with a black handkerchief, and having pinioned his arms behind him, led him to the head of his coffin, on which he was made to kneel with body erect, awaiting the volley which was to despatch him. What a moment of awful suspense and anguish to the sufferer, and breathless anxiety to the spectators; but it was but for a moment, for on a signal being given, eight muskets were pointed at his body, and at another silent signal, the triggers were simultaneously pulled, and the loud report followed. But, lo! the *victim* still retained his erect position, his limbs writhing and his flesh quivering with intense suffering and pain from three wounds, from which the blood oozed and ran in crimson streams down his white habiliments. A moment of intense pain and suffering to him, and suffocating anxiety to the spectators; the provost presented a pistol to his head, and the *victim* to the inhuman, barbarous, and cruel martial law of his country, fell a mangled and disfigured corpse, his skull blown to atoms, and his brains spattered on the Indian plain[4]. 'Twas not enough that we, his companions in arms, were made the involuntary witnesses of the legalized murder of a fellow soldier; but with an insatiable and refined species of cruelty, we were made to march in slow time close by the mutilated and disfigured corpse, with the command 'eyes right' given as we passed, that being the side on which the body lay. Of all the scenes I had witnessed this was the most heart rending.

I could, with sorrow and regret, see the last struggles and sinking for ever of a comrade beneath the briny waves of the ocean. I could with pity and grief see many of my comrades dying around me from some pestiferous disease, or watch the last struggles of a companion as the expiring embers of life quitted his body; these were natural causes, not so the one I had just witnessed. They died a natural death, a fate which myriads have done before them, and which is the common lot of man. I could with sympathy and heart-felt sorrow witness the sufferings of the wounded, and calmly, when divested of all extraneous excitement, contemplate the havoc that ambition had made on the corse strewn plain; but this was the freak of war! – war, which may sometimes be necessary for the establishment of permanent peace, and as such is a necessary evil to obviate one of greater magnitude. All these are the natural consequences of the mutability of human affairs, over which man has but little control. But to witness the legalized murder, in cold blood, of a man innocent of anything worthy of death, and that man in every sense a *brother*, as well as a countryman. I say to witness this without a feeling of sorrow and compassion for the *victim*, and a disgust, to say the least of it, for the inhuman authors of its execution, a man must be divested of humanity and all the better feelings of his nature. The solemn sound of the Dead March had scarcely died away, and the rattling volley still seemed to ring in our ears, when the troops were again assembled to witness a similar tragedy. The second *victim* was John Palmer, one of my own regiment. He suffered death for – can it be credited by an Englishman – *throwing his cap at his Commanding officer*. Having committed a minor offence, Palmer was taken before the Major, who awarded him six days extra drill, which excited the man's anger, and in his passion he threw his cap at the Major, saying, 'There, take that, you ———.' For this latter offence he was tried by a General Court Martial, and sentenced to be *shot*.[5] From the time of his trial to the execution – about a month – he was lively and in good spirits, and used to tell his comrades on guard that he should only be transported.* Poor fellow, his death warrant was then being signed, and soon the awful truth was to be revealed to him. In the service, when a soldier is to receive corporeal[sic] punishment or death, all hands parade to witness it, even the prisoners in the cells, hence Palmer, who was in custody at the time, was marched to be an involuntary witness of Atkin's execution. It was here the awful truth of his own fate seemed to burst in on him. In Atkin's sentence and death he read that of his own, and a total change came over his mind. He returned to his cell with a full conviction that he was a doomed man; and he was not deceived, for at 4 o'clock in the afternoon of the same day, the chaplain entered his cell, and communicated the fatal truth to him, informing him that but three days were permitted him to prepare for that awful change. He was not surprised, and received the news with apparent composure; but shortly afterwards broke out in a passion of grief, and his tears flowed copiously. It was a burst of filial affection and grief for his only parent, at the thought of the bitter cup she would have to drink on hearing the fatal news; and he exclaimed in the bitterness of his soul, 'Oh, my poor mother, God help and support her under this trial!' He shortly afterwards composed himself, and wrote an affectionate letter to his mother full of repentance for the wrongs he had done her, and the sins committed against God. This done, he devoted the brief time allotted to him in preparation, and I believe he became a true penitent.

Our commanding officer[6], though as a soldier he was sometimes severe in his punishments, yet as a man was of a kind, tender, and humane disposition; hence the respect and honour he felt for the service, rendered him strict in the performance of what he deemed his duty, and sometimes the man was lost in the strict disciplinarian. No sooner did the sentence arrive from head quarters than he resolved, if possible, on obtaining a reprieve for Palmer. To this end a letter of intercession was addressed to the Commander-in-chief, and despatched by double *dak* to head quarters at Simlah. But as well might he appeal to an adamantine rock as to the hearts of men steeled against humanity; the fatal decree had gone forth, and like the laws of the Medes and Persians, was unalterable.

At 3 o'clock on the fatal morning Palmer arose, washed, cleaned, and dressed himself as if for a parade, after which he partook of a cup of coffee and a small portion of bread and cheese. At a quarter before five he was conducted from his cell, and a *dhooly* being there for his conveyance, he was expected to get in, but respectfully declined, though the distance to the spot was nearly a mile. With a firm and soldier-like step, he marched to that spot where four days before he had witnessed the death of a fellow soldier. As Atkins had done, he was

---

* His sentence, according to custom, not being communicated to him until just before it was carried into execution. [Gilling's note.]

Colonel James Hope Grant (1808-1875). He served in the First China War, the Sutlej and Punjab campaigns, commanded a cavalry brigade in the Indian Mutiny, and commanded the British forces in the Second China War. He ended his career as a Major General and GCB. (Private collection)

made to march along the front of our regiment, amongst whom were his boon companions and comrades, some with whom he had spent many a jovial and pleasant hour; many were in tears, nay, the feelings of some were so intense, that they were obliged to fall out from the ranks and turn aside from such a scene, amongst whom were the Adjutant and other officers.

The culprit marched along the front of the three sides of the square with the same firmness and fortitude as his unfortunate predecessor; the same ceremony was performed, his eyes bandaged, and kneeling on the head of his coffin, his manly breast was presented as a target for the bullets of his own countrymen. Several shots pierced his body, and he fell lifeless on the ground. Again we were formed into open column; again were we commanded 'eyes right' as we marched in slow time past our unfortunate comrade. Many a suppressed curse, many an imprecation was uttered on the authors of this unjust and barbarous punishment, and many now began to feel a disgust for the service, and not a few to dread the horrors of martial law and tremble for themselves; for we knew not to what lengths it might be carried now its severity had commenced[7].

Palmer was a native of London, of respectable parents, and had received an education superior to the common class of men; but, like many others, he had in his young and foolish days made 'one false step,' which led to others. He was what in military parlance is termed 'a random shot,' of a wild and roving disposition, and fond of change and excitement. The dull routine of barrack room life in India, and the restraint imposed on his actions, were uncongenial to his temperament. In 1843 he deserted from the regiment at Calcutta, and managed to elude the vigilance of those in search of him. Engaging himself on board a vessel

Captain Richard Freer Thonger c.1860. Thonger, born in Boston, Lincolnshire in 1819, enlisted in the Ninth Lancers in 1841. A man of obvious ability, he rose quickly through the ranks to become a troop sergeant major in 1849, and regimental sergeant major in 1851. He was commissioned in 1857 and retired as a captain in 1865. Here he is wearing mess dress, with the ribbons for the Sutlej, Punjab and Indian Mutiny medals. He died in 1906. (By courtesy of the 9th/12th Lancers Museum, Derby)

he made his way to the Cape of Good Hope, where, by his genteel appearance and good address, he soon managed to ingratiate himself with an opulent merchant, and obtained a good situation, and might have done well, had not his natural waywardness destroyed his prospects and lost him his liberty; for while drinking one night at a tavern, a quarrel ensued betwixt him and some sailors, one of whom went out to India with him, and recognizing him, reported him as a deserter. The consequence was that on the following morning he was taken prisoner, and eventually forwarded to his regiment in India. He was tried by court martial, flogged, and received twelve months' imprisonment.

It would seem at this time that the shrine of Mars was never to be satiated with human sacrifices, for ere another week had passed, another victim was to be immolated. This was a soldier of Her Majesty's 32nd Foot[8]. His offence was *striking and abusing a Sergeant* when in execution of his duty. I was not present at this last execution, being on duty, but I heard the fatal volley; a sound which brought the whole ceremony vividly before my imagination. He was an Irishman and a Catholic. Of his former character and habits I knew but little, but I believe he had been an indifferent soldier. He did not bear his fate with that fortitude which distinguished the others. He was supported with much difficulty along the front of the ranks. It is worthy of remark that the sergeant who was made the inadvertent and unwilling cause of the fatal court-martial, grieved to the heart, at being instrumental in the death of a fellow-soldier, became a prey to melancholy, and finally committed suicide by jumping down a well, thus adding another victim to the catalogue. It is not less remarkable, too, that the sergeant who was appointed Provost, and had to shoot with his pistol poor Atkins, the first victim, committed suicide in the same manner three years afterwards.

Taking a review of this painful subject, we assert, without hesitation, that no reasonable man can justify the perpetration of such black and foul destruction of human life. We find that three men have been *shot* for offences which, in civil legislation, would hardly be constituted a crime, or at least would be expiated by the payment of a few shillings, or at most a few months' imprisonment. These, too, were committed under somewhat palliating circumstances; the poor victims had been subject, in a greater or less degree, to the perpetual persecutions of petty tyrants, until their better feelings had become blunted, they had lost all respect for themselves, had little respect for others; and were finally exasperated to the commission of that offence which proved fatal to them.

These men, in the waywardness of youth, and deluded by the vain pomp and show of military spectacles, had quitted their homes, and all that was dear to them, had voluntarily embarked their youth and manhood, and even life itself, in the service of their country. They were expatriated from their native land, and doomed to drag through the best of their days in a withering and pestiferous climate. This was not all; like true patriots they had nobly fought, perhaps bled for their country, and had contributed to gain honour, rank, and titles for their commanders. What was their reward. How many generals – nay, how many of our aristocracy owe their rank and titles to the *common soldier.* 'Tis the *common soldier* who toils through his long and arduous marches, who suffers fatigue, hardships, and privations in his incessant watchings, who advances to the charge 'midst showers of grape and musketry, fearlessly braves the imminent breach, and jeopardizes his life in a thousand different ways for his country and his generals. But does he reap the reward of such conduct. Alas, the truth replies 'no,' 'tis his generals who reap the reward to a greater or lesser degree; and it is at the caprice of these very generals that he is doomed to an unjust and ignominious death. The savages of the wilds of Africa could not be guilty of a blacker piece of ingratitude.

During the Hungarian war all England was in a ferment of horror, and shuddered to hear of Hungarian prisoners being shot in cold blood by their remorseless persecutor, Haynau[9]. Not an editor of a newspaper or periodical but took up his pen to champion the cause of the unfortunate patriots, to cast such opprobius epithets on the inhuman Haynau as he deserved, and to compassionate the poor sufferers. This was truly worthy of a great nation, and may Englishmen ever be prepared to take the part of the oppressed patriots of other nations. But so strangely incongruous is an Englishman, that while his whole energies are directed towards a suffering foreigner, his own countrymen – *his country's protectors* – may be *shot* without giving him the least concern to know the reason why, or how justly, or otherwise they suffer death. 'Tis enough to him that they are *common soldiers*; two words implying mere animals, distinct from human kind, and only used as tools to carry out the work of their Generals. These, too, have *willed* that it should be so, and there the matter rests. The tale is recited in England as a mere matter of course, and the next topic, or a visit to a ball or theatre, totally erases it from the minds of those who have heard it, and thus the matter sinks into oblivion. Had these military executions occurred in any other country but our own, or rather in any other army, under the same circumstances, the people of England would have shuddered at the bare recital of the fact, and rivers of ink would have flowed in the cause of the unfortunates; but as they were but British *common soldiers* they were not worth an evanescent thought[10].

The victims, poor fellows, were not the only individual sufferers. How painfully revolting was it for their fellow comrades who were made the involuntary witnesses, and ten-fold so those who were compelled to be their executioners. And how poignant would be the grief of fathers, mothers, brothers, and sisters, on receipt of the sad news.

It may be urged that the increasing offences for which they suffered demanded the extreme penalty of the law for its suppression. Such an assertion, however, I am convinced, would never be made by the right minded and philanthropic. That this may be a palliation on the part of the Commander-in-Chief I admit; but I think that no one will allow the cause to *justify* the effect. Other feasible, equally as effectual, and less barbarous modes of suppressing the evil might have been resorted to; methods which would have had the desired effect, and have at least redounded more to the honour of a nation which boasts of freedom, justice, and mercy. These men were not guilty of spilling man's blood, hence, according to the laws of both God and man, their blood should not be spilled. If we trace ancient history we cannot find one single instance where a soldier suffers death for 'striking a superior officer,' and yet the ancient Greeks and Romans always maintained a super-excellent discipline in their phalanxes and legions; such deeds are only worthy of a Nero, Tiberius, or Sejanus, a Robespierre, or a Grouchy.[11] They cast a stain on the otherwise lustrous character of one of the greatest generals of the day, and will be a dark spot on the page of military history.

Having treated on a subject so sternly savage, I will say a few brief words on another mode of military punishment, almost equally inhuman, and shamefully degrading, flogging. A man for a trivial offence is tied up to the halberts[12], and his comrades are compelled to use the lash until his back is excoriated in a most revolting manner, while his fellow soldiers are made the witness of the disgusting scene. In England there is a society, whose principles are to protect *animals* from cruel treatment, and if a man is seen to ill treat his own horse, ass, or dog, he is fined, or otherwise punished as an inhuman wretch. But Englishmen are such a strange inconsistent people, that while they forbid a beast to be hurt, they look with indifference on the torture of their fellow countrymen inflicted by the degrading lash. Flogging produces effects the reverse of what are intended. Once subject a soldier to the 'cat' and he loses all respect for himself, and consequently all respect for his officers; he becomes reckless of all consequences, and, like a hardened gambler, plunges deeper and deeper into military crimes, until either death or the penal settlements rid the service of a bad soldier. Out of upwards of two hundred I have seen flogged during my military career,[13] only in two instances has it produced beneficial results. Those whose propensities are naturally evil the 'cat' will never improve, and such should not be permitted to contaminate the others by their evil practices, but should be summarily ejected from the ranks. If this was done the army would soon become a respectable and well conducted class of men, and at least the barrack room would be more endurable to the quiet and well conducted. Many a soldier may trace his disgrace and ruin in the service to the lash, and not a few have either died under it, or at remoter periods, from its effects. The case of the poor soldier of the 7th Hussars, in 1846, which created so much excitement in England[14], was but one out of many more which have been carried from the halberts to the hospital, and from thence to the grave, many unthought of, uncared for, and unknown.

Since the above mentioned exposure of this torturing system, flogging has been limited to fifty lashes[15], but the flogging is more severe and equally as degrading as ever, and even that limited number, under some circumstances, may prove fatal; an instance of which occurred during the present year, 1850, at Allahabad, on a recruit just arrived from England, who sunk under the lash and extreme heat combined, the day after the punishment was inflicted.

It is highly essential that the discipline of the army should be maintained with the utmost strictness. Were it otherwise insubordination and demoralization would soon supply the place of discipline. But we know that the cat-o-nine tails, though a torturing instrument, is not a weapon of so much terror in the eye of the soldier as to keep him in the pale of military law. In Russia, Austria, Prussia, and France, the lash is unknown[16]; and yet where are there better troops, or men in better discipline than in these countries. England stands alone as favouring this horribly degrading punishment. It is the only land where the blood of man gushes forth on the application of the knotted lash. Such brutality is unknown in any other country, except amongst slaves.

The barrack room in India seems to claim a passing remark. It may safely be designated a mirror, where all the varieties of human life are reflected. No two blades of grass, no two speeches from the throne, no two peas are exactly alike; how much wider and more curious a difference might the nicely observing eye detect between any two soldiers. Like the debtors in prison, the paupers in the poor house, they resemble each other in one point only, and differ on ten thousand. Debtors by merely occupying one prison together; paupers by simply occupying the lowest place in the social scale; but there ends the likeness. Let those who walk about the open world troubling themselves in vain, or wearying out their days in shadowy pursuits, just take a survey of the matters going forward in this noisy region, where they will see traits of human life not to be witnessed elsewhere, and where the beings fret and fume away their time, with fully as much anxiety as their brethren of the wider sphere which they have quitted. Irritated, vexed, and annoyed almost beyond endurance by flies, heat, and dust, during the day; robbed of natural rest by a stagnated and suffocating atmosphere at night, almost devoured by mosquitoes, sand flies, bugs, &c., the soldier's situation is far from enviable; and to crown the whole, tormenting jealousies, the pride of office, the love of rank, the overweening airs of your would-be great men, and your little great men, with a whole catalogue of petty nuisances, invented as if by patent, for the express [gap in text] person of common sense from the profession. The soldier who goes out to India often curses his own folly in entering the service. He lingers through the early and best years of his manhood in tasteless dislike of the monotonous routine of regimental duty, and in gloomy despondency amidst the blighted prospects of his youth. From his brothers and relations in Europe he perhaps seldom hears, and their letters are but wormwood to him. They have toils there it is true, but are they not at, and have not they the comforts of *home*?

Aye, and in that one word, home, lies all the earthly happiness which an exiled soldier sighs, and hourly pines for in vain. He has out lived many of his comrades in arms; has followed them to the scattered tombs of our up-country cantonments, or has seen them fall beneath the sword or bullet on the battle field. He is a martyr to a broken constitution, and his yellow and wasted cheek gives token of withered health. He is alone in the world; his native country has long ceased to hold out charms for him; he is unknown there, and his friends have either ceased to exist, or care not for the expatriated soldier in the East. Is not this a gloomy picture? I could point out many who might sit for it, and who, ere they give their bones to moulder beneath the sun of Hindostan, would feelingly bear testimony to the truth of its description – yet this is 'life in India.'

Having made these observations, I will now return to passing events. A sad and melancholy event befell one of our men in the cold season of 1847, by which a check was put to our occasional country sports or gypsy parties. Some half dozen men had obtained leave of absence one Sunday, and resolving to have a spree, had hired a small pony each, and rode out into the country to a grog shop, where they spent the day and their money, and got inebriated. On returning to quarters they must needs race each other, and away they went flying like a lot of Gilpins[17] through the jungle; one of them it appears, a newly arrived recruit, tumbled off his horse, but the remainder laughing and calling him a 'joskin,' kept up the chase and left the poor fellow to his fate. His 'Rosinante' it appears gave him the slip, and after walking some distance – for he was not hurt by the fall – he lay down to sleep. The next day he was found by the natives a black and swollen corpse, having been bitten by a venomous snake. That which seemed to increase the melancholy fate of the youth, was the fact that he had just become the owner of £6,000 in property and money in England, by the death of a relative, and an order for his discharge came immediately after his death. Scarcely a brake, jungle, or ruin, in India but abounds with snakes of the most poisonous description, with numberless other venomous and noxious reptiles, which are at all times a just dread to the sportsman, and an alloy to the pleasures of the excursionist. Some months prior to this occurrence two natives were sleeping under some mango trees adjoining the grave yard, as is usually the custom here during the hot season. It was their last sleep. They were bit by a cobra do capello, and within two hours their bodies were changed into loathsome corruption. I saw them about eight hours afterwards, lying side by side on the grass, a few yards removed from where they received the fatal bite. They were the most frightful and disgusting objects I ever saw, hardly a semblance of the human form could be traced. Their bodies resembled the carcase of a large black buffalo which had been drowned and become swollen and putrid from being a long time in water. It seemed as if their whole bodies were inflated with air and in a state of fermentation, while the outer surface was covered in blisters. The bites were, one on the middle finger, and the other on the arm, and so small that they could hardly be seen.

10

The Punjab Campaign: Ramnuggar

And there was mounting in hot haste: the steed,
The mustering squadron, and the clattering car,
Went pouring forward with impetuous speed,
And swiftly forming in the ranks of war.

The state of affairs in India now rendered it necessary that all the disposable force of the British army there, should assemble at certain points in the Punjaub, in November, 1848. The base and treacherous murder of our envoys, Vans Agnew, and Anderson, at Mooltan, is fresh in the memory of all who took interest in those revolutionary times in India. But this was only a prelude to the storm which shortly afterwards burst out and spread itself throughout the Punjaub, causing a fearful effusion of blood, and at one time seeming to threaten the subversion of the British Empire in India. The open disaffection of Shere Sing, the Commander-in-Chief of the Sikh forces, together with the *Sirdars* and soldiery, speedily manifested itself. Then followed conspiracies and intrigues, for subverting British authority in the Punjaub. We were ordered to march on the 29th September. Our route from Meerut to Ferozepore, 22 days, lay through the same country as that through which we marched in 1845, to join the army on the Sutlej. The days being yet extremely hot, our marches were accomplished generally before sunrise. Of all the harassing and wearisome marches a soldier can know, that during hot weather is the worst. The heat is so suffocating in the tents, and the flies so fierce in the day time, that you are vexed beyond endurance. Then at night when you should be enjoying rest, you have scarcely stretched your weary limbs on your pallet, ere you are aroused by the trumpet. You must turn out, pack up, mount and off for the road, while all the world beside are enjoying sound repose. Being thus incessantly deprived of our required rest, drowsiness irresistibly steals over all to a greater or less extent in these nocturnal marches, and, like the mariner, we could 'ride and sleep.'

As we again passed over the ever memorable fields of Mudki and Ferozeshah, I could not but remark the pleasing change which had come over those scenes of blood and strife. The villages were again inhabited by the peasantry, and patches of corn, indigo, and sugar cane, were waving in their full luxuriance. Under British protection the peasant followed his peaceful avocations unmolested, and where but three years before were heard the loud clang of battle, the thundering cannon, and the rolling volleys of musketry, was now all quiet and tranquillity, and nature herself seemed to smile, as if to bury in oblivion the havoc that ambition had made. Happily hardly a vestige of the former fearful devastation was now visible, save the clustering graves and the piles of whitened bones and skulls of the slain, which had been gathered by the cultivators, and thrown in heaps together as encumbering the ground. Such is the soldier's end who falls on the battle field, and such is his *honour and glory*. In a solitary and almost isolated spot, about a mile from the village of Ferozeshah, stands out in bold relief an obelisk of snow-white *chunam*. A marble slab about a foot from its base bears the following inscription:

TO THE MEMORY OF
SIR PETER COLNETT LAMBERT,
WHO FELL IN ACTION AT FEROZESHA, ON THE
22nd DECEMBER, 1845.
THIS IS ERECTED OVER HIS REMAINS BY HIS
BROTHER OFFICERS.
Requiescat in pace[1].

We reached Ferozepore on the 21st October, and in consequence of grass being scarce on that station, we quitted it the following morning. Ferozepore was our extreme frontier station prior to the annexation of the Punjaub, and as such was used as a depot for stores and ammunition. A low but massive mud wall protects the arsenal and munitions. When the Sikhs invaded our territory in 1845, they first threatened this fort, but subsequently took up a position around Ferozeshah, a village about twenty-six miles from Ferozepore, thus throwing themselves betwixt the fort and the British army that was marching up to its relief; hence the battle of Ferozeshah.

On the 26th we crossed the Sutlej and again entered the Punjaub amidst rain and thunder; a natural enough course of the elements, yet such would have been pronounced an unlucky omen by the ancients. It certainly was so to us, inasmuch as we got a good drenching, and consequently were in much discomfort. We encamped about two miles from the river, and remained in a state of inactivity until the 8th of November. Two regiments of native cavalry here reinforced us, and on the 1st of November, Brigadier Cureton reviewed us.

Brigadier Cureton was every inch a soldier, having seen much hard service. He had known what it was to do a private soldier's duty, having obtained his first commission from the ranks, consequently he generally dispensed with unnecessary pomp and ceremony when only rough and ready service was required. As a soldier, none could be more brave and intrepid, but as a leader he was too impetuous; hence the almost fruitless effusion of blood at Ramnuggar, as the reader will see in a following page.[2]

On the 8th of November, our brigade was put in motion, and moved towards Lahore. Our first march in brigade order gave us a prescient of that which afterwards really resulted from our feeble Brigadier,[3] an imbecile who was destined, by his want of tact or generalship, to bring an indelible stain on as brave and distinguished a corps as ever drew a sword. Brigadier Pope was one whose personal appearance and pusillanimous conduct, was ill calculated to inspire the soldier with that respect and enthusiasm which he should entertain towards his leader. So enfeebled and stiff was he that he had always to be lifted into his saddle, and when there, in his padded coats and wrappings on a cold morning, he wanted but a peruke to make him the exact personification of 'Dr. Syntax astride his 'Grizle,' in search of the picturesque.'[4] He was quite a valetudinarian. In this state then how absurd to enter a campaign, where activity and excitement is the order of the day.

We reached Lahore on the 10th, and this time I was more fortunate in viewing this fortified city. The capital of Lahore is undoubtedly one of the great wonders of the East. It is enclosed by well constructed fortifications, a strong and handsome wall forming a sweep of eight miles, and armed enclosure seldom rivalled. There are twelve gates, and as many wickets, each of the former having a double entrance, so that if any adversary did force the outer gate, he must pass through a flanking fire before reaching the second. The wall is, throughout the greater part of its extent, fronted by a *fausse-braze*, and a deep and broad ditch. The interior of this *fausse-braze* now forms comfortable barracks for Sepoys, and some alterations have been made in the flanking towers to make them suitable for officers' quarters. Her Majesty's 53rd Foot[5] occupied the north-western corner of the fortress, near to the Palace, part of their barracks very pleasantly overlooking the river Ravee, and a large sweep of country beyond. A spacious, clean, and paved square, formerly used by the Sikhs on occasions of great religious festivities, served them for the double purpose of barrack yard and drill ground. In the centre of this square stands the famous Hazareh Baguh, with its high minarets and shining domes. This is a noble looking edifice and formerly was the Sikh's principal *samee dukhan* or place of worship. It is now however devoted to the use of the *Feringhee's* munitions of war. In September of this year, 1848, a plot for its destruction and the utter extinction of the Europeans from Lahore, was discovered in time for its frustration, or terrible would have been the catastrophe. One of our irregular cavalry, a shrewd fellow, pretended to join the conspirators, and attended several of their meetings. Having obtained a true knowledge of the plot he made it known to the British governor of Lahore, for which he was highly praised and duly rewarded by government. About a mile distant from the city runs the Ravee, the Hydraotes of the Greeks, and on the opposite bank of which stands the monuments of the Moghul Emperor, Jehangeer and his consort, the celebrated Noor Jehan. They are worth a traveller's while stopping to look at them, if it were only on account of the historic recollections of those who have long since mouldered into dust beneath them. They are the greatest architectural wonder I have seen, but I believe are far surpassed by some of the magnificent tombs at Agra. Although many ages have passed away since their erection, they are quite fresh in appearance.

At one o'clock on the morning of the 12th October, we struck camp and marched in a north-westerly direction. Our route lay across a vast, uncultivated, and wild looking plain, thickly studded with prickly bushes. The moon was shining and a sharp nor-wester was streaming over the plain, and we felt it most piercingly cold. We did not pull up until we had marched about twenty-four miles, and then encamped on a large grassy plain. Here we halted about five days. On the 17th to Groganwallah, distance unknown. Here we joined Brigadier Wheeler's brigade. About two miles from camp stood a large picturesque looking town.

18th to Guzenwallah, a large and well-built town. About half a mile north of it stands a strong built and formidable looking mud fort. It forms a square, covering an area of about an acre of ground. It was at this time in the possession of Utter Sing, a young *Sirdar* of nineteen years of age, professing alliance with the British, and in consonance therewith he had hoisted the British colours from the ramparts. As we passed under its walls the *Khalsa* soldiers flocked to the ramparts, and many came out of the fort to scrutinize the *Feringhees*, with whom they were destined in a few weeks to measure their strength as enemies. They were men of athletic frames, and looked as if they were capable of any desperate service. Some concealed a lurking treachery in their hearts, but others more palpably manifested hatred and resentment in their ferocious countenances.

About ten days subsequent to that of which I am now writing, their treachery broke out more openly, for our siege train, which was marching up to join the army, was attacked by this same garrison. However, their designs having previously been communicated to the Commander-in-Chief by a spy, Brigadier Wheeler, with a formidable little force, was detached from the main army, and came up with the siege train just in time to save it from falling into the hands of the treacherous garrison. They, however, nearly all made their escape, and managed by a detour to form a junction with Shere Sing, and they afterwards figured at Chillianwallah and Goojerat.

On the 20th we joined the Commander-in-Chief, with staff and three battalions. 21st formed a junction with the advanced divisions, under Major-General Gilbert, Brigadiers Cureton and Wheeler. The forces now concentrated amounted to about 18,000 of all arms. Hitherto we had met with no enemy to oppose us; however today we felt a powerful influence of their proximity. Extra pickets, patrols, and reconnoitring parties were thrown out along the front of our lines on our part; and the enemy, as if to convince us of their whereabouts, were firing at intervals throughout the day, seemingly at no great distance, and direct to our front. All hands were on the *qui vive* and looking to their arms and ammunition in anticipation of a closer acquaintance with our long bearded friends of 1846. No one need be told that a multiplicity of rumours, reports, and speculations, most of them vague, contradictory and unfounded, are the forerunners of the advance of an army. 'The enemy is in position at such a point with so many thousand men, his front covered by a deep and impassable river,' declares one; 'We shall soon have a brush with them,' says a second; and so on, every man conjuring up something wherewith to throw a light, not only on the intended operations and movements of his own army, but moreover on those of his enemy. The *on dits* on the present occasion were by no means few; yet we were not left long to conjecture, for at two o'clock on the following morning (22nd) the 3rd and 14th [Light] Dragoons[6], with 5th Light Cavalry[7] and a Light Field Battery, were detached to the front as a feeling party. At seven the desultory firing of cannon to our front intimated to us that the hornet's nest had been disturbed, and immediately afterwards the trumpet sounded to horse, and though we were just getting our breakfast we left our gastronomic avocations until we had more time, mounted, and in less time than it has taken me to write it, were advancing at a brisk trot to join in the strife. Away we dashed past artillery and infantry, each battalion cheering us as we passed them. We cheered in turn, and never, I believe, were troops more eager for the fray. However, we were destined not to 'go in' as soon as we expected; for having got a little in advance of our brethren on foot, both our speed and ardour received a check, as we dropped into a steady walk.

In the mean time the firing in front alternately increased and abated, and it sounded as if it were at so little distance from us that we expected every minute to come up with the combatants. Our march was directed over a vast ocean-like plain, dotted here and there with villages, *topes* of trees, and patches of sugar cane. The sun was powerfully hot, rendering the *mirage* strong and delusive, for a broad and clear stream seemed to be at no great distance from our front. This we thought was the river Chenab, on whose banks we knew the Sikhs had taken position, while the dark patches of sugar cane seemed to complete the illusion, by presenting to our eyes the exact appearance of columns of infantry. As we advanced, these columns with the river receded, which soon convinced us of our error, but about noon stern reality confronted us; for as we debouched from behind the town of Ramnuggar, a long line of turbaned heads, glittering bayonets and swords stretched along our front as far as the eye could reach both right and left. The 14th were just retiring from their charge, and the 3rd Light Dragoons and 5th Light Cavalry, were a little in advance, supporting a Light Field Battery, which kept up an occasional fire, smartly returned by the Sikhs. Some of the killed and wounded had been borne from the scene of strife, and were stretched in *dhoolies* in a ravine just out of cannon range of the enemy. Having crossed the nullah we drew up in line; the officers grasped their swords more firmly, and we took up our reins preparatory to an expected charge. The enemy, jealous of our proximity, began to bang off their nine-pounders, which rattled amongst us rather unpleasantly. It appeared that this firing was but a ruse for their cavalry to retire across the river. After waiting some minutes in this very unpleasant situation for the order to advance, we were ordered instead to 'take ground to the right,' and there form a main picket.

This convinced us that there would be no more fighting today, and we could soon perceive the Sikhs retiring very orderly to their camp on the opposite side of the river, where they were strongly posted along its bank. Thus a broad, deep, and rapid river lay betwixt us and our foe, along the opposite bank of which cannon and *jin-jowls* bristled everywhere, forming a formidable opposition to an opposing force. The army now retired out of possible range of the Sikh guns, and took up lines for encampment. My squadron, now on picket, had just dismounted, and were stood to their horses, when all at once our Major shouted, 'Three or four men of you mount and gallop to the rescue of yonder officer!' In a moment a greater part of the squadron was mounted and galloping to the support of Lieut. Williams of the 24th Foot[8], who having foolishly gone out and approached a *tope* of trees between us and the river, was suddenly pounced upon by a dozen Sikh horsemen from their ambush, and he being mounted on a small pony, they were fast gaining ground on him, but as we approached to the rescue they fired a volley into us and wisely retired to their ambush. This same officer had ample revenge afterwards, for the mean advantage they had attempted to take. He was an excellent shot with the rifle, and throughout the campaign subsequent to this, adopted their own mode of retaliation whenever he could see a chance. While we were at Ramnuggar he was perpetually out in advance of the videttes, either concealed in a patch of sugar cane or under the edge of a *nullah* opposite the said *tope*, from whence the Sikhs would steal to fire on our videttes. In this manner he picked many of them off, and taught the rest that our videttes were not to be annoyed with impunity. At Chillianwallah, this brave man received no less than thirteen wounds in the fearful melee of his unfortunate corps, and it was only by dint of cool and intrepid courage that he succeeded in fighting his way out from amongst the enemy. Though he suffered much from this fearful mutilation, and his life was sometime despaired of, he ultimately recovered and I trust is alive while I am writing this[9].

In the affair at Ramnuggar, Colonel Havelock, of the 14th, fell at the head of his regiment, with many others, in a ravine. It appears that when Brigadier Cureton first came up with the foe in the morning, they had very strong outposts on this side of the river; he fired into them and a smart cannonading occurred on both sides, and continued for some time, the enemy in the meanwhile bringing reinforcements from the opposite bank. At length about 11 o'clock, Brigadier Cureton ordered the 14th and two Regiments of native cavalry, supported by a light field battery, to charge.

A body of Sikh cavalry waited to receive them. They advanced at a trot under a heavy shower of round shot and grape, and when at a proper distance from the foe, spurred their horses for the charge; but just as they approached the front ranks of the Sikhs, they found themselves on the edge of a deep *nullah*, under the shelving bank of which were a number of Sikh infantry; many fell headlong with their horses into the midst of the *Khalsa's* bayonets and *tulwars*, and fearful was the slaughter of the dragoons. It was here that Havelock, while tally-hoeing like a huntsman, fell pierced with a dozen musket balls. His body was not discovered until the enemy vacated their position twelve days afterwards. Brigadier Cureton was killed in the onset by a cannon shot, also Captain Fitzgerald of the 5th Light Cavalry[10], with many men. Besides the loss of two field officers and a great number of men and horses, a gun stuck fast in the sand, and was abandoned to the enemy – rather an unpropitious opening of the campaign. Its moral effects at such a time, when the whole Punjaub was wavering and ready to throw off its allegiance to the British, soon became visible.

The British arms have been so long used to one continued stream of conquest in India, that anything short of a decisive victory is at once construed by the natives into a defeat, hence the British lose their prestige – that which enables them to rule over sixty millions of Asiatics – and the real sentiments of the disaffected openly manifest themselves by joining the ranks of the enemy. Such was the inimical results of this abortive affair at Ramnuggar. Shere Sing caused it to be proclaimed throughout the country that he had obtained a glorious victory over the British; this induced the *Sirdars* (petty chiefs) as also the Afghans – who before hesitated from fear of the British arms – to join the rebellious standard, and from that day Shere Sing's forces augmented, until from about 20,000 they numbered more than 60,000. That the brave Cureton acted too precipitately in charging against such fearful odds, and over ground of which he was perfectly ignorant, is indisputably true; but whether it was on his own responsibility or not is a matter known but to few[11]. Some have gone so far as to say that in charging he acted contrary to orders, and that he was simply to reconnoitre the enemy's position. Cureton's error, however, if it was one, was one of which some of the cleverest generals have been guilty. Had the result been adequate to the intrepid *coup de main*, which he made, it would have been worthy of so brave a leader, and his memory would have been justly lauded as a 'Moore' or a 'Wolfe,'[12] for like them he fell in the midst of the fight, though victory did not render his death so illustrious. Yet his intrepid and cool courage alone should immortalize his name, and class him among England's bravest soldiers. His form, once so noble and manly, now lies mouldering with two brave companions who fell with him (Colonel Havelock and Captain Fitzgerald) beneath the shade of some citron and orange trees, in a garden at Ramnuggar, once the property and shady lounge of Shere Sing, and in which stands the house in which he first breathed. A snow-white obelisk, with the names of the three inscribed thereon, points out the spot where they are interred.

I now return to my note book. My squadron, as I have said before, was posted on picket, and this night our lodging was on the cold ground, for in the hurry to mount in the morning our camp and luggage were left standing in the last camp ground, and it was not until the following day that they came in. The night passed in quiet, but it was evident that the Sikhs, from their continuous stirring to and fro near their watch fires, were uneasy at our proximity to them, and were on the alert.

The greater proportion of the 23rd was occupied in taking up our position, and we had just pitched our tents, and were congratulating ourselves on having a little rest and a meal – for we had had none since the morning previous – when the 'turn out' sounded, and we found, to our vexation, that our opposite neighbours had commenced their old mode of annoying us; but on our advancing up to the front, they, as usual, retired. The Chenab (Greek Ascesines) here runs directly east and west, and our encampment extended about two miles in a line parallel with it, and exactly opposite to that of the Sikhs; but their camp considerably out-flanked ours on each side, extending almost as far as the eye could reach on the left, and far in the distance on the right. Our pickets were posted about fourteen or fifteen hundred yards from those of the Sikhs, who formed an extensive chain on the same side of the river as ourselves. Thus confronting each other, no one could move in front of either camp without being seen by the pickets of the opposite one. Our duty here was very heavy. Europeans[13] alone formed the main pickets, which were posted opposite the ford of the river. There being but three dragoon regiments on the ground, it of course came to our turn to furnish a squadron every third day, and that with a squadron in front of our own lines, together with furnishing guards, patrols, &c., hardly allowed us a whole night in bed once a week. However there was no use in murmuring, for as the sergeant of my tent used to say: 'More duty more honour,' a charming consolation for a night on the cold sand and sometimes a fast for a day or two. On the 24th I was on main picket. About 9 o'clock in the morning, a party of Sikh cavalry sallied from the *tope* before spoken of, and taking a sweep along the right front of our pickets killed one *Sepoy*, wounded another, took a European prisoner, and captured some camels which had gone beyond the videttes. At sun-set, just as the videttes were being doubled, we seized on a native who had just come over from the Sikh camp. On his person being examined, some papers rolled up like cartridges were found, offering inducements to our *Sepoys* to desert. He was a wily grey bearded old gentleman, and when seized by the vidette, and while being examined, he, pretending to be a padre, was counting his beads[14], and to our interrogations only answered '*ace, doe*,' (one, two) and so on. However his *ace* and *doe* would not do for old soldiers, and he was forwarded to the Commander-in-Chief for further examination. How he with many other prisoners we sent into camp at different times, were disposed of, I never heard; but on more than one occasion it was whispered that a hempen rope cut short their traitorous career. This circumstance reminds me of a trait in the character of the *Sepoys* which is worthy of notice here. I mean their undeviating faith and fidelity under all circumstances and changes. After the battle of Mudki, and while the Sikh hosts at Ferozeshah menaced the British forces, the Sikh emissaries had spread themselves throughout the English camp, offering large rewards, high rates of pay, and all the liberty and licence of the Sikh soldiery, to induce them to come over to their service; our force consisted of less than 20,000, and out of that only about 6,000 were Europeans, while the Sikhs numbered more than 50,000; add to this the fact that the Sikhs, through a long stream of conquest, had inspired the natives of Hindostan with the idea that they were invincible, and their numbers and name had produced a moral dread throughout India.

Thus our cause, under such a combination of formidable foes, seemed desperate; yet spite of all this the *Sepoy* was impervious to bribes, and true to his colours. 'No,' he would say to the seducer, 'I have eaten of the Company's salt, and how can I desert.' Before Sobraon too the Sikhs tried every stratagem to alienate our native soldiery from their colours, but with very few exceptions they were unsuccessful. Few mercenary troops, as they are termed, could be more staunch and faithful, and on the whole more compliant than the British *Sepoy*, and though they may have occasionally shown a spirit of mutiny and revolt, yet it has not been without a real or imaginary infringement of their rights or religious prejudices[15].

An European gunner, in a mad fit of drunkenness, went over to the enemy, and it is said, challenged Shere Sing out to fight, but his illustrious opponent not seeing fit to accept the challenge, he became infuriated, and struck a Sikh soldier, who immediately cut him down. Throughout this day the Sikh horsemen kept us perpetually turning out and mounting. The *tope* served for an ambush from which they would occasionally sally and drive in our videttes, just as if by way of diversion and amusement. One fellow in particular, who was very conspicuous from riding a milk white horse, had become most vexingly daring, and had commenced his delectable pastimes early this morning by knocking over one of our videttes. However he did not long revel in these diversions with impunity, for a rifle bullet from the piece of Lieut. Williams cut short his career and relieved us from so annoying a neighbour.

25th. The man who was taken prisoner the day before yesterday was sent back to his camp, and brought the account I have just related of the man who foolishly challenged Shere Sing to fight. He says he himself was well treated by Shere Sing, but the soldiery handled him very roughly while in the guard. 26th nothing important. 27th on main picket. Two natives came in bearing intelligence from Lieut. Abbott, who had been obliged to shut himself up in the fort of Attock, on the banks of the Indus, where he was now besieged by the Hazarians[16]. He was subsequently betrayed into the hands of the enemy. These messengers being suspected as British emissaries, had been retained in Shere Sing's camp all night and strictly examined, but no papers being found on them they were liberated. They had shrewdly enough placed Abbott's dispatches between the soles of their shoes. We took several prisoners during the day. The Sikhs, as is usual, ushered in the new moon this evening with a *feu de joi*. The whole line of their encampment seemed to be one continued blazing of musketry; every one seemed to be firing away *ad libitum*. It being nearly dark, it seemed as if the whole country in our front was a general blaze of squibs and crackers.

30th. My squadron formed a reconnoitring party. We took a sweep along the front of the Sikh camp and marched some distance beyond their extreme right. As we neared the line of videttes they seemed to fear contamination from us, for they retired as we approached, and ridiculously kept up a continuous pop, pop, pop at us, but did no harm.

1st Dec. At one o'clock this morning a division under General Thackwell[17] moved off to the right towards Wuzeerabad, with instructions to cross the Chenab by a ford to be pointed out by a guide, and, if successful in this, to take the enemy in flank, while the force left here was to threaten them in front, and if possible effect a passage across the river, and thus bring on a general engagement in front and flank. In furtherance of this, every man was served with half rations for the following day. Long before the break of day we were mounted and in position to the front, awaiting the signal from Thackwell's force to commence action. We were all excitement and full of conjecture as to the work laid out for us, which seemed to be a diversion of no very pleasing character, seeing that we had to force a passage across a deep and broad river in the very teeth of a host of bayonets, showers of musketry, grape, and other missiles. However, every man's courage seemed screwed up to the sticking point, and the desperation of the anticipated adventure seemed to give an interest and stimulus to the enterprise; but after awaiting the expected signal for some hours, we were ordered to turn in; thus our visions of *honour and glory* were not yet to be realized. It subsequently appeared that Thackwell's division had found that the ford was impracticable, consequently they marched further up the river, and did not cross until the following day. Tonight at sunset I was one of a party on advance outpost. We had just taken our position for the night, dismounted and stood to our horses, when flash went a gun, followed by half a dozen more direct to our front. One of the party had just cried out, '*Kobadar* boys, here come some *bobera wallahs*,'[18] when sure enough they did come in the shape of 12-pounders, striking the ground first and then flying over our heads. This was a treat we had not bargained for, and having no particular desire to sup off such indigestible food, we shifted ground a little to the left. They continued blazing away for some time afterwards, doubtless chuckling to themselves at their cleverness in thus surprising us. Perhaps they fancied they had quite destroyed us. But I think we had the last laugh at them, for they threw away their shot uselessly. About nine o'clock a party of sappers and miners with their implements and accompanied by some *Sepoys*, were ordered to proceed to the *tope* and throw up some defences. But as it was supposed that a Sikh picket occupied its interior, it was necessary first to cautiously reconnoitre it. It was thought that a single horseman would execute this the most successfully, and he was to be a volunteer from our party. The moment the proposition was made half a dozen offered their services; but they were overruled by the sergeant objecting to either horses or men. At length I was picked out, as having a horse which would go anywhere in the dark, and consequently was well qualified for such an enterprise. For my part I felt not a little proud that I had been chosen, though rather uncomfortable at the idea of so hazardous an expedition. However with seeming satisfaction I prepared by first taking off my sword and muffling some of my horse's head gear to prevent the clattering and tinkling noise it would occasion.

This done I mounted and pressed my horse towards the *tope*. The night was calm and serene, a light vapoury dew was hanging over the plain like a thin cloud; the young moon had just sunk in the horizon, and the stars shining brilliantly produced a sort of twilight. The strangeness and novelty of the enterprise, together with an undefinable curiosity to peep into a *tope* which had had so many little adventures connected with it, at first stimulated me on. Its distance from where I started was about a quarter of a mile. Suddenly I was startled by a rush, as if of a pack of wolves, just ahead of me. I looked in the direction and saw a fleshless skeleton before me. It was that of the poor *Sepoy* who was cut down by the Sikh horseman a few days before, and the noise I heard was the sudden retreat of the jackals I had just disturbed at their banquet. This sad sight almost unnerved me for a moment, but I looked forward to the *tope,* and having reason to fear more from the living than the dead, I left the corpse behind me. I approached to within about fifty yards of the *tope*, and halting, listened with breathless silence for some moments. As I thus sat on my horse I could distinctly see the Sikh pickets round their watch fires on the river bank, and could hear the sentries challenging their patrols. I fancied also that I could hear a murmuring of voices from the *tope*, and gazing intently in that direction my imagination conjured up a mounted Sikh just emerging from it. I now felt the loneliness and peril of my situation, and for a moment I hesitated whether I should proceed further, or return without having executed my mission. But at that moment a greater moral fear came over me, that of being laughed at if I returned; so pressing my horse on a few steps at a time, listening at each halt, I was soon under the looming shade of the little wood. Still fearing to trust myself further, I again halted, and listened with a suffocating breathlessness, but all was silent as the grave, when I was startled by the howling of a pack of jackals in the interior. Though this for a moment disturbed my confidence, yet I took it as a good omen, for I felt convinced that if the jackals inhabited the tope, the Sikhs did not. Feeling assured now that the enemy was not there, I circled round the *tope* at a quick pace, and soon turned my back on it to return to my picket. But here again my courage was tried, for I could hear the clatter of horsemen to my right front as if emerging from a patch of sugar-cane in that direction. At the same time I could discern two mounted men making over towards the very direction that I was going, as if to intercept me. I paused for a moment not knowing what to do. I hoped they were some of my comrades, yet I dare not challenge; they halted, and the same moment I heard a low whistle; I knew it to be from my comrades and whistled in return, and pressing my horse forward soon joined two of our party, who were waiting for me, and I communicated the result of my mission to the sergeant.

11

Pursuing Shere Singh

Suspense, my breathing thickens, and my heart
Beats heavily, and with remittent throb,
As like to lose its action.

The next morning daylight developed to the Sikhs what they had never dreamed of – some breastworks and epaulments thrown up, and bristling with 18 and 24-pounders, and threatening the destruction of a portion of their camp. In the meantime Thackwell was crossing with his troops to the right. To divert the enemy then in front, the troops here were again out at daybreak on the 2nd, threatening a general assault. I remarked here that our opposite neighbours never required calling up by us in a morning. They had taken a cautious lesson from Sobraon in 1846. Every morning, long before dawn, drums were beating to arms, and when the morning broke forth it revealed to us the long dark line of Sikhs in battle array. This morning, as usual, as the mist cleared from the river, a long and formidable line of glittering steel, interspersed everywhere with wide-mouthed guns, confronted us on the opposite bank, ready to oppose our passage should we attempt it. They seemed not a little alarmed however for the safety of their camp, as soon as the daylight developed our field works to them, and they began in right good earnest to take ground to the rear. However, by some unaccountable circumstance, we allowed them time to retire without molesting them. But about noon the heavy guns opened fire on them, and the shells soon made great havoc amongst the tents; however we were not to have all the fun to ourselves, for the Sikhs opened their batteries in good earnest, but [gap in text] some fell short and others flew over our heads. The only injury done to us was the blowing up of one of the tumbrils[1] by a shell, and wounding three gunners. In return for this our twenty-fours opened in earnest, and the Sikhs tents were knocked over like nine pins.

In the meantime breast works and parallels were progressing on our side towards the river's edge, as a covering fire for our passage over the river. But it was now evident that Shere Sing began to 'smell a rat,' or rather that he had received intimation of Thackwell's movements, for a great portion of his camp was struck, and dense clouds of dust rising on his left, denoted that a portion of his forces were on the move in the direction that Thackwell was to attack him.

Early on the morning of the 3rd we were again ready to act in concert with Thackwell. We remained standing, or rather lying, to our horses throughout the morning, in anxious expectation of the preconcerted signal from him. About two o'clock p.m. a smart cannonading commenced at some distance from the enemy's left, which convinced us that our brethren had come up with their foe. We seconded them on this side of the river by opening our heavy batteries and menacing the ford, but our opponents were no wise slow in returning the compliment. Several times we advanced towards the ford under our well served batteries, but as often were forced to retire. It were madness to attempt to cross it under such an enfilading fire as was kept up by the Sikh battalions. In this manner the night stole on us and put an end to the strife on our side of the river, and it was evident that it had abated on the opposite side also, as we could only hear occasional shots. We returned to camp, but hardly to rest, for about midnight we were suddenly aroused by a terrible report which shook the ground under us. This was followed by other reports not so loud and which seemed to be from the firing of artillery in the enemy's camp, and then all was quiet. We of course turned out and prepared for a night attack, but after shivering in the cold for some time we again turned in and rested in our clothes until five o'clock. At that time we were again out to the front and expecting something very extraordinary to be done; and many were the reports and opinions as to the terrible explosion I have just mentioned, among which was one that the Sikhs had 'hooked it.' In this manner we remained anxiously waiting for the mist to clear from the river and clear up the mystery at the same time. About eight o'clock the sun began to disperse the mist; we strained our eyes over toward the spot where we last saw the Sikh encampment; it had vanished, and nothing now remained but the naked field works. Here then the mystery of last night's explosions were explained; for they had amused themselves with blowing up their charged mines before they retreated.

I will now inform the reader how Thackwell's division fared. He crossed with his force late in the afternoon of the 2nd, and bivouacked that night a short distance from the ford. On the following morning he advanced in battle array, parallel to the river, towards the Sikh encampment. Shere Sing in the meantime had detached a strong force from the main army to intercept him, and about two o'clock p.m. they came in collision, some four or five miles to the left of the Sikh camp[2]. A brisk cannonading on both sides ensued, and several feints were made by our cavalry, but no general attack was made. In this manner the afternoon was passed, and night found the two armies bivouacked just out of cannon range of each other. The following morning Thackwell was not less surprised than we were to find that they had decamped.

As soon as the fact of their departure was known, we at once marched down to the ford, leaving tents and baggage behind us, and headed by Major Gilbert commenced the passage of the Chenab. We found the river here about a quarter of a mile broad, with a sandy bed now dry about half way across, and forming a little island. The current was very rapid, and being too deep in many places for our horses to bottom, it was with difficulty they were managed. Yet, under the instructions of our judicious leader, who warned us to give our horses a loose rein and follow in his track, we fortunately got to the opposite bank without sustaining any loss. The native troops and camp followers, however, were not so fortunate, as several horses and riders were carried down with the stream, and the men being crippled with their tight uniform and accoutrements, perished.

The passage of these rivers is seldom effected without loss. The 16th Lancers, in crossing the Jumna, on the Afghan campaign, lost fifteen men and horses[3]. A dragoon, with being so crippled with his arms and dress, is quite helpless in the water, hence if once his horse becomes unmanageable, and he gets carried away from the track, it is all over with him.

Having arrived on *terra firma* in the Jetch Doab, a reconnaissance was made of this new country, but no enemy was visible in any direction, and we appeared to be the undisputed possessors of the soil. They had made a clean retreat of it; not a vestige of anything was left behind but the naked breastworks and defences. No less than six batteries had commanded the ford, so constructed that they could throw out an enfilading and cross fire at the same time, and thus threaten almost certain destruction to any force that should attempt its passage. The Sikhs had not been idle while here, for epaulments, abattis, and entrenchments commanded the whole front of their camp along the river's edge, thus evincing a tact and judgment in field works far from contemptible, and which even our Generals could not but admire. Some charged mines had been exploded; and a monster one just at the landing of the ford, convinced us that this had produced the terrible explosion which so unceremoniously aroused us at midnight.

We crossed a broad tract of sand, which in the rainy season, is part of the bed of the river. We then came to another river, or rather a branch of that we had just crossed; we had also two other branches to cross ere we found ourselves in the open country. My regiment being the first in the Doab, we did not wait for the others to cross, but in hopes of coming up with, and annoying the fugitives, we gave rein to our horses. Being headed by a guide we marched over many miles of flat country, but interspersed at intervals with wood and patches of sugar cane, and dotted here and there with mean-looking mud hamlets. However, no enemy could be seen; but that we were on his track we were convinced, from the marks of gun-carriage wheels and other signs of the march of an enemy. We bivouacked on an open plain, near a patch of sugar cane, and having no commissariat with us, we made our breakfast, dinner, and tea, by chewing the cane. During the night several other regiments came up with us, and at daylight on the following morning my regiment, the 14th, and the 5th Light Cavalry, marched in search of the foe. The 14th, after marching with us about two miles, broke off to the right front, while we, with a Light Field Battery, inclined a little to the left. The morning was clear and sharp, producing a transparency in the air seldom known in the humid climate of England. Direct in our front, and apparently within half an hour's ride, arose the barren and rugged mountains, like a thunder cloud from the horizon, called the Salt range, and to the north-east the mountains of the eastern districts of Cashmere – the Peer Pinjal range probably – arose in lofty grandeur, exhibiting

Robed snow wrought and hoar'd with age.

Our route lay through an open uncultivated country for about three miles, when all at once we entered a vast, and almost impervious jungle. We were again guided by a villager who knew the road, or rather track of the retreating army. As we penetrated into the heart of the jungle, we again came upon the tracks of gun-carriages, and soon had other signs of being on the right scent, for several wounded stragglers were taken, from whom we learnt that Shere Sing was now in full march, and but a few miles in advance. In hopes of coming up with him we broke into a brisk trot, but in so doing we broke our ranks also, for, owing to the thick jungle, combined with the dense clouds of dust we made – it being excessively dry – it was impossible for us to keep together. This dust, and the clattering noise we made, soon betrayed us to our foes, of whose proximity we now became certain, from the stray shots which dropped amongst us from his skirmishers, followed by a brisk cannonading, which brought us to a halt. We formed up in the best manner the jungle would permit, and our commanding officer desired the guns to be brought forward and opened in return. But the artillery officer, thinking it unwise to attack the whole Sikh force with a handful of cavalry, objected, saying 'he would not be responsible for his guns if they were thus jeopardized.' Hence we were obliged to return, having obtained nothing but a knowledge of the enemy's position. Harassed, tattered and torn by the jungle, and almost dying with thirst, we returned from the chase, and found the army were pitching camp near to the spot on which we bivouacked last night. On our return, I witnessed a barbarous act, in which was evinced that strong antipathy the Hindoos bear towards the Sikhs, and which makes them such enemies to each other.

A poor Sikh soldier, whom the fortune, or rather misfortune of war, had placed in our power, being badly wounded, was by order of our commanding officer, conveyed in a *dhooly* along with us; but the cruel bearers, having carried him some miles, refused to carry him further, and hurled him out of the *dhooly* on to the narrow path on which we were marching; thus two regiments of cavalry rode over him, few being able to avoid trampling on him from not seeing him, on account of the dust, while the poor wretch's cries were most piteous. The inhuman bearers were subsequently punished for their cruelty.

The 14th and 5th Light Cavalry did not return to camp until midnight, having also picked up several prisoners. My squadron was ordered out on picket here, so that we had to pass another night without the luxury of changing our clothes, which had been thoroughly wetted in the passage of the river on the previous morning. The next morning the ground was taken up for permanent encampment, about two miles from the jungle, and formed a long continuous line facing it. Here we remained for about a month, during which the cavalry were by no means idle, having to furnish strong pickets, reconnoitring parties, escorts, &c. The Sikhs, like foxes, had taken cover in the jungle, and as if we feared losing the game entirely, parties were sent every day to ascertain their whereabouts, so that we became thorough bush rangers, and in some of these expeditions we had no scarcity of adventure and excitement, for we would suddenly surprise a covey of *black birds*, or they would sometimes surprise us, by making a predatory excursion on our cattle while it grazed in the jungle, which would cause a sudden 'turn out' to the rescue. But when we were not engaged by our friends, we were not killed by *ennui*, though I have heard some men say that Englishmen seldom make themselves at home in camp like the soldiers of other nations. However that I will be bold enough to refute from experience. For a short campaign the camp is in every sense of the word the Englishman's home. There are seasons, it is true, when a soldier, worn out and harassed by incessant watchings, hardships, and privations, ardently wishes himself in quarters. But there are few campaigns but have their occasional sunshines, their momentary respites from severe toils and battles. So it was with us here. Though the enemy were but a day's march from us, and were constantly reminding us of their proximity by firing salutes, *feu-de-joies*, &c., and the occasional appearance of cavalry parties; this did not deter us from seeking such diversions and amusements as we could find. Horse and foot racing, hopping, jumping, and other athletic exercises, were performed with true English spirit, and, owing perhaps to the extreme uncertainty of everything, even life itself in camp, gives an interest to its most trivial enjoyments, and makes us grasp at the very shadow of pleasure as it flits by us. These sports were entered into with as much spirit, and more zest and pleasure, than those of the like nature in Europe. The same men who were skirmishing but yesterday in the jungle, today were racing, jumping, or throwing the sledge hammer. An English soldier is never out of his sphere in camp; he is pliant and conformable to circumstances, and can enjoy himself in camp as well as in quarters. Thus Christmas was enjoyed with us in the good old English style. The enemy might fret and fume themselves as they liked, we were determined not to be done out of our old English custom; and as far as circumstances would permit we enjoyed ourselves. I mention these trifles merely to show that British soldiers, contrary to certain fire-side writers, are, either in camp or in quarters, in their element. 'Tis true the camp, like all other scenes of life, has its grumblers, men dissatisfied with everything and everybody around them; yes even with the very order of nature. I believe, however, that they too are happy in their own way; have a heartfelt pleasure in venting their spleen, and feel, by comfortable experience, that grumbling, like virtue, is its own reward. To reason with such persons would be a waste of time; but while pouring out their vials of wrath, and storming the gentle ear of some experienced campaigner with their vain complaints, I have frequently known the torrent of their eloquence suddenly and effectually stopped by the old stager's whiff of cigar, accompanied by the cool and very pertinent question, 'Why did ye list?' There are many occasions, however, on which we are all grumblers, for the life of a soldier teems with annoyance.

This little philosophising brings me to the last day in 1848. Our regiment, with two native cavalry regiments, and two light field batteries, formed a 'flying brigade,' under Brigadier White, for a secret expedition. Various and contradictory were the rumours concerning it, and many were the opinions as to its destination. The latter mystery, however, was soon partly solved by our striking off to the left rear of the camp in a south-westerly direction towards the Chenab. Having proceeded some miles, scouring parties and skirmishers were thrown out, and the brigade assumed an attitude of caution and defence, denoting anticipations of meeting with a foe. A vast level plain lay before us, admirable for cavalry manoeuvres, and we secretly wished we might meet with the Sikhs on such a spot as this, that we might show our prowess on fair and equal terms. Having marched some fourteen or fifteen miles, we halted between two villages, from the inhabitants of which we learnt that some ten or twelve thousand Sikhs had passed there about two hours before our arrival. Thus the game again slipped through our hands, and that day Shere Sing's army received a reinforcement of about 12,000 disciplined troops under Narain Sing.

On the 8th January, 1849, we shifted camp about six miles to the right of the old camp ground. It was now evident that there was a move on the board. Ammunition was renewed, pistols looked to, and swords freshly sharpened. In short everything denoted the approach of a grand struggle. The reason of our long inaction prior to this was owing to our small force and the enemy's strength, with the almost inaccessible jungle in which he had taken his position. We mustered but about 17,000, while the Sikhs were 52,000. Hence we were waiting for reinforcements ere we attacked them. However from some reason, which I have no right to question, Gough determined with this little band to risk a battle. On the 10th he reviewed us, and as he moved down the line he was received with loud and enthusiastic cheering by all ranks and colours. Such demonstrations of confidence in their leader, and enthusiastic ardour to be led to battle from that gallant little band, among whom were many tried veterans whom he had led to victory before, was calculated to cheer the heart of the veteran chief, and make him feel within himself that with such he could conquer the Punjaub. At daybreak on the 12th we were put in motion, and shortly entered the jungle, which we found in this quarter by no means so impervious as that portion we had penetrated before. After marching some hours with difficulty, for want of proper roads or tracks, we emerged into an open cultivated plain, in the centre of which stands the village of Dinghee. On our advance party approaching this place, a number of Sikh cavalry decamped in double quick time; but several infantry and some camels, being less swift of foot, were captured. Here we encamped. Our right flank was bounded by a low range of dark hills, which, running along to our right rear, in a south-easterly direction, increased gradually in magnitude, until they are lost in the vast Himalayas. But in the opposite direction they ran some seven or eight miles to our right front, and suddenly forming an obtuse angle, seemed to form a junction with the Salt range, of which I have before spoken. It was under this Salt range that the enemy swarmed like bees, and along the lower range they had formed their outposts. At night the hills offered a scene quite picturesque. Watch fires kept blazing up at intervals all along the range to our right front, looking in the distance like so many stars of large magnitude sinking in the horizon. However the night passed off without a visit from any of the enemy, as they did not choose to come down from their high places. This night a mystery seemed to hang over the camp. That the enemy were but a few miles from us we had ocular demonstration, and that we should ere long come in collision with them, every man in the camp felt convinced.

However hardly a doubt was left on our minds the following morning, for we were aroused at half past three, without the sound of bugle or drum. Half a *rooty* (loaf) was served to each man, with a dram of grog – a certain forerunner of something very extraordinary. The camp was struck, baggage packed, and we were mounted at day-break. It was a dark and dreary morning, the muttering of distant thunder was heard rolling amongst the mountains to our rear, and the damp chilly wind, and dark surcharged clouds, seemed to portend a coming storm; while the Hades-like expanse of jungle before us looked gloomy and dark, and all nature seemed pervaded with a general gloom. But though all around seemed drear, it was not so with British hearts; for as our veteran chief rode down the line, loud and simultaneous cheers from each corps rang through the welkin and were re-echoed from the mountains. Our commanding officer[4], having formed us in close column, harangued us in the following words:

> Now, my lads, I expect we shall have some sport today; it is expected that we shall meet with the Sikhs, and if we should, 'charge,' I hope you'll keep your horses well in hand, and above all keep together men; don't allow yourselves to become separated, for most assuredly if you do you'll have each a dozen Sikhs pounce on you. If we charge through their ranks, I'll merely give the word 'three's about,' and the rear rank will then charge back. Do this, and be steady and cool, and no enemy can rout us.

This harangue was responded to by loud and repeated cheers, and each soldier felt resolved to conquer or die. At length 'forward' was the word, and the infantry in columns of divisions, and cavalry of squadrons, with artillery interspersed along the line, advanced at a slow and cautious march towards the enemy. We found the jungle in some places thin and scattered, and in others almost impervious, so that we were obliged to march in sections and threes. We had marched about four miles when we emerged on an open space, where we halted for upwards of an hour. Here, on this wild and barren spot, we received letters from Europe[5]. Those harbingers of love, and life's enchanted spring, of hopes born rainbow-like, of smiles and tears; bearing tidings of home and friends – that home and those friends, which under the present circumstances, it seemed very probable many of us would never see more. Many felt the sad conviction that this might be the last home messenger that would ever gladden their eyes, and with such reflections, how many agonizing thoughts would fill the breast.

Yet this did not unman the true British soldier. No, while his bosom swelled with emotion, and perchance a silent tear trickled down his cheek, he would feel all his native courage and patriotic spirit burning within him, and would feel resolved to maintain the honour of his country to his last life's blood.

12

The Battle of Chillianwallah

Mark you war-worn man, who looks on high
With thought and valour mingled in his eye;
Not all the gay revels of the day
Can fright the visions of his home away;
The home of love, and its associate smiles,
His wife's endearments, and his baby's wiles;
Fights he less brave through recollected bliss,
With step retreating, or with sword remiss.
Ah, no! remembered home's the warrior's charm,
Speed to his sword and vigour to his arm;
For this he supplicates the God afar,
Fronts the steeled foe, and mingles with the war.

The reconnoitring party which had been sent out when we first halted, having returned, we again moved off at a tardy pace. Like benighted travellers we had now to feel our way with scouting and reconnoitring parties, and every one felt, by that secret and indescribable sort of feeling, which pervades all grades on the near approach to an enemy, that we were drawing close to them, and we expected every moment to disturb the hornet's nest. Suddenly we emerged on to a small cultivated plain, just where the low hills formed the angle I have before spoken of. Immediately on rounding this, a camp, of no great magnitude, burst on our view, standing very conspicuously on a flat topped hill, or eminence, about two miles from us. This, of course, was a portion of the Sikh camp, the remainder being lost to sight in the jungle. For some time we halted and gazed over toward the camp, watching the manoeuvres of large bodies of cavalry at the verge of the low hill to our right front. Hitherto not a shot had been fired, and a treacherous silence reigned over the dark jungle. Soon, however, this was disturbed, and from a quarter we least expected.

The Sikhs had taken advantage of an eminence, or mound, near to a village called Chillianwallah, and had formed a very strong outpost, their guns cannonading an extensive sweep of a portion of the open plain I have just mentioned, and in the direction that our left centre advanced; hence, the moment they emerged on the plain, these guns opened a smart fire on them. This being to the left, we on the right were not a little surprised to hear that the Sikhs extended so far on that side. A heavy British battery was brought up, and after some ten minutes firing, the picket retired, taking their guns with them. This was all the Commander-in-Chief desired today, hence he gave immediate orders for the lines to be taken up for encampment. But the foe, like the wolf disturbed in his lair, was determined not to permit us to do so quietly. Shere Sing knew Gough too well to remain long quiet so near to him. That it was Gough's intention to encamp here, reconnoitre the Sikh position, make his dispositions, and attack them on the morrow, there is no doubt; and that Shere Sing seemed to know this, is most probable too, as he determined to take advantage of Gough's ignorance of the Sikh position, and the half harassed state of the British troops, and himself become the assailant. Thus, while our camp colour men[1] were engaged taking up the camping ground, he boldly advanced some heavy guns and suddenly commenced a vigorous cannonading, the shots flying on to the very ground taken up for encampment. For some minutes they had it all to themselves, until at length a ball pitched close to his lordship. Convinced that now no alternative was left but to *fight or retire*, he resolved on a *coup de main*. This was undoubtedly a fearful hazard against such odds as he had to contend with. About 4,000 men were absorbed for baggage and hospital guard, therefore not more than 14,000 British troops were available for actual engagement, while the Sikhs numbered at least 45,000; and being in a dense and intricate jungle, every yard of which they were intimately acquainted with, they had a double advantage over us. This favoured them materially in another respect, inasmuch as undisciplined troops, which might be easily dispersed on an open field, would fight here with the greatest obstinacy, from the confidence they would feel in the jungle being a cover for them. On the other hand, the same cause which favoured them was unfavourable to us, in consequence of the impossibility of troops acting together with that machine-like exactness which distinguishes disciplined from undisciplined troops. That which told against us too most fearfully was our commander's ignorance of the extent of the Sikh line – for he could not see a single corps of them – nor how far they out-flanked us. But, as I have just remarked, no alternative was left except the disgraceful one of retreat – the very last thing a British army thinks of – hence the brave chief, trusting to the valour of his handful of men, sent forth the word, 'to battle.' The brigadiers, being summoned to his presence, he ordered each to lead on his brigade, when the time should come for them to do so, and, once on the move, each was to act discretionally as circumstances required. This done our artillery advanced, and soon the wild forest rang with the thundering cannon's roar, and was re-echoed in rolling peals from the adjacent mountains. At first but a few straggling guns opened from the foe, the smoke from which alone directed the aim of our artillery – for the jungle still concealed the Sikhs – but ere long full one hundred pieces of cannon belched forth their angry missiles, developing, as the smoke rose up in curling wreaths, a line of some three miles along our front. In this manner each army blazed away for more than an hour; it being all guess work on our side, our loss was already considerable, and the foe evidently advancing his line, Gough at once ordered a charge.

> *Then shook the hills with thunder riven;*
> *Then rushed the steed to battle driven,*
> *And louder than the bolts of heaven*
> *Far flashed the red artillery.*

While the thundering cannon rends the air, and the British divisions are advancing to the attack, I will relate the manner in which my own regiment was disposed, with some incidents which came under my own notice. We, with the 6th Light Cavalry[2], and eight guns, were posted on the extreme right, with our left abutting on the British line, forming an [gap in text] I have before mentioned. More technically speaking we were 'the right thrown back.' I should have said that the left wing of my regiment had been withdrawn from the right at the commencement of the battle to join their own brigade, under their Hudibras-like leader, leaving us with the native cavalry; in all eight squadrons and eight

The Battle of Chillianwallah. The scrubby jungle and pools of water that covered the battlefield, compounded by the low evening light and musket smoke, made it a very unsuitable place for cavalry to deploy. (Anne S K Brown Military Collection, Brown University Library)

guns[3]. Our attention, from the first, was drawn towards three separate and large bodies of *Goorchurras* (Sikh cavalry) who hovered about in advance of their camp and under the brow of the low hills to our right front, menacing our right flank, and seeming to have some designs on our baggage. For a time we remained dismounted, but carefully watching their every movement. As the battle increased in the centre of our line, they began to assume an offensive attitude, and made several good attempts to get round our flank. However, by some dextrous manoeuvres on our side, we managed each time to foil them. Had they succeeded, God only knows what a fearful result would have followed. At length the British line, having advanced far into the heart of the jungle in their attack, and consequently left us in an isolated position, our commander found it necessary 'to take ground to the left,' to co-operate with them. This manoeuvre being executed under a steady trot, we were soon enveloped in a cloud of dust. We were still trotting, when suddenly one of our scouts galloped in, crying out, 'The black d——s are coming upon us at a charge!' A stentorian voice, from the officer of artillery[4], now shouted, 'Halt, front, unlimber – stand to your guns!' Every man of us, sitting firmly in his saddle, and grasping his lance firmly under his arm, calmly awaited the shock. Thinking to cut us off from the British line, three bodies of Sikh cavalry had united themselves, and now came sweeping through the scattered jungle like a mountain torrent, and threatening to sweep us from the face of the earth. Shouting like furies, and brandishing their swords, they were approaching fast to a collision with us, while we felt that strange undefinable half suffocating sensation one feels at the sensible approach of a catastrophe. Just as we were expecting them to close with us, the same stentorian voice which cried out, 'Stand to your guns,' now vociferated, 'Ready, fire!'

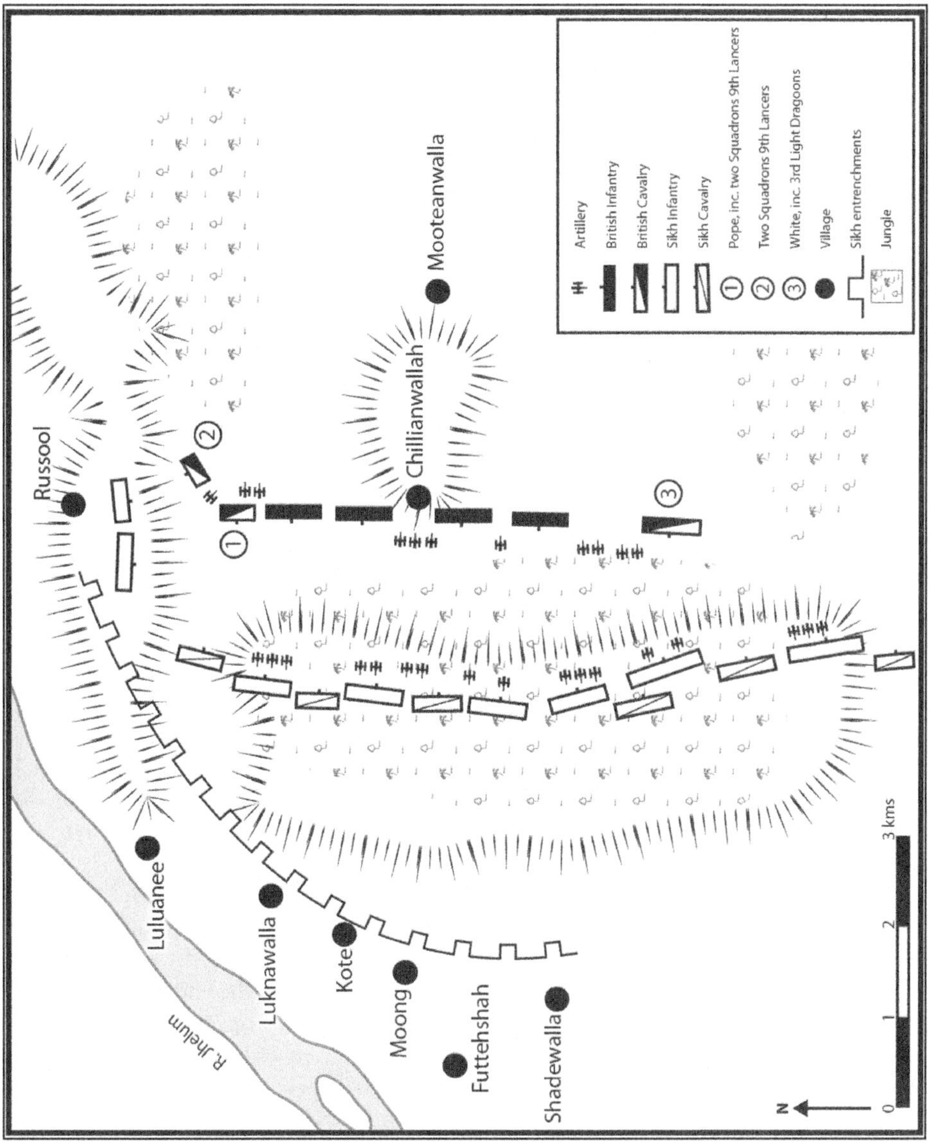

The Battle of Chillianwallah

Simultaneously the eight guns vomited forth their double charges of deadly grape, which at a distance of not more than twenty paces, made fearful gaps in the ranks of the astonished *Goorchurras*, and being smartly followed by a well directed fire, they at first wavered, then recoiled, and taking a panic, fled. That they suffered most fearfully from this fire was certain, from the numbers I saw strewn about that spot the next day. We had scarcely repulsed this swarm, when other bodies from the left approached us, but like their predecessors, were permitted to come 'thus far and no further,' for a galling fire of grape and canister toppled many of them out of their saddles, and sent the rest to look after their equally unfortunate comrades. During this last affray some stray cannon and musket shot came whistling rather unpleasantly about our ears, but fortunately did little harm.

Throughout this affair I was not a little amused at the cool indifference and merriment of one of our gunners. With a short pipe stuck in his mouth while he rammed home, he seemed to enjoy his 'bacca' with the greatest zest, while between each whiff of his pipe or discharge of his gun, he would pass off such jokes on the Sikhs, as even in a time of so much danger, did not fail to excite the risibles of those who heard him. 'You'd better sheer off, Mr. Shere Sing, or you'll soon have to sing small,' said he. 'There's pepper for your curry, you black d—-s. That'll shave your beards for you, my boys.' Such were the sallies made on our enemies by this cool and intrepid Englishman, in the most appalling scenes of battle and strife.

I will now carry the reader to a more sanguinary part of the field. While we on the right flank, by a bold front and destructive cannonade, had repulsed a body of *Goorchurras* six times our number, a fearful tragedy was being enacted on our left by the attacking battalions. On the British extreme left were the 3rd Light Dragoons, with the 5th and 8th Light Cavalry,[5] under Major-General Thackwell. With nothing short of rashness, one squadron of the 3rd supported by the 5th Light Cavalry, were ordered to charge a body of Sikh cavalry about five times their number. The 3rd, with their usual bravery, obeyed the command, under their gallant leader Captain Unett[6], and charged into the midst of the Sikhs, who first opened out and then closed around them. What could a single squadron do against thousands. Without effecting anything more than displaying to their foe British courage and intrepidity, they cut their way back through the Sikh ranks and retired. But they paid dearly for their temerity by the loss of nearly half their squadron[7].

Her Majesty's 24th Foot – for the first time in action – eager for fame, rushed to the onset with a mad impetuosity, far outstripping the supporting regiments on each side of them. For more than half a mile they advanced at the double, thereby exhausting all their animal powers, so that when they should have closed in with the enemy's ranks, they were utterly helpless. The *Khalsas* were here in vast strength, and from twelve guns poured amongst them a most terrific storm of grape and musketry, at only a few yards distance, sweeping them down by hundreds. I should have said that their approach was over a spot almost free from jungle, thus exposing the whole of their line to the Sikh batteries, which being covered by thick jungle, and barricades of trees felled and thrown crosswise, rendered their capture almost impossible. The enemy was not long in discovering the error the British had made by their impetuosity, and his cavalry poured upon them in overwhelming numbers, literally cutting them to pieces. In this fearful dilemma they retired as fast as they could. This gallant and superb regiment marched into the field nearly 1200 strong, but scarcely one half that number returned. A Lieut. Colonel took them into action, and a young Lieutenant brought them out. Scarcely an officer was left of that unfortunate corps. Their Brigadier, Penichuite, and his son, a young Lieutenant, fell in the outset[8]. The circumstances connected with the death of these brave, and devoted men, is one instance among many others on record, of patriotism and filial love combined. The brave veteran fell, with many others, from a volley of grape. The young and devoted son, who had never lost sight of his parent, seeing him fall, in a moment sprang towards his now bleeding form, threw himself upon him, and in a phrenzy of grief embraced and called upon his dying and unconscious parent, endeavouring in vain to stem the crimson stream which was saturating the Indian soil. Heedless alike of the strife around him, and of the approaching enemy, the heartbroken son still clung, even after death, to the inanimate form of his father. Side by side we found the sire and his son, hacked and mangled corpses.

The brigades forming the centre and right centre, under their brave and distinguished leaders, Gilbert and Campbell, were more fortunate, notwithstanding that they had to contend with vast numbers, and those rendered desperate by fanaticism. With a steady and undaunted spirit they cautiously felt their way through the jungle, until they came in collision with their foe. Wherever opposed they gallantly closed in with them, driving them from position to position and battery to battery, spiking their guns as they drove them from them. Like the 28th[9] and 50th Foot, who when in Egypt had to fight the French cavalry front and rear, so was it with these brigades today, for the *Goorchurras* had boldly galloped through the intervals of brigades and attacked the rear, hence our gallant foot soldiers found it necessary for the rear ranks to face about and engage with the cavalry, while the front ranks engaged the infantry. Thus while the brigades on the left had been repulsed by their own precipitancy, those of the right, through cool and unyielding courage, were driving all before them, and night alone prevented them from following up their advantages, and most probably robbed us of a decisive victory.

That which I have just related will raise feelings of pride and enthusiasm in the heart of every patriotic Englishman, I feel assured. Such Spartan-like courage is worthy of that nation under whose banners such soldiers fight. Having related the glory, would that I could, for the honour of British arms, throw a veil over the shame which unfortunately, like a drop of ink mixed with pure water, seemed to cast a stain over the whole. Would that with one dash of my pen I could for ever obliterate the stain of dishonour cast over British arms by the flight of a British regiment. But the harsh, the unjust, and the superficially judging world knows it, hence I develope no secret. The reader, if a military man, will discern ere this the corps I allude to[10]. Though within a few hundred yards of them at the time, I saw no more than they who were by their fire-sides in England. Even in the most open battle field no man knows, during the conflict, what his right or left hands' corps are doing; how much less then were we to see how others were engaged in a thick tangled jungle like Chillianwallah. So complicated and confusing were some parts of the scene of this dreadful conflict, that many poor fellows, who in the heat of the contest, had got separated from their corps by the bushes, never saw them again until the next day, and many, alas, never; for the *Goorchurras* were galloping about in every direction, sparing none who fell in their way. Moreover, if once you lost your corps, you knew not which way to turn, whether to the right, left, front, or rear; for you would reasonably fancy you were going to your own rear when you might be going directly into the enemy's batteries. Thus the reader will perceive that I know no more about this matter, that what I learnt on the spot afterwards. My object on writing on this subject is not to add even a shade to the stain, and the knowledge I possess of it will not enable me to diminish it materially, though it would give me pleasure to do so,

Sikh 9-pounder cannon, captured at the Battle of Chillianwallah. Cast in the Mogul fashion in about 1800, but with a British style carriage. Its performance would have been equal to those of the British-Indian artillery which confronted it at Chillianwallah. (Copyright Royal Armouries collection, Fort Nelson)

for the sake of that fine corps.

I have said before that the left wing of my regiment was detached from the right, in the commencement of the action, to join Pope's brigade, which was posted on the right of the infantry, in line of attack, in the following order. The -th [14th Light] Dragoons on the left, four squadrons of native cavalry in the centre, and our two squadrons on the right. A line such as this might have looked imposing enough on a parade ground, but any soldier who has been in the field can at once discern the want of generalship in attacking with his whole force, and thus leaving himself without a reserve in the event of a repulse. In this manner they were advanced to the attack, but here that decision and spirit which distinguishes good generalship seemed wanting. Confused and undecided, the Brigadier ordered them alternately to trot, walk, and halt, when the enemy were seen in masses but a short distance from them[11]. And even when the bullets were flying among them, and the men were panting to get at the enemy, he gave not the word to charge.

The Sikhs, seeing their indecision, became themselves the assailants, and the Brigadier got a sword cut on the head, and it is asserted that when smarting from his wound, he gave the word 'Threes about and retire.' The retire became a panic-stricken flight[12]. Our two squadrons on the right, having become separated some distance from the rest in their advance, fortunately heard not this command, and knew not, until they themselves retired, that the rest of the brigade had done so, hence they still kept advancing on until they found themselves fired upon in every direction, and soon were hand to hand with the Sikhs, who, brandishing their swords, were cutting and slashing in a most furious manner, accompanying each stroke with a contemptuous, *'Bog Feringhee Cootah – Feringhee bian.'* ('Run away, or hook it, you English dog.') A few minutes' wild and irregular fighting served to disperse these hordes, but clouds of cavalry still hovered about them. However the Brigadier's Aide-de-Camp galloped up, and ordered them to retire in the best manner they could. They did so, and most opportunely to save four of our guns; for the artillery who had advanced with the brigade had been abandoned by the cavalry and left to the mercy of the Sikhs. They had got safely off with two guns, and were just about capturing the remaining four, when our squadrons came upon them and recaptured them. In this unfortunate affair nearly the whole of two gun crews were cut up[13].

During the whole of this fearful and irregular struggle, the chaotic din and clattering of arms, together with the dark Hades-like scene of action, produced an effect, to anyone not actually engaged, terribly sublime. The occasional glittering and flashing of steel; the gleaming of turbaned and long bearded masses moving to and fro through the dark forest; the simultaneous and thunder-like British 'hurra' or Irish 'Faugh-a-ballagh;'[14] the wild and demoniacal *'Wah purakjee'*[15] of the fanatical *Akalies*; the sounding of trumpets; the beating of tom toms and gongs; the rolling musketry; the booming of cannon; the rattle of gun-carriages; the galloping of fiery steeds; the clang and clash of arms, mingled with the groans, curses, and prayers of the wounded and dying, formed a scene truly appalling at the moment, and too fearful for the mind to contemplate in after years.

> *Night, however,*
> *Closed around the conqueror's way,*
> *And lightning showed the distant hill;*
> *When those who fought that dreadful day*
> *Stood few and faint, but fearless still.*

Although we gained some advantages over the enemy by driving him from his original position, and spiking many of his guns, these advantages were lost through the density of the jungle, and the scattered state of our army when darkness threw a veil over the scene. The Commander-in-Chief found it necessary to sound the 'recall,' and to withdraw his scattered forces from the thick jungle, and concentrate them on the open space I have before spoken of near Chillianwallah. There we were formed in such order as the darkness and locality would permit, and a bugle was sent out a little in advance of our bivouac to sound the 'assembly,' in the hope that the wounded and stragglers might thereby be guided to the spot. But, alas! few indeed were permitted to do so, for the exulting Sikhs had returned to the field, and demon-like plundered, hacked, and mangled, both the living and the dead who had fallen in the fight[16].

Dismounting, but retaining order, so that we could mount again at a moment's notice, with the reins on our arms, we stretched ourselves on the cold ground, and with our lance caps for pillows, many of us soon forgot in sleep our awful situation. Being wearied, hungered, and fatigued, nature was not the less kind to me. It was not long, however, ere we were all suddenly aroused from our repose by the booming of a gun, followed by others, from the brow of the low hills, which at first we thought was a cannonading opened upon us, but our experienced ears soon convinced us that they were not shotted, and it subsequently turned out that Shere Sing was firing a salute in honour of the victory which he claimed to have achieved[17]. A chilly and hollow wind was now blowing from the south-east, and heavy spattering drops of rain were falling, threatening to render our night's lodgings very cheerless. However, as a temporary fortification against the cold and wet, we had a dram of grog and half a loaf of bread served to us. As water to the thirsty soul, so was this to me, and after partaking of it, I wrapped my military cloak around me, and getting under the shelter of a bush, again lay down to sleep, heedless of the cold and wet. The rain and wind, however, increasing, I awoke about midnight, most miserably wet and shivering. Tying my horse to a bush, I endeavoured to shake off the cold by pacing to and fro; and while doing so I fancied I could hear the moans of some one to the front. Believing it to proceed from a wounded comrade, I called the attention of one of our men to the sounds, and he at once agreed to accompany me to the spot from whence they proceeded. We had not gone far when we discovered something crawling on the ground, which turned out to be a *Sepoy* of the 30th Native Infantry[18], who having been severely wounded by a shot in the thigh, and awfully cut and hacked by the *Goorchurras* – his body being literally scored – presented a most painful sight. Poor fellow, on seeing that we were 'brothers,' as the *Sepoys* generally designated us, meaning brother soldiers, he was in a transport of joy, and called on Allah to confer a thousand blessings on us. We of course got a *dhooly* for him, and he was conveyed to the field hospital. Whether he recovered or not I never knew. We could not think of laying on the cold wet ground again, and I now felt a strange desire partly from the love of adventure, and partly in the hope of assisting some poor wounded comrade, who might perchance have escaped the merciless *tulwar*, to go over the field of battle. Having prevailed on a comrade to accompany me, we stole away from our bivouac unperceived, armed with our pistols, in the event of meeting with some ugly customers. A cold drizzling rain was falling, and the hollow wind rushed with a sighing sound through the bushes, while the moon, which was but a few days on the wane, and was now high in the heavens – for it was about three o'clock – cast a pale light through the fleecy clouds as they scudded by, and every now and then the jungle rang with the dismal howling of troops of jackals and wolves. The hour, the gloomy and mysterious jungle, each bush of which might contain an enemy, the beasts of prey prowling about, together with the dead strewn everywhere, rendered our enterprize one of danger and fear, and more than once we had nearly given it up at the commencement; but curiosity and adventure prompted us on still further. We had threaded some distance into the jungle, every now and then halting and listening, when we were suddenly startled by a rushing sound, which proceeded from a pack of jackals we had just disturbed at their feast, and we saw a *Sepoy* stretched lifeless before us; he had already been stripped of his cloth trousers, and his coatee was opened, and the amulets he wore had been stripped from his arm. The jackals had devoured the greater portion of his legs, and the flesh was gnawed off his ribs; but his face uninjured, looked calm and placid as if he was only sleeping. His pouch was on him, and one solitary shot remained in it, so that the poor fellow must have fired fifty-nine rounds before he fell. Stealing onward a little further, a most awful and melancholy spectacle revealed itself. Months and years have rolled by, and I have removed far from the theatre of that fearful tragedy to an English fire-side, yet so deep is the awful picture painted on my memory, that neither time nor change can efface it. Promiscuously scattered, and in some cases literally piled on each other, were thousands of slain. Englishmen, Hindoos, Afghans, and Sikhs, were indiscriminately scattered over the jungle. The merciless plunderers, and the fierce and demoniacal *Akalies* had done their work, and most of the corpses were partially stripped, those of my countrymen nearly all totally naked, and cut and hacked in a most frightful manner. Here was a leg, there an arm, here a head, and there a body frightfully gaping with deep wounds, while their rigid and marble-like faces looked ghastly in the pale moonlight.

In contrast to these last were the dark and grim-visaged Sikhs, with their long flowing hair and beards. These thousands of human beings, thought I, were all life and animation a few short hours ago, but the sword and bullet have made a fearful levelling. Friend or foe, 'tis all the same now. Death has made all alike. Sikh and Britain now lay side by side in the calm repose of death. What an awful lesson for the human passions! We glanced around the sickening scene, then gave a half-repressed whistle, and listened to hear if anyone should answer it. But, alas, the sound died away unanswered. Not one of the thousands around us had been spared. All had been butchered by the prowling plunderers and the Sikhs. Our contemplations were interrupted by hearing some stray shots, and soon a murmur of voices not far distant from us. This undoubtedly came from the prowlers, and as it [gap in text] in contact with them, [gap in text] confronted by a Sikh. Under the impulse of the moment, not knowing how many companions he had at hand, we thought to despatch him for our own safety, and my comrade in a moment pointed his sword at the fellow's breast, at the same time interrogating him as to who he was, and what he was doing there. Seeing himself in our power he supplicated mercy, saying he was a poor villager and so on. We first searched his person, and found on him many amulets and other silver and gold ornaments, besides money, which he had taken from the dead. There was no time for parley, for the prowlers were now close in our vicinity, and they seemed to be amusing themselves by firing at the dead, so we ordered our prisoner to lead the way to the mound, and to prevent any treachery, we gave him to understand that the moment he deceived us, he would be a dead man. To let him see that we were in earnest, we presented our cocked pistols at his head, and in this manner moved on, when after some little turnings and windings, to avoid the prowlers, we ultimately succeeded in extricating ourselves from this dangerous and puzzling dilemma, and our guide having proved himself faithful, we dismissed him uninjured.

The day was breaking when we came up to our regiment, and fortunately our absence had not been noticed. We had just time to get up to our horses when the order was given to mount. In my adventure I had picked up a *tulwar* and several other trophies, but I found them now cumbersome to me, so cast them away. Having mounted and formed up, I could perceive that our army was all on the *qui vive*, and everything denoted preparations for another day of battle. However we were again dismounted, and ordered to feed our horses as they stood, but just taking the bits out of their mouths, and we also refreshed ourselves with a dram of grog and crust of bread; the officers also, joining in with the soldiers, seemed to relish the hard crust. Indeed it is not the least remarkable trait in the character of the aristocratic English officer, that a little of the up hill work of campaigning generally takes down his pride and imperiousness. It is the finest thing in the world to tame the old martinets for the time being, and even cools the ardour of the proud young aspirant. It is in such rough and stern scenes as Chillianwallah offered that the officer knows the intrinsic value of the *common* soldier, and he will then make him, as far as is compatible with his rank, his fellow soldier and comrade. Such circumstances as these seem to produce quite a republican spirit in all ranks and grades, and a mutual good feeling and consistent equality invariably exists so long as bullets keep flying about. But, as one of our old soldiers used drily to remark, not sooner is the 'shooting' season over than the 'hunting' season commences, meaning that fighting being over, a system of rigid discipline, arrogance, and petty tyranny follow.

But to return to the morning of the 14th. While we were thus regaling ourselves the infantry and artillery were being formed into brigades, and the British army began to assume a menacing attitude, and though fearfully reduced in numbers since the previous morning, still presented a formidable front. The Sikhs too seemed to be preparing for a crisis, and were moving to and fro like rolling billows at the foot of the hills. Our position now was really a desperate one, and but this alternative seemed left for us – either to hazard another battle or to retreat on Dinghee. It has since transpired, that in a council of war held that morning, the latter was advised by some of the council, but for the honour of that army and the British empire in India, our chief opposed such an unwise measure, and resolved on standing his ground so long as he had a British soldier to stand by him.

Our army being formed into line, the brave chief rode along its front, and was received with loud and enthusiastic cheers from right to left. Alas, the voices of thousands who cheered him in the same manner but yesterday, were now hushed for ever in death. The rain, which had been falling more or less throughout the night, now began to descend in torrents, and we could perceive the Sikhs dispersing in different directions, and soon a large camp, as if by magic, arose up on the brow of the low hills. Right glad were we to see this, wearied and harassed as we were, for we desired to rest. The Commander-in-Chief now gave orders for our lines to be taken up, and about noon the two camps were fully developed, that of the enemy looking frowningly on our small but majestic little camp. The rain descended in torrents as we were pitching our tents, so that we had but uncomfortable quarters, for our bedding, which by the by had been on the camels' backs during the last thirty hours, was drenched through with rain. All these circumstances combined, offered us but sorry comfort after our recent fatigues and privations.

Many of our dead having been brought in during the day by fatigue parties, at four o'clock the sad and affecting burial service was performed by the Commander-in-Chief's chaplain. The dark and dreary expanse of jungle everywhere surrounding us; the gloomy heavens pouring forth torrents of rain 'midst thunders and lightning; the hundreds of corpses, white and black, many wholly naked and covered with gaping wounds, all contributed to render the scene one to make an impression on the mind which can never be forgotten.

13
Battle of Gujerat and Home

The drenching rain in torrents poured
Upon the battle field,
While with the sudden lightning's flash
Alternate thunders pealed.

While the rain is rattling like shot over our heads, and dribbling through the roofs of the tents, accompanied by an occasional burst of a flood of water through the sides, and teaching our beds the art of swimming, I will, by way of forgetting these hardships, relate a few hair-breadth escapes which I heard related at different times, and cherished in my memory. Two men of the 24th Foot having in their advance received shot wounds, were assisting each other to the rear, when three *Goorchurras* galloped towards them, brandishing their *tulwars*, and threatening to cut them down. But, with admirable presence of mind, they struggled into the midst of a bush, just as the Sikhs were about to cut at them, and each man raising his firelock fetched down his opponent; the third, exasperated at the loss of his comrades, rode furiously at them in the bush, when one of them receiving the blow on his bayonet, knocked him off his horse and then ran him through. They then quietly retired to the field hospital where they got their wounds dressed, and are I believe still living.

Lieut. Cureton, son of the Brigadier Cureton whom I have before alluded to, had vowed to be revenged for the loss of his father. On advancing up to the attack with his regiment, he clapped spurs to his horse and dashed into the midst of the Sikhs' ranks, exclaiming, 'Revenge! revenge!' striking terror into the hearts of the astonished enemy, and cutting down with his sword many of them before he himself fell. He had penetrated so far into the enemy's ranks, that his body was not discovered until a month afterwards, when the Sikhs evacuated their position, though subsequent to the battle search was made for it as far as we dare go towards the Sikh pickets. It is not a little singular that the means of his discovery was a small portion of the cuff of his jacket, with the gold lace and button belonging to his corps, still clinging to his shrivelled and skeleton wrist[1].

A sergeant and corporal of my own regiment, being on the rear guard, were thus deprived of the honour of participating in the fight, which it seems was not agreeable to their aspiring notions, for on seeing their squadron advance to the charge they put spurs to their horses and galloped to join them, but before they could do this the squadron had come to close quarters with the *Goorchurras,* and our two heroes found themselves surrounded by mad and infuriated enemies, who were charging about in every direction, brandishing their swords, and threatening destruction to every *Feringhee* dog who should fall in their way. Several attacked them, and in the struggle the corporal drove his lance through the body of one of them, but before he could extricate it he was attacked by a second, whose cut however he avoided by leaning over the opposite side of the saddle; but the Sikh, rushing at him, grasped one side of his double breasted jacket with his left hand, while with his right he prepared a second time for a cut, but the corporal, with presence of mind, dropped his lance, and in a moment drew his pistol from the holster and shot the Sikh through the head. The serjeant during this time had two to contend with also, but, being a clever swordsman, he managed to disable one and parried the cuts of the other until the corporal came to his assistance, when the remaining Sikh fled. No injuries were sustained by either of our men, further than that the serjeant's cap lines were cut in two, and the brass part of the scales of his left epaulette, while his horse had received a gaping wound on the left haunch. They immediately joined in with their squadron and took part in the struggle which followed.

In the *melee,* a private, named Johnson[2], rushed at a Sikh with his lance, which gliding off his breast plate took its course between his arm and side, and by this means they rushed into each other's arms, the impetuosity of the charge having brought them unavoidably into this position. For some moments each hugged and tugged at the other, during which the Afghan, for such he was, succeeded in extracting his sword arm, and was endeavouring to disable his foe, when one of our men, coming to Johnson's aid, ran the Afghan through with his lance.

Another, named Hunt[3], drove his lance furiously at an Afghan, but here again a breast plate resisted it, and both combatants were nearly unhorsed. The Afghan now fired his piece at Hunt, but fortunately missed him. Although his lance blade was almost doubled by the resistance it had met with, he again lunged it out at his foe, unhorsed him, and finally gave him the *coup de grace.*

The following narrative of two men, which is not without parallel in the British service, is illustrative of a trait in the character of the true British soldier, as shewing the desire which he has to participate in the honours and *éclat* of war.

A private of my regiment, and a gunner of the artillery, having been left behind in quarters from sickness, and having recovered, were marched up the country with detachments of other corps to join the army. On arriving at Lahore, they were ordered to remain there to augment the little force in that garrison. The two men however of whom I now speak, taking deep interest in all news which came from the seat of war, and hearing that another engagement was about to be fought, mutually agreed to steal off to their corps. They had to travel nearly one hundred miles, to cross two broad rivers, with but a few *pice* to purchase rice or grain, and to traverse a country unknown to them, every inhabitant of which was an avowed enemy. However, with that good fortune which sometimes attends bold adventurers, they both arrived with the army a few hours before the commencement of the battle. But the same good fortune did not attend them here, for the gunner had hardly unlimbered his gun for firing, ere a shot came and almost severed his body in two. The man of my regiment had also well nigh lost his life, for he was unhorsed in the melee, and received a severe wound in the sword arm.

Our camp here took a triangular form. The north-eastern face being overlooked by the low hills, was occupied by cavalry and artillery; the other two faces had infantry in the centre and were flanked by cavalry. The rain having continued incessantly for three days after the battle, subsided on the evening of the 16th, and the following morning broke forth with brightness and sunshine, cheering our drooping spirits and dispelling the gloom which had hung like a cloud over the camp. As the sun broke forth, a long line of canvas, now white as the driven snow, developed itself to our view, apparently about one and a half miles to our front, the whole defended by field works and batteries.

We had anticipated that the clearing up of the weather would bring on a renewal of battle; but it was now evident that our chief felt himself in a position unable to attack. [He was] almost surrounded by an innumerable and formidable foe in the midst of a difficult jungle defended by field works, having but 14,000 fighting men at his disposal to bear arms against them. On the other hand, to remain here until reinforcements could arrive from Multan, which might be weeks, or even months, would subject the army to constant and harassing attacks from the enemy. In addition to this, starvation or a plague seemed to threaten us, for only one line of communication was open, and to preserve this, absorbed one half of the cavalry; and the putrescent vapours arising from the dead bodies on the battle field, and from the hundreds of cattle that died every day, produced an extremely unpleasant and dangerous stench. However, spite of all these difficulties, our chief resolved unflinchingly to maintain his ground, were it at the point of the bayonet. To this end dispositions were made for strengthening ourselves in position, and all hands were employed night and day, amidst deluges of rain, (for rain came on again,) in throwing up defences, and in about four days every angle and tangible point was commanded by breastworks and redoubts, bristling with cannon and bayonets. At the same time the attendants on the sick and wounded were decreased so as to fill the ranks as much as possible, while the cavalry were instructed, in the event of a night attack, to turn out dismounted, and to fight as infantry, and to prevent a false alarm, three distinct guns were to be fired from the mound, on which we had planted a heavy battery.

I must now allow our field operations to progress while I relate another incident. Two men of my regiment, named Sinclair and Walter[4], went out in search of a missing comrade two days after the battle, and were suddenly pounced upon by some Sikh horsemen, who made them prisoners, but not before Sinclair had been severely wounded on the back part of the left shoulder. The fellows who took them, stripped them of their jackets and the little money they had on them, and being taken to the enemy's picket, they were severely maltreated and insulted by the common soldiery. More than once they had nearly fallen victims to the vindictive Afghans, and they expected to meet with a torturing death, or to be shot from a cannon's mouth for the Sikhs' amusement. However, on the morning after their capture they were ushered into the presence of Shere Sing, and after answering several questions they were removed into a clean tent, and were somewhat better treated. In four days afterwards he caused them to mount on the back of an elephant, and taking them to the highest elevation of his camp, which commanded a view of the whole, desired them to view his colossal army, telling them that Gough had better give up the contest, for if he conquered that army, he, Shere Sing, would have another one as formidable in less than a week. He then told them to look at the diminutive looking English camp, and contrasting the size of the two, seemed to treat the English with contempt. This done, he presented each with a scarlet scarf, such as the Sikhs form into turbans, and sent them off to the English camp bearing a letter to our chief. We were not a little surprised to see them return alive, for they had been given up and their kits disposed of. Sinclair suffered very much from his wound, for it had been unskilfully sewn up by a Sikh doctor, and when he rejoined the regiment our surgeon undid the Sikh's work and re-sewed it. His life was for some time despaired of, but a strong constitution ultimately ensured his recovery.[5]

On the 22nd dark and heavy clouds again obscured the sky, and in the afternoon the rain descended in torrents, continuing for three consecutive days, deluging our camp, floating our beds, and everything belonging to us. Embankments and trenches were dug round each tent to keep the water out, but our lines being low, the water rushed from the upper part of the camp and burst upon us in floods. If ever soldiers were in woeful plight my regiment was on this occasion. On picket or guard we had to stand or sit on horseback at our posts for two hours, in the cold and pitiless rain, and sorry was the comfort awaiting us on returning to our tent, everything we possessed being floating, and we were fortunate if we could find a dry place to stand or rest on until it came to our turn to go on vidette again. In this state of misery and suffering, many thought that by drowning their senses in drink, it would render them less conscious of their sufferings, and those who could procure liquor intoxicated themselves, reckless of the dangers around them. Such rash foolishness produced its natural consequences, for many of the poor fellows who thus indulged, lay about in the wet, and thus brought on themselves diseases which in a few months subsequently told fearfully on our regiment. Such are the soldier's woes and sufferings in the field of 'honour and glory.' Thank God the rain ceased; and the morning of the 25th broke forth with warm sunshine, and we began to think again that life was worth living for. All disposable hands of my corps were now set to work to dig a tank, to receive the water, which lay in large pools in our camp, and by strenuous efforts it was finished, and our camp soon assumed an air of regularity and comparative comfort, the sun aiding us in drying our bedding and clothing.

On the 26th we received the cheering news of the fall of Multan, for which we fired a salute of twenty-one guns[6]. The Sikhs shortly fired twenty-two guns in derision of us. The enemy acquired more strength and consequently audacity, and knowing that a few weeks would bring us relief from Multan, he took advantage of our present paucity of numbers. He had not the boldness to make a general attack, but tried every stratagem and provocation to draw us out from our lines, but our chief's policy being simply the defensive, he avoided a general engagement. Hence our foe attributing this to fear, became insupportably annoying and insulting, firing on our pickets, making feints, sallies, and pretended attacks; thus alarms and turn outs were frequent both night and day. Frequently we were aroused from our sleep at midnight, and more than once from false alarms. Two of the latter I well remember, and will briefly relate them as an illustration of these contingencies which are the usual concomitants of the pleasures of campaigning. One night, just as the clocks had struck twelve, being myself on vidette, I was suddenly startled by the sound of horses' hoofs galloping along our front; at the same time I could catch a glimpse now and then of a horse galloping along towards our right. I challenged, but no answer being returned, prepared to receive a foe; presently I heard others challenge, and the next moment off went a pistol, followed by others along the line of videttes to my right; this was succeeded by a whole volley on our extreme right, which I well knew was from a party of infantry posted in a village. In less than five minutes from this the whole army was under arms, and forming to the front, in the full expectation of a nocturnal engagement. Things had proceeded thus far when the officer of the main picket sent word to the Commander-in-Chief that 'It was only a horse which had broken loose.' The next occurred a few nights afterwards. The *Sepoy* picket in the village to our right front, seeing objects moving to their front, challenged, but receiving no answer, fired; a loud groan was heard, mingled with the smart return of some dozen shots from the same quarter, and all was hushed in silence. The firing had been heard throughout the camp, and during the remainder of the night all were under arms, but nothing more occurred to disturb the silence of the night. The light of the morning revealed the cause of this disturbance. The dead bodies of three Sikhs were seen lying on the very spot where the firing took place. It has subsequently transpired that a night attack was premeditated, and a party had been sent to cut off our *Sepoy* picket as a prelude to their further designs. How they succeeded, we have seen.

Some young officers used to amuse themselves with rifle shooting, to the no small danger of themselves and the jeopardy of the videttes. Posting themselves near to a vidette they would commence popping away just as if they were partridge or snipe shooting. Such a practice cannot be too much censured, and thanks to Lord Gough, it was soon put a stop to. Theirs was the fun, ours the greatest danger; for they could advance or retire at discretion, while we poor fellows, the videttes, had to stick there like targets, while the balls whew'd and whistled about our heads in a most unpleasant manner. But for me two of these sporting gentlemen might have lost either their lives or liberty on one of these occasions. It was one evening just as the sun was sinking behind the Salt range, two officers had penetrated far beyond the line of videttes, and having deliberately dismounted in front of a party of Sikh horsemen, were popping away at them *ad libitu*m. The Sikhs in return alternately fired and then retired some paces, thus gradually drawing the English officers from the British lines. I watched them attentively for some time, then withdrawing my eyes from that direction, perceived the figures of some half dozen red jacketed Sikhs, stealing from bush to bush, along my front, in the direction the officers were. Being convinced that they intended entrapping them, I signalled for the sentry of the picket to intimate that I wanted to communicate with the officer. The next moment the corporal was galloping towards me, to whom I communicated my fears respecting the officers. He, perceiving their danger, and that there was no time to be lost – for the Sikhs would be betwixt them and our lines in a few more minutes – galloped out towards them, pointing out their danger, when they instantly mounted their horses and galloped over in a diagonal direction to our lines, followed by a shower of musketry from the now chagrined and disappointed Sikhs.

Of the many situations a soldier is placed in on a campaign, none can be conceived more dangerous and disagreeable than videttes, and particularly at Chillianwallah. The jungle in the immediate vicinity of our camp had been cut down, and the space from the camp to where the line of videttes was posted was comparatively clear, while thick jungle filled up the space between them and the Sikh camp. Hence the Sikhs were enabled to approach with impunity under cover of the bushes, and shoot the videttes at discretion. With their long matchlocks too they had double the advantage over us with our pistols, for which they cared no more than a snap of the finger. Had they been better marksmen I should not have been left to tell the tale; for one day, during the whole hour I was on vidette, the balls whistled about my head most alarmingly; but fortunately a large tree was close at hand, behind which I took shelter, the balls several times grazing the bark of the tree.

This species of annoyance was endured without a murmur until several of the videttes were 'knocked off,' when it was complained of to the Commander-in-Chief, who immediately took steps to obviate it to some extent, by supporting each vidette with two riflemen, who being all picked marksmen, soon toppled over some of the red jackets, and gave a considerable check to their amusements. The enemy being frustrated in his attempts to bring on a general action, at length resolved on cutting off our only communication, and consequent supplies, by blockading the road to Dinghee. These designs, however, being anticipated by our chief, some half dozen squadrons and a light field battery were detached from the camp every day with the object of checking and counteracting their manoeuvres. It was on one of these detached parties that I had well nigh lost the number of my mess[7], and the English government a shilling's worth of human flesh, in the following manner. I was posted on vidette, and a thick jungle stretched out along my front to the foot of the low range I have before mentioned; while about twenty yards to my right front stood a small mud village. The slope of the hill was literally alive with Sikh horsemen, moving to and fro, and every now and then a group of turbans, surmounted by glittering bayonets glancing through the trees, announced the near proximity of bodies of infantry. My attention was directed towards a party in my front, who seemed to advance in a hostile manner, when all at once a rustling and crackling amongst the bushes to my right rear startled me, and at the same moment I was horror struck to see some half dozen Sikhs, who had most unaccountably placed themselves between me and our troops, thus cutting me off from any support. I had no time for reflection; the next moment I should be in their hands, either alive or dead, so with pistol in hand, I put spurs to my little charger, and taking a diagonal direction to avoid my intending captors, galloped off for my troop. Two of them, however, more expert than the rest, made a dash to seize my reins; I discharged my pistol at them, one fell, and the next moment I was out of the reach of the other, but with a dozen bullets whizzing after me. Scarcely a day passed here but some such skirmish occurred, which not only seemed to keep us on the alert, but from the excitement and consequent interest they occasioned, every day a new feature to campaigning life.

Up to the 11th of February the signal guns had not been fired; however about 11 o'clock that morning, the fatal signal rang through the camp, and the next minute the whole army was prepared for action. That this was no false alarm we were convinced as soon as we had mounted. The enemy were in advance of their camp, presenting everywhere a formidable front. Look which way we would a forest of steel and hosts of turbaned heads seemed to frown destruction on us. In short we were literally surrounded by them. Every heart beat high for the result of such a threatening crisis. We however remained *in statu quo*, only waiting the word 'To battle.' Two hours passed and still the two armies looked frowningly on each other without coming to blows; at length some guns were moved up towards us, and the round shot soon rolled about our horses' feet. Retiring just out of their reach we dismounted, thus seeming to treat them with contempt. They were evidently trying to allure us from beyond our defences, but our chief being on the defensive, kept his ground, and the enemy being thus foiled in their attempts to draw us under their batteries, retired to their camp, about 4 o'clock.

Long before daybreak the following morning we were aroused from our beds, with orders to prepare for action, there being an extraordinary stir in the enemy's camp. As we turned out a magnificent scene presented itself to us. The whole line of the Sikh position, as far as the eye could reach, from right to left was one continuous line of fires, the hills being so illuminated that we could almost fancy that we were near a large city, and that it was illuminated for the celebration of some great event, were it not that the illusion vanished as every now and then the dim outline of groups of soldiery were seen moving around the fires. A continuous hum of mixed and indistinct sounds reached us from the Sikh camp; sounds which a practised campaigner knows usually attend the striking of a camp, while looming in the distance could be distinguished, by night glasses, bodies of Sikhs moving along the verge of the hills, in a direction towards Dinghee.

Shivering with the cold and full of conjecture and anxiety as to the result of all this, the morning gradually broke, and right glad did we welcome the light. But what a change it revealed to us. The Sikh camp had vanished. We were astounded – nay, it seemed so much like a dream, that it was some minutes ere we could credit our own eyes. Where were the thousands of warriors too who but yesterday seemed to make the hills, nay, the very bushes our enemies? They too were gone. It seemed so much like magic, that we were almost persuaded that we were under some enchantment. However, further reconnoitring confirmed the fact that the Sikhs had fled, but where was yet a mystery. Though the sudden disappearance of our enemy was pleasing to us in general, yet a sort of disappointment seemed to pervade all hands; the most fascinating feature in campaigning life seemed gone from us; the excitement and interest of those skirmishes and other enterprises which gave a sort of charm to life in the field.

The day after their departure, I stole over to the enemy's now evacuated position; on reaching it, I soon discovered that rumour had not belied its strength and formidableness. A deep ravine ran zig-zag along the front of their first line of defences; there were several mud walls and artificial embankments, with numerous embrasures for guns, the approaches to which were protected by large prickly bushes, which had been stuck vertically in the ground, and so close that one could not penetrate them without difficulty and punishment. In some places a treble line of breastworks and entrenchments, intersected everywhere with loaded mines, presented themselves. The whole position was traversed, like the labyrinths of a spider's web, with deep precipices, wide chasms, and nullahs, with the edges of those facing the British camp, commanded by batteries. On the whole a more formidable position could not have been selected. It is fearful to contemplate the carnage that would have been the consequence of an attack on a well defended position like this; for, supposing the first line of defences taken, the attackers would find themselves opposed to a second, and in some instances, a third and fourth, with deep and wide chasms between them and the enemy's destructive artillery and musketry; and many must have been inevitably precipitated headlong over the precipices. The next day, the 14th [February], I strolled over the field of battle, having no fear now of being disturbed by the prowling enemy. Sad, sad was the spectacle I there witnessed. Arms, legs, and carcasses, protruded everywhere from their thin covered graves, all now in various stages of decomposition, some swollen and bloated, others shrivelled and blackened in the sun, while others again had been torn up from their temporary graves by the voracious jackals and birds of prey, and thus severed limb from limb. Here lay a fleshless leg, there an arm, and there a head or carcase, their bones left to bleach in the sun. Some too I saw with their uniforms on, as when last they joined the ranks; they fought and fell, and as they fell so they were lightly buried. The spot where a Sikh had perished could well be distinguished even at this period of time from the battle; for whole fleeces of long black hair strewed the ground round about the disjointed corpses.

The thought came home to me that I might have been the same inanimate corruption, and I felt that I knew not even now the day or hour I might, like them, meet the soldier's fate. A soldier at such times as these, had need have something better to support him than the mere love of glory; he ought to have the consolation of knowing that he has fought in a just cause, and that it is his country's good, and not his own, that he aims at. In my time perhaps I have run after the bubble glory as ardently as the boy pursues the butterfly; but there are seasons – I speak from experience – when the heart of a soldier is sick of war, and then he muses and moralizes like other men. When harassed day after day, and night after night; when bivouacking on the cold ground, or watching by the dying embers of the camp fire, and especially when lying among the dead and wounded on the battle field, he sees friend and foe around him who have been swept down by the sharp scythe of war, he yearns for the calm quiet, the soothing comfort of a happy and peaceful home; and then, like others, he can break out in ardent exclamations against mad ambition, questioning the value of mere glory, and even doubting the lawfulness of making earthly honours an object of his desires. The good of his country and the real welfare of those around him is a better motive to move the soldier's heart than all the glory that can be acquired.

Early on the morning of the 15th we struck camp, and at daybreak quitted that scene of so many events, a spot with which is associated so striking a mixture of thrilling interest, ardent excitement, stirring strife, sorrow, and misery, and for which I shall ever feel a melancholy interest, knowing that many of my fellow comrades perished in that wild and isolated jungle. After about four hours marching we emerged from the dark jungle on to a fine plain, and about mid-day we encamped near to the village of Lussoorie, where little more than a month before we encamped some 4,000 stronger than now. On the 16th the march was again resumed in a southerly direction. Our route lay through beautiful and luxuriant corn and cotton fields; the morning was clear and pleasant, and all nature seemed cheerful and gay, circumstances so delightfully contrasted to our previous confinement to the dismal jungle, that it seemed to have an exhilarating effect on all hands, nay even our horses, by their frisking and playfulness, seemed to enjoy the change, while we ourselves began to think that life was yet worth cherishing. From the 13th up to this date many and various reports had reached us as to the whereabouts of the enemy, but no definite knowledge could be obtained. Tonight it was current in camp that they were now posted around a city called Gujerat, some twenty miles to our front. On the 17th we advanced about six miles in the same direction as yesterday, but on pitching camp, we changed front to the left, thus facing an easterly direction, instead of south as yesterday. On the 18th we advanced about five miles to the front. The country still presented a beautifully luxuriant appearance, and it was really grievous to witness the unavoidable devastation of the crops caused by our march. In battle array we formed a line extending for about three miles; thus for a sweep of that extent right and left, every blade of corn or vegetation was utterly destroyed; for that which the tramp of battalions trod not down, did not escape the thousands of cattle and camp followers coming in their wake. Little rude hamlets, the habitations of the industrious peasantry, dotted the country here and there, many of which, I regret to say, were ravaged and sacked by the native camp followers, although strict injunctions had been given to all grades against plundering, and the provosts vigilantly prevented it where it occurred in their immediate jurisdiction.

About ten o'clock in the morning we were rejoiced with the first division from Multan, and late at night the second division joined us. On the 19th we halted, and on the 20th removed camp about three miles to the front. In the evening the third division from Multan arrived. The whole of the Multan force had now joined us, augmenting our force to about 35,000, hence we all felt that Gough would not be long ere he measured his strength once more with our long-bearded foe[8]. That night my troop was on outlying picket; I was posted on vidette at one o'clock, and on returning to my tent at three, after being relieved, one of our sergeants from the camp was serving a dram of grog each and half bread [sic – half a ration?]; a fact which at once convinced me that we were going to fight today; a conviction which was immediately confirmed by the sergeant in question. Strange though it may appear this information produced no very different sensation from an order for a march or a parade; for there are times when a soldier, wearied and harassed by long and arduous campaigning, feels almost sick of life; and would willingly exchange the strife and toils of war for the peace and rest of the grave, more especially in a country like India; where from the day you leave your quarters until the day you return, campaigning is one continued warlike and rugged path, and a friendly face is not seen beyond your own camp. Hence it is that from a long continuance of such occupation and the consequent waste of physical power, the soldier's life becomes of little value to him, and he thus becomes reckless of the dangers of the battle field. It was thus I felt on the morning of the battle I am about to relate.

At daybreak the troops were marshalled in array of battle, the cavalry in column of troops, and companies of infantry, with guns of different calibre, interspersed at regular intervals. Thus disposed the whole army could, at a given signal, deploy and form a compact line. The morning air was cool and bracing, and a light mist hung like a curtain over the extensive flat country around us, rendering distant objects dim and obscure. In stately order we moved on, and soon the sun springing up unclouded, together with a light breeze from the north-west, just sufficient to flutter our flags, dispelled the mist, and disclosed to us vast fields of luxuriant corn waving in the breeze, diversified by beautiful groves of shady trees; in short, the scene before us seemed purely English; but far distant be the day when her fertile fields are made the theatre of such carnage as these were.

About half past seven o'clock the booming of cannon towards our centre announced the proximity of the enemy, yet their shots convinced us that they were still beyond cannon range. A simultaneous and deafening shout, enough to strike terror into any but British hearts, accompanied the first shot. About eight o'clock, as we debouched from behind a village, a dense cloud of dust presented itself, about a mile to our front; it immediately cleared away and revealed to us, as if by magic, a vast host of Sikh and Afghan horsemen; and the next moment the welkin rang with their deafening '*Wah purakjee,*' which was responded to by a British 'hurra.' Half a minute more served to deploy us into line, thus presenting a stern front of glittering swords and lances. The enemy were as usual the first to commence by sending sundry whizzing and fizzing shots amongst us, which however we evaded by continually changing ground, and thus preventing them getting correct range of us. They were permitted to fire away for a length of time without our guns returning a single shot, the time having not yet come to open fire on them. In the meantime their cavalry had thrown back the flanks of troops, and made several judicious attempts to outflank us, but each attempt was foiled and counteracted by several quick and well executed manoeuvres on our side, and they found that though they were three to one of us, General Thackwell, who commanded our brigade, was one too many for them[9].

A sort of artillery fight was carried on until about ten o'clock, when an extraordinary activity of the whole body of the Sikh cavalry gave evidence that they were gathering the whole of their strength to attack us. And now came the time for us to act a part. The four squadrons on the left advanced in *echelon*, left in front, bringing up their right flanks, thus performing precisely the same manoeuvres as the Sikhs themselves had been several times foiled in. Simultaneously the whole brigade moved on to the attack, and our artillery alternately advancing and firing over our heads as we proceeded, the shot and shell pitched into the Sikh ranks, striking terror and confusion amongst them. Still however the two armies advanced to meet each other, our squadrons wall-like and unflinchingly cool, but the Sikhs more like the chaotic eddying of light and buoyant rubbish in a whirlwind. We did not move out of a walk until within about one hundred and fifty yards distance from their front, they all the time peppering away at us most fearfully. The two left squadrons fired their carbines[10] and the ominous words 'trot,' 'charge,' followed in quick succession afterwards. And now followed a clashing of swords and lances, accompanied with a loud 'hurra!' mixed with the Afghan curse of '*Feringhee* dog!' and the Sikh '*Feringhee brian*!'

followed by other imprecations, and the groans of the wounded; and in about the space of two minutes our foes turned their backs upon us and fled like chaff before the wind. We pursued them until coming up with a gun they had abandoned, we were ordered to halt for the remainder of our artillery to come up. Two of their colours had fallen into our hands in the first onset, and now we captured a nine-pounder gun, which, strange to say, turned out to be one that was taken from us at Chillianwallah.

While we were harnessing a couple of horses to this gun, and turning it on to a body of Sikhs who had retreated to the opposite bank of a broad ravine, I will return to the proceedings of the other portion of the army on the right, and by quoting some passages from the Commander-in-Chief's despatches, I shall carry the reader better through the details of operations which I could not see.

> At half past seven o'clock the army advanced in the order described, with the precision of a parade movement. The enemy opened their fire at a very long distance, which exposed to my artillery both the position and range of their guns. I halted the infantry just out of fire, and advanced the whole of my artillery, covered by skirmishers. The cannonade now opened on the enemy was the most magnificent I ever witnessed, and as terrific in its effects. The Sikh guns were served with their accustomed rapidity, and the enemy well and resolutely maintained his position, but the terrific force of our fire obliged them, after an obstinate resistance, to fall back. I then deployed the infantry, and directed a general advance, covering the movement by my artillery. The village of Burra Kalia, in which the enemy had concentrated a large body of infantry, and which was apparently the key to their position, lay immediately in the line of Major-General Gilbert's advance, and was carried in the most brilliant style by a spirited attack of the third brigade under Brigadier Penny, which drove the enemy from their position with great slaughter.
>
> The heavy artillery advanced with extraordinary celerity, taking up successive forward positions, driving the enemy from those they retired to, whilst the rapid advance and beautiful fire of the horse artillery and light field batteries, broke the ranks of the enemy on all points. The whole infantry line now rapidly advanced and drove the enemy before it; the *nullah* was cleared, several villages stormed, the guns that were in position carried, the camp captured, and the enemy routed in every direction, the right wing, Brigadier-General Campbell's division, passing in pursuit to the eastward, the Bombay column to the westward of the town. The retreat of the Sikh army thus hotly pursued, soon became a perfect flight, all arms dispersing over the country, rapidly pursued by our troops for a distance of twelve miles, their track strewed with the wounded, and their arms and military equipments, which they threw away to conceal that they were soldiers. Throughout the operations thus detailed, the cavalry brigades on the flanks were threatened and occasionally attacked by vast masses of the enemy's cavalry, which were in every instance put to flight, by the steady movements and spirited manoeuvres of our cavalry, most zealously and judiciously supported by the troops of horse artillery attached to them, from whom the enemy received the severest punishment. On the left a most successful and gallant charge was made upon the Afghan cavalry, and a large body of *Goorchurras*, by the Scinde Horse[11], and two squadrons of the 9th Lancers, when some standards were captured. The brilliant service they have performed in so signally defeating so vastly superior a

The Battle of Gujerat. The British commanders cluster under a tree as an aide-de-camp gallops up with a message. Although fanciful in places, this contemporary print does convey something of the crowded nature of a battle fought with short-range weapons, and the confusion resulting from clouds of gunpowder smoke from cannon and muskets. (Anne S K Brown Military Collection, Brown University Library)

force, among whom were the *elite* of the old Kalsa army, making a last united effort, will speak for itself, and will, I am confident, be justly estimated by your lordship.

In the charge I had received a slight sword cut in my left arm; but the wound being of no great magnitude, and the excitement of pursuit seeming to divest it of pain, I kept along with my troop throughout the day.

To return to my brigade; we now wheeled to the right, for the fugitives had retired in that direction, and after driving away the body of cavalry who had made a stand on the opposite side of the *nullah*, we managed, after a little difficulty, to cross it; and now a magnificent sight was before us; the vast and vari-coloured camp of the enemy, many of whom were fleeing from it in the greatest haste and confusion. We soon had possession, and at a steady walk we passed through one portion of it without interruption, for not a single Sikh remained in it, except the dead and wounded, who had been abandoned to their fate by the panic stricken enemy. Rich and magnificent tents, chiefly of scarlet silk, with blue stripes streaking the exterior, and the interior of richly embroidered Persian brocades; silken beds and costly carpeting for the floor, all manifested the luxurious display of Sikh wealth and splendour. Everywhere *attah*, *ghee*, grain, and all the appurtenances of an eastern camp scattered about, gave tokens of the confusion and hurry of their flight; while large *dexees*, or camp kettles, still seething over expiring fires, convinced us that they had left their breakfasts behind them.

As we emerged from the camp in an opposite direction to the one we had entered, some wild shots came flying amongst us from a thicket close by, but our skirmishers soon dislodged those bush rangers. Shortly after this we came to a village, the inhabitants of which, fearing that they would be mercilessly massacred, had all assembled on the tops of their houses, from which in piteous tones they supplicated mercy, and happy I am to say that they were left uninjured. Round the village were high and thick hedges of prickly pear, a plant of the cactus tribe, with long and exceedingly sharp thorns, yet many of the Sikhs had thrust themselves into the interior of them to conceal themselves from us, a plan which would have succeeded had they not indulged in their propensity of firing at us as we approached. They were hunted out like foxes, and by the aid of a bullet, were deprived of further opportunity of injuring us. Leaving this village behind, we soon captured a prize, two 18-pounders, as fine pieces of brass ordnance as ever fired a shot. A little further on was a tortuous and narrow *nullah*, under the shelving bank of which were great numbers of the fugitives, many of whom were concealed in the folds of bedding, tents, and other baggage, which had been abandoned by the cattle drivers. Their places of concealment did not save them, for few escaped the shots of our skirmishers. While we were thus hunting them, a division of infantry came up, and we were ordered to gallop off at once in pursuit of the retreating enemy. Away we went, alternately trotting and galloping, a light field battery accompanying us. We had thus proceeded about five miles when we sighted the enemy retreating without order or regularity. However, as we approached, the cavalry formed up, and wheeling about presented a formidable front to us. But they would not risk a charge of our lances a second time, for as we approached them they faced about and fled. From this time the first instinct of nature seemed to predominate, for they never afterwards made a stand. A fresh impetus was also communicated to them, by an additional reinforcement to us; the whole of the cavalry that had been engaged on the right of the British lines came sweeping round a *tope* of trees to our right rear, and by inclining to the left formed a junction with us. Thus formed we were truly a magnificent and imposing force. A splendid line of cavalry extended, like an edge, for about a mile from flank to flank, and rolling on like a mountain torrent, driving all before it. And now was exhibited all the terrors and chaotic confusion of a panic-stricken army, the horrors of retreat, and the vengeance of a justly exasperated soldiery. Our artillery, galloping up to within a score of paces of the flying fugitives, suddenly wheeled round, and pouring amongst them shot, grape, and canister, made most awful havoc. Like as shocks of corn before a mower's scythe, soldiers, camp followers, and camels laden with baggage, were swept down in masses. Numbers cast away their arms to expedite their retreat, and many divested themselves entirely of their uniforms, and assuming the peasant, fled to the adjacent villages. Many, unable to outdistance us, strove to conceal themselves in the high standing corn, while others took shelter in the midst of large trees. Some there were who bravely met their fate, and springing up from their hiding places, fought desperately single handed. Many, too, trusting to the clemency of their conquerors, which they had so often experienced before, threw down their arms and supplicated mercy; but shall I say it? yes, the truth compels me, they were answered by cold steel or a bullet. The reader will, perhaps, at such an assertion, deem the heroes of Gujerat inhuman and merciless wretches; but ere he comes to such a conclusion, let me refer him to the previous events of the Punjaub War. Let him feel the intense sorrow that we have felt at witnessing the merciless and vindictive work of the Sikhs during the time of, or after a battle. Did they not at Mudki, Ferozeshah, Aliwal, Sobraon, and Chillianwallah, cruelly butcher, in cold blood, our helpless sick and wounded, who by the fortunes of war, fell into their power; and did they not cruelly use and insult those prisoners whose lives they thought fit to spare, and this in return for the kind treatment their wounded had always experienced at our hands. Hardly a soldier in our ranks but had lost a beloved comrade, friend, or brother, and not all in fair fight; hence a general feeling of reprisal and vengeance seemed to pervade the breast of every British soldier, and especially of our native troops. Another reason, more weighty than that of revenge, self-preservation, induced us to give no quarter. From our sad experience in two campaigns with the Sikhs we knew that to pass any of them without giving the *coup de grace*, would render us subject to be shot at immediately our backs were turned on them. The following incident is an illustration. In the pursuit today, at Gujerat, a soldier of the 14th Light Dragoons was about to despatch a Sikh who lay under a bank apparently wounded and without arms, which an officer of his troop seeing, prevented, saying, 'it was a disgrace to the British soldier thus to kill a fallen foe.' The wretch's life was spared, but, no sooner had they turned away to leave him, than he drew a firelock from under him, and firing at the officer, wounded him so severely, that he died the next day[12]. Such was the Sikh's gratitude.

To return; the enemy being now closely pressed, abandoned gun after gun, and the track of retreat exhibited a strange and chaotic mixture of the material of an Indian army. For miles the country was strewed with cannon, gun-carriages, arms, ammunition, *hackeries*, *palanquins*, tents, and bedding, intermingled everywhere with the dead and wounded, while camels, elephants, horses, and bullocks, now let loose and abandoned by their drivers, galloped about the plain, or quietly grazed in the corn fields around us. Our irregular cavalry, being mostly Rajputs, a tribe retaining an hereditary hatred of the Sikhs, wreaked their vengeance on them most terribly. Entering the villages in small parties they hunted them out from their hiding places and butchered them without discrimination. Such were the horrors of this vengeful, and of necessity unsparing pursuit. Humanity, ever the English soldier's predominating feeling to a vanquished foe, might prompt him to spare and pass by the fallen Sikh, but our own safety demanded the disagreeable and revolting alternative of no quarter. In this terrible retreat many camp followers and villagers were either shot down or put to the sword in the common havoc, and it is to be feared that women and children too, did not all escape the sweeping scythe of war.

It is in such scenes as these that war assumes its really hideous character, and presents the field of 'honour and glory' with such grim visaged features. Our pursuit was continued until darkness put an end to it, when we wheeled about and returned over the ground we had come, and reached Gujerat, near which our infantry had already encamped, about ten at night, ourselves and horses completely worn out. The following incidents which came under my own cognisance, are descriptive of that day's warfare.

About four o'clock in the afternoon we halted for a moment to allow the guns to come up with us, and it happened that a stagnant pool of water was at my horse's feet, and although the bodies of two Sikhs, from which the life's blood was just oozing, were laying partially in the pool, so intense and painful was our thirst, that we hastily dismounted and drank from the pool, which seemed to be the very elixir of life to us. An officer too availed himself of the same draught, thus showing that in moments of intense suffering from thirst, we eagerly drank a liquid which at other times would create feelings of disgust.

During the pursuit several Sikhs, springing up from their lurking places, sold their lives as dearly as possible, one instance of which I will relate, as evincing the unyielding

The Surrender of the Sikhs. The reverse of the Punjab Medal depicts the scene as Sikhs lay down their firearms, swords and shields at the feet of a British general. (Private collection.)

spirit of that warlike race. On our right, a regiment of irregulars, a few of whom were elated with success, occasionally broke from the ranks and rushed at the poor fugitives, cutting them down. A Sikh, eyeing one of these little parties from behind a bush, where he was concealed, marked the leading man and shot him dead from his horse; at the same moment he rushed on the others with his sword, cut one down, and succeeded in wounding several others before he was himself killed. A trooper of the same corps, a Rajput, having hunted a poor fellow from a village, commanded him to give up his arms, at the same time promising to spare him. He, the Sikh, surrendered, and the Rajpoot then told him to go away, but no sooner was his back turned than he shot him down.

About four o'clock in the evening the horses of one of the guns were quite fagged out, so my troop was ordered to remain in charge of the gun. We dismounted in the midst of high standing corn, about sixty yards from a mud village. Being fond of adventure, and having perhaps a little desire for plunder, I, with a comrade, named Bill Budgen[13], stole off to the village. On approaching it we perceived two Sikhs lying in the corn apparently dead. We were in the act of rifling them when they proved not only to be living, but unhurt, and were lying on their swords to conceal them. I immediately placed the point of my sword to the breast of the one I was rifling, and gave him to understand that he must yield up his sword to me. He did so, begging for mercy, and it was granted; my comrade did the same with the other. I still retain possession of the sword or *tulwar*, and the poor Sikh, I hope, still lives. Proceeding on to the village we found that Rajput irregulars, like Prussians at the retreat of Waterloo, seemed to exult in revenge on their now vanquished enemies, and were dragging them out of the huts and shooting them down with unrelenting cruelty. Prying about in the huts we had well nigh lost our lives for our cupidity; for, as we entered one of them, we were attacked by two stout Sikhs sword in hand. I had but just time to evade a cut he made at my head, when the next moment I fired my pistol and he fell dead. As for my companion I know not how he managed it, but when I had time to look round he was plunging his sword repeatedly through his opponent's body, the poor fellow showing a strong tenacity to life. On their persons we found four gold mohurs which we divided[14]. Bill's expression on joining the troop is well remembered to this day. Like many other soldiers he had sold his box and kit, except what was absolutely necessary for the march, before leaving quarters; thus when he had secured the gold *mohurs*, the first thing that suggested itself was the purchasing of a box and kit with the money. 'Wah, wah, box and kit, box and kit,' says Bill, in his usual quaint manner, as he approached his comrades. The sequel of this, however, was that Bill converted the *mohurs* into liquor the first opportunity, and instead of purchasing a box and kit he was soon boxed up in the guard tent and punished for insubordination; and alas, for poor Bill, a few short months afterwards he died of fever, and was boxed up in a box six feet by two, and carried to his last quarters.

In the early part of the pursuit one of our men, seeing a Sikh concealing himself in a prickly pear bush, galloped at him with his lance, to run him through. The poor fellow, who was already bleeding profusely from a bullet wound, bared his breast and directed his victor where to make the thrust. So magnanimous a resignation to death was not lost on the Englishman, who not only spared his life, but protected him from the fury of our irregulars, who came up immediately; and he afterwards conducted him to our field hospital, where his wounds were dressed and attended to.

It is generally known that the Asiatics, from their religious prejudices, never eat or drink from the same vessel as an Englishman, as they say 'It would break their caste.' However I saw many today, several of whom I myself administered to, eagerly drinking from the Englishmen's bottles, thus shewing how exquisitely painful is the thirst proceeding from loss of blood, that the Mussulman or Sikh will risk his caste for the sake of a drop of water on such an occasion as this[15].

In this decisive victory the enemy lost his camp, fifty-two guns, a vast number of camels, swivel guns, some standards, a great quantity of ammunition and arms. The number of killed and wounded is beyond any definite calculation; but it was estimated at more than 10,000, which I fear is under the mark, for the country and villages for many miles around, were literally covered and filled with the dead bodies. History records but few such signal overthrows of so powerful and numerous an army with so little loss on the side of the victors. But 121 were killed and about 200 wounded on our side[16]. Our chief determining not to give the enemy time to recover from the shock he had received, divided the army the following day, and General Gilbert, with a strong force, marched on towards the Jhelum, while another portion of the army took a direction towards the Beembur pass. General Gilbert's division, after four days' forced marching came up with them, when some shots were fired on both sides; but soon the Sikhs ceased firing, and one of the Singhs was seen approaching our army with a flag of truce. The sequel is that the Sikhs ultimately surrendered at discretion, and upwards of 20,000 *Khalsas*, the remainder having fled to the hills to join the hill chiefs, laid down their arms, or rather surrendered, for many of them had none. The surrender is described as an affecting ceremony, and one that evinced the spirit which had made them a dreaded and formidable nation. As the grey haired veterans of Runjeet's *Kalsas* cast down their arms one by one, resentment and revenge flashed from their eyes, and many smashed their arms into pieces before our eyes, muttering their offended feelings.

The Punjaub was finally annexed to the East India Company's territories, and on the 18th March the army was broken up, and each corps returned to its quarters. Military stations were established at advantageous distances throughout the Punjaub, and it happened that my regiment was chosen to cantone one of the new stations called Wuzeerabad.

The locality selected for our cantonment was on the left bank of the Chenab, and about two miles distant from that stream. It was a flat level plain; and during the hot season was literally a sandy desert. As soon as possible temporary barracks were erected, but during their progress, which was throughout the hot season, we were necessarily encamped on the burning sands; an evil from which we suffered most terribly. None can truly conceive the pain and suffering occasioned by the glaring of a noon day sun. The effects of this, together with the hardships of the recent campaign, soon manifested themselves. Diseases which were partially generated on the campaign, now broke out in all [gap in text]

It is no less remarkable than true, that for a brief campaign, the Europeans in India, from their energy, and from a certain original vigour of constitution, will endure hardships and exposure to the sun, better than the majority of the natives, but afterwards they pay a heavy penalty for their exertions. When the excitement has passed away they often sink into supineness, disease invades them, and the gallant fellows wither into yellow and bloodless men, and whilst scarcely at middle age they die. It is well to remark these things, for thousands upon thousands of soldiers in all armies, and in all countries, sink down into early graves, which their own services have dug, without the *éclat* of battle, without one leaf of laurel to mingle with the cypress.

I must now bring my narrative to a close, for I have little more to relate which would be interesting to a reader. The death of a comrade and intimate friend severed the last remaining link of friendship that I had in India. The country became distasteful to me, and my only and constant thought was of my native home. After contending with many obstacles and difficulties from my commanding officer, for they part with good soldiers very reluctantly in India, I obtained my discharge by purchase in September, 1850[17].

I quitted the regiment in company with a detachment of invalids in October, and after four months toilsome marching and sailing in boats down the Sutlej, we arrived at Bombay in January, 1851. From thence I took passage in a first rate sailing vessel, on the 15th February, and after four months tossing about, the first lights which mark the coast of Cornwall, were hailed by the 'look out.' All on board crowded on the deck straining their eyes for the welcome sight. 'Land on the larboard bow,' was shouted from the mast head, and almost immediately afterwards the blue mountains were seen looming in the distance, and England, old England, was said and repeated from mouth to mouth; the very name seeming to produce a magic influence on all. Long after dark did I linger on deck straining my eyes to catch the dark outline of the coast, marked out as it was by lighted beacons.

This, I thought, is the land of my birth, which contains all that is now dear to me, and which many a time I thought was lost to me for ever. This the land of my dreams in the bivouac and on the battle field. That land to which they so oft have transported me, only to tantalize me with vain hopes.

In two days more I trod its soil, and in less than a week I revisited the home of my childhood.

Appendix I

Military executions at Meerut 1847: Major James Hope Grant's account

The *Act for Punishing Mutiny and Des*ertion, read out to all troops, stated clearly:

... that if any Person who is or shall be commissioned or in Pay as an Officer, or who is or shall be listed or in Pay as a Non-commissioned Officer or Soldier, ... shall strike or use any violence against his Superior Officer, being in the Execution of his Office ... [he] shall suffer DEATH, or such other punishment as by a Court-martial shall be awarded.

The power to award capital punishment for such offences was therefore in legal force, but the reluctance of commanding officers to carry it out to its full rigour had led some soldiers to doubt that such executions would ever be inflicted.

This account of the affair provides a different view from Gilling's, by the officer most closely involved in the affair.

About this time there had been a great deal of irregularity in the army, - men knocking down non-commissioned officers, and men striking their officers. The bad characters had an idea that they were gainers by committing some crimes which would involve them in transportation to Van Diemen's Land, rather than by continuing serving in a country where they would be in constant scrapes and under constant punishment. Many, in fact, were transported, but others were flogged and imprisoned. They also began to fancy either that no court-martial could award the punishment of death, or else that the Commander-in-Chief would not carry such a sentence into effect. An infantry regiment at Meerut had lately come from New South Wales, and had excited the minds of many wild reckless fellows by their accounts of the delightful climate, and the easy treatment accorded to convict soldiers. A bushranger's life was also thought by many an enjoyable existence, and the prospect of travelling seemed a pleasant change to many. So some resolved to get sent out of India. Consequently the crime of insubordination had become so prevalent throughout the whole army that a commanding officer never knew when he might be insulted, and the mere awarding of punishment became an exceptionally disagreeable duty. There had been very little of this sort of crime in my regiment, but the contagion of bad example was now to be illustrated. One day a soldier of the name of Palmer was brought before me for absence and selling his kit. He was a good-looking young fellow, but had a sullen, scowling look about him. I was reading his crime, and had not even spoken to him, when I received a blow on the face from a forage-cap which had been thrown at me. At first I could not make it out, and thought I had been struck by some accident, until I heard the exclamation, 'Cut him down! cut him down!' when I saw one of the escort on the point of making a cut at the prisoner, who, however, was collared by the sergeant-major and removed. He was tried by general court-martial, and during the interval between the confirming of the sentence, the whole of the troops were paraded to witness the execution of an artilleryman for striking one of his officers. The poor prisoner of my regiment was obliged to be present at the terrible scene. We were formed up on the plain at daybreak, and the gunner was marched round the parade. His sentence was read out, his eyes were bandaged, he was made to kneel on his coffin, and a firing-party from the Queen's 32nd Regiment fired a volley at him at twelve yards' distance at a signal from the provost-sergeant, - apparently, however, without effect, for the kneeling prisoner remained motionless, although a subsequent investigation showed he had been struck by three bullets, one of which had passed through the centre of his body. The provost-sergeant, see the volley had not been immediately fatal, instantly went forward and fired a pistol close to the prisoner's head, but by some mistake he had been posted within the flank of my regiment, and the provost, in the excitement of his act, was heedless of the direction in which he fired. Consequently the bullet, after passing through the prisoner's head, whistled past me, pierced the cap of a soldier standing behind, and further passed through the cap of his rear-rank man, without, however, inflicting any additional damage. My own unhappy prisoner was a spectator of the execution, not yet aware of his own sentence; but that very morning it was notified to him that his fate was sealed, and that in three days' time he must suffer a similar death. Next day he sent a request that I would come and see him. Accompanied by a clergyman, I went to his cell. I shook hands with him, and tried to say something consoling, but he burst into tears and was for some time unable to control himself. At last he spoke, and begged that I would not for one moment consider he had any intention of injuring me; that he had acted solely with a view to being transported; and that he had been urged to the deed by another man in the regiment, who suggested that they might get sent out of the country together. "Oh, sir," he concluded, 'can you not save me from this terrible death?' I told him I had no power; that his punishment was not for striking me as an individual, but for having used violence against his superior officer. He said, 'Well, I thank you for telling me in a straightforward way.' He murmured to himself, 'Oh, if only I could live! But to be cut off in this way!' and once more his emotion overpowered him. It was heart-breaking, and the only relief to this dreadful scene was a beautiful prayer from the clergyman. I went to see the poor fellow several times before his execution, and he confided to me his sad story.

He was about twenty-seven years old, and having been left an orphan at an early age, had been brought up by an uncle, a distiller in London. He turned out wild and extravagant, and this uncle had, as a last resource, sent him out as a settler to New South Wales. After he had been there for some time, he became acquainted with a handsome young convict girl who had been transported for stealing, and fell in love with her. He obtained the sanction of the authorities to marry her, and they lived together in harmony until he suddenly had suspicions that she was untrue to him. Maddened with jealousy, he could, he said, almost have murdered her; and at last, fearing lest he should commit some desperate act, he secretly fled the country and returned to England. Shortly after landing, he enlisted in the 9th Lancers, then on the point of embarking for India, but on arriving at Calcutta he deserted and took passage on a homeward-bound ship. Ere reaching the Cape [of Good Hope] his identity was discovered by some person on board, and he was sent back to India.

[After rejoining his regiment, he was sent some correspondence from New South Wales that convinced him of his wife's innocence, and made him frantic to rejoin her.]

Poor Palmer died very penitent, trusting fully in his blessed Saviour ... At daybreak there was once more a general parade on the plain, and as the sun rose the poor fellow was marched in slow time round the three sides of the square. The provost-sergeant, mounted, headed the procession; then came the band, playing the 'Dead March in Saul'; next the coffin, carried immediately in front of the prisoner; then the prisoner, accompanied by the clergyman; and finally the firing-party. When Palmer came opposite his own troop he said to the men, 'Farewell, comrades! I hope this will be a warning to you. I can only say I trust in the mercy of God through the merits of Jesus Christ,' and when opposite me he bowed respectfully. The march round completed, he was moved to the centre, where his coffin was laid down; the Assistant Adjutant-General read the sentence, and the prisoner advanced and knelt on his coffin. A black handkerchief was then tied over his eyes; the firing-party, consisting of twelve men from his own regiment, were marched on this occasion to within six yards of the prisoner; a volley, and all was over. The scene was concluded by the troops marching past the body in slow time. [A soldier from the Thirty-Second Light Infantry was similarly executed about the same time.]

Thus in eight days three men suffered death in this shocking manner. But these punishments, though awful and severe, did great good, and we had no more disgraceful cases of insubordination. Officers no longer had any difficulty in commanding their men. The bad characters arrived at the conclusion that there was little satisfaction in running the risk of being shot for the satisfaction of being transported. In fact, this latter punishment was found to be so little of a deterrent that it was abandoned, and in lieu large prisons were built in different districts where proper restraint could be enforced.

[Knollys, *Life of Grant*, pp. 110-6.]

Appendix II

The actions of Pope's Brigade at the Battle of Chillianwallah: Major Grant's report

This account shows how the strung-out formation of the brigade, and the dust and confusion of the battle, prevented the officers of the Ninth Lancers from exercising any control on their men, who progressively followed the collapsed centre of the brigade in its rout. Grant's career did not, as he feared, suffer from the incident; his account was regarded by Thackwell as satisfactory, and was favourably received at the Horse Guards.

> Chillianwallah Camp, 15th Jan., 1849.
> Sir, - I have the honour to report, for the information of Major-General Sir Joseph Thackwell, K.C.B., that two squadrons of the 9th Lancers, in the action of the 13th instant, were in line on the extreme right of the four regiments constituting the 3d brigade of cavalry. The other two squadrons were detached on another duty to protect Colonel Lane's troop of artillery, which was thrown back to cover our right flank. The two squadrons which I took command of, on the right of the 2d brigade, were proceeding on steadily, and changing their direction a little to the left, when the native cavalry began to cheer and charge. I confess at the time I could see no enemy, except a party of about fifty horsemen a good deal to our right flank, which, from having red coats on, in the distance I took to be some of our own Irregular Horse, as they were apparently going in the same direction with ourselves. The 9th Lancers were dressing upon the 6th Light Cavalry, I think, and they of course increased their pace and brought their lances down to the guard. There were some few of the enemy now seen in our front, but nothing in the force to stop any body of Europeans; and I had an encounter with one of them, and received two blows with a sword, but not sufficient to cut through more than the *murzir* which I wore. The two squadrons were going along with the line steadily, and no hesitation was evinced; on the contrary, the flank-men were engaged with some of the enemy, and doing their duty, when the whole line checked and went about from the left, and my squadrons, certainly without a word from me, turned round too; but the jungle and dust might make some excuse for the men, as it was difficult to hear, and in many cases to see. The dust upon this movement became very great, and the men of my regiment got mixed up with the other regiments; and though I did all in my power to stop them, ordering them to halt and front, and many of the officers in the regiment did the same, it was useless. They would not turn round; they appeared, after having gone about, to have got panic-struck. I grieve greatly to make this report of my regiment, as I did consider them, and even do so still, as fine a set of soldiers as there are in the army. But it was one of those wonderful coincidences which there is no accounting for. I grieve too for myself, as it must ruin my prospects in life.
> I have the honour to be, &c., &c.,

J Hope Grant,
Lt.-Colonel, &c., &c.
To the Assistant Adjutant-General, Cavalry Brigade.

[Knollys, *Life of Grant*, pp. 136-8.]

Appendix III

The actions of the cavalry on the left flank at the Battle of Gujerat: Major-General Sir Joseph Thackwell's account.

This account demonstrates clearly the highly successful use of horse artillery, which having all its men mounted, was able to keep up with the cavalry and support them to break up any attempt by the Sikhs to rally after their defeat on the battlefield. Major Yule of the Ninth Lancers later wrote a book on the integration of cavalry and horse artillery which probably drew on his experiences at Gujerat.

> Large bodies of Sikh cavalry showed themselves in front and on the rising ground on our left flank, and this occasioned the cavalry to form line, as the infantry had already deployed. ...this induced the enemy to open fire from four guns, which obliged White to retire his left. I, however, soon remedied the mischief by directing Duncan's troop to advance within four or five hundred yards of the enemy's cavalry, and he opened a well-directed fire upon them. Huish's troop also advanced and opened fire, and as the enemy's cavalry were advancing to outflank my left, the [9th] Lancers, who had thrown back the left, were formed to the front, and I ordered the Scinde Horse and a squadron of Lancers, supported by another squadron in echelon to the right, to charge the enemy's right, which they did in fine style, and drove this Afghan body and Goorchurras opposed to them back with considerable loss. During this time our line and guns were advanced, and cannonaded the enemy with good effect, and the Sikh cavalry were driven with loss beyond the Bara Darri, losing a gun which had belonged to Captain Huish's troop. The infantry of the left being well up, I continued my movement to the left of the above place, where the tents of Shere Singh and others, with their entire camp, were left standing, and opened my twelve guns upon the retreating enemy, and continued thus, inclining well to the left, by which movement an immense body was cut off from that to Bimber. They were several times charged by the 9th Lancers and 8th Light Cavalry, and a good deal cut up by Duncan's, Huish's, and latterly Blood's battery, until the horses had no longer a trot in them. A great number of men were killed in the pursuit, which lasted for nearly twelve miles from the Bara Darri, and ended at twenty minutes after 4 p.m., when no enemy was in sight, and the villagers reported that they had taken away only three horse artillery guns.

[Thackwell, *Military Memoirs*, pp. 337-8.]

Notes

Chapter 1 (pp 41–42)
1. Royal Horse Guards.
2. The Regiment's full title at this period was 9th (The Queen's Royal) Regiment of Light Dragoons (Lancers).
3. Esculapians: i.e. doctors, followers of the Greek god of medicine, Aesculapius.
4. Recruits received a 'bounty' on enlistment of £2-12s-6d; as Gilling says, ten shillings of this was paid in cash, which was usually spent on 'treating' the recruiting sergeant and his friends. The rest of the bounty was not seen by the recruit: it was taken to pay for his uniform and kit.

Chapter 2 (pp 43–49)
1. The draft with which Gilling embarked on 4 September 1843 consisted of the newly-commissioned Cornet Robert William King, the much more experienced 473 Sergeant John Williams, 1272 Corporal George F Jackson, and ninety-eight private soldiers. The survivors of this draft finally joined their regiment on 28 April 1844, after a journey of eight months, not untypical for troops stationed in Bengal. [TNA WO 12/891.]
2. Newly-commissioned junior officers of the East India Company's army.
3. At least sixteen of the draft died of disease before the end of 1844, many at Calcutta before they had even joined the Regiment. Others were invalided out, purchased their discharge (like Gilling and Corporal G F Jackson) or soldiered on until they had served their full twenty-four year term of enlistment.
4. The East India Company's rule excluding missionaries from its territories had been overthrown by Parliament in 1813, the debate being led by William Wilberforce, who summed up the attitude of the Christian reformers towards Indian religions with the remark 'Our religion is sublime, pure and beneficent. Theirs is mean, licentious and cruel.' The missionaries' bigotry and contempt for Indian culture and learning made them unpopular with soldiers and civil administrators. Captain Ouvry of the 3rd Light Dragoons complained in 1847: 'I feel very much annoyed at times with ... the English missionaries in particular; they are ten times worse than the natives, many of whom have really good intellects. All missionaries should be prohibited and sent out of the country. They bring discredit on the English name by their folly.' [L James, *Raj: The Making and Unmaking of British India* (New York, 1998) pp. 223-30; H A Ouvry, *Cavalry Experiences and Leaves from My Journal* (Lymington, 1892) p. 9. See also the introduction by M A Laird to R Heber, *Bishop Heber in Northern India: Selections from Heber's Journal* (Cambridge, 1971) pp. 2-13.]
5. The sailors' term for Petrels, a group of small sea-birds.
6. In 1848, 3rd (The King's Own) Regiment of Light Dragoons; in 1861 they became Hussars.
7. George Baker was born in St John's parish, Leeds, Yorkshire, and was a carpenter when he enlisted in 1843. He was drowned in the Bay of Bengal 29 December 1843. [TNA WO 25/3251.]
8. Robert William King was born in London 5 May 1821. He purchased a commission in the 9th in June 1843. He was promoted to Lieutenant in 1847, and served in the Sutlej and Punjab campaigns. He returned to England on leave in February 1851, and retired in June 1854. [TNA WO 76/538; WO 12/891.]
9. The *Sundarbunds* (from Bengali meaning 'Beautiful Forest') are the huge tracts of marshy mangrove forest forming the delta of the Rivers Ganges, Hooghly and Brahmaputra. The shifting nature of the muddy river channels and sandbanks makes it a treacherous approach to Calcutta for shipping.
10. *Leptoptilus dubius*, a large bird of the stork family. Its popular name came from its military gait, likened

by soldiers to the adjutant, the regimental officer who had charge of drill and discipline. It feeds mainly on carrion, but will also eat snakes, and for this reason was protected, as Sgt MacMullen of the 13th Light Infantry discovered when he was at Calcutta about the same time as Gilling:
> Many of these birds were stalking quietly around, utterly regardless of my approach, their tameness resulting from the protection afforded them in consequence of their being excellent scavengers. No soldier is allowed to hurt one of them; and should injury be wantonly done them, the delinquent, besides other punishment, is obliged to pay so much per diem, until the bird, which is placed in the charge of some native, recovers.

[J MacMullen, *Camp and Barrack Room; or the British Army as it is, by a late Staff Sergeant of the 13th Light Infantry* (London, 1846) p. 73.]

11 Fort William, founded in 1696, guarded Calcutta, seat of the Bengal Presidency and major centre of British power in India.

Chapter 4 (pp 52–56)

1 The first month of the Muslim New Year, applied in this instance to the period of fasting and public mourning to commemorate the deaths of the brothers Hassan and Husain. They were the sons of Ali, nephew of Muhammad, who is regarded as the Prophet's rightful heir by Shi'ite Muslims.
2 The *tazzees* actually represented the tombs of Hassan and Husain. Here as well as elsewhere Gilling confuses Islamic and Hindu practices.
3 At this period diseases such as malaria and cholera were commonly believed to spread through the air as 'miasmas,' detected as foul smells. The sun was also often blamed for causing disease:
> The Commanding Officer cautions the Men against exposing themselves to the Sun, as well as against the Morning and Evening Dews, as nothing is more likely to bring upon them that fearful scourge the Cholera, to which so many Men of the first division have already fallen victims, and by which he laments to add he has lost some of the best men in the Regiment.

[DM Regimental Order Book p. 66, Bhangukpore 20 November 1842.]

4 In 1848, 50th (The Queen's Own) Regiment of Foot; in 1881 it became 1st Battalion The Queen's Own (Royal West Kent Regiment).
5 In 1848, the 75th Regiment of Foot; in 1881 it became 1st Battalion The Gordon Highlanders.
6 Cholera is a bacterial disease of the gut, symptomised by violent purging and vomiting which cause extreme dehydration and painful cramps and convulsions. Death, as Gilling remarks, often followed quickly, and this was to many the most shocking aspect of the disease. Cholera is spread by drinking water contaminated by infected faeces, a common occurrence where wells and cess-pits were often in close proximity. The disease was endemic in India, and had spread across Asia and Europe in the 1820s, to reach Britain in 1831. There were many theories of treatment, ranging from bleeding to wearing flannel belts. In 1854 Dr John Snow, investigating an epidemic in London, proved that cholera was water-borne, but it was a number of years before his theory was accepted.

[W L MacGregor, *Practical Observations on the Principal Diseases affecting the Health of the European and Native Soldiers in the North-Western Provinces of India* (Calcutta, 1843) pp. 65-73 discusses the various theories on the causes and treatment of cholera. See also the letter to the *Military Spectator* (1844) copied into papers on cholera, BL L/MIL/5/419 (355), and treatments advocated by A Wynter, 'The Lodging, Food and Dress of Soldiers.' *Quarterly Review* 105 (1859) p. 171.]

7 This was probably 732 Edward Willoughby, who enlisted in about 1841 and travelled to India in the same draft as Gilling. He died at Calcutta 15 March 1844. As a slightly more experienced soldier than most of the draft, Willoughby may have been an acting sergeant on board; he was listed as a private when he died.
[TNA WO 12/891.]

8   In 1848, 62nd (The Wiltshire) Regiment of Foot; in 1881 it became 1st Battalion The Duke of Edinburgh's (Wiltshire Regiment).
9   During this voyage, the 9th Lancers lost one officer, five sergeants, two trumpeters and 83 rank and file, besides fourteen women and eight children, a total of 113. [Reynard, *The Ninth Lancers*, p. 39.]

Chapter 5 (pp 57–60)
1   Lord Cornwallis was Governor General of India from 1786 to 1793.
2   Now Varanasi.
3   'Ranee Chundar' is Gilling's transcription of the name of the Maharani Jind Kaur, also known as Rani Jindan. Born in 1817, she was the youngest wife of the great ruler of the Punjab, Ranjit Singh. After his death in 1839, she skilfully wove a way through the murderous intrigues of the various courtiers striving to place themselves on Ranjit's throne, attempting to have her son, Duleep Singh, recognised as the legitimate heir. In 1846, after the First Anglo-Sikh War, she was placed in custody by the British, first near Lahore and then at the Chunar Fort. She escaped on 19 April 1849, and fled to Katmandu. In 1860 she was allowed to travel to Britain to see her son, who was living the life of an English gentleman. She died in London in 1863.
4   A British cavalry regiment stationed in India at full establishment contained 45 officers, 9 warrant officers, 71 NCOs and 621 privates, although anything up to half the officers might be on leave in England, and sickness depleted the ranks. The regiment was subdivided for administrative and command purposes into eight troops, lettered A to G, with an additional depot troop at home for receiving and training recruits. Each troop was commanded by a captain, with two lieutenants, one cornet, a troop sergeant major, four sergeants, four corporals, a trumpeter, and approximately 75 privates. (The term 'trooper' for a cavalry private was just coming into common use in the 1840s; previously it had more often referred to the regiment's horses.) Squadrons, consisting of two troops acting together, were at this period mainly used as tactical units on the battlefield. [Sheppard, *Ninth Queen's Royal Lancers*, p. 101.]

Chapter 6 (pp 61–66)
1   One problem of riding in a hot climate was the constant perspiration, which caused the skin of the legs to soften, and become raw from friction with the saddle and stirrups. [QRLA, Thomas, Diaries, 1840s p.6.]
2   This man was possibly Pte Joseph Slone [sic], buried at Meerut, aged 35, on 2 December 1847, although if so Gilling is mistaken about the date. Sloane was one of at least seven men of the 9th Lancers who committed suicide in India in the 1840s. In the mid-nineteenth century, cavalry soldiers in India had the highest suicide rate of any comparable group in British society. [A Harfield, *Meerut: The First Sixty Years (1815-1875)* (London, 1992) p. 122; J H Rumsby, 'Suicide in the British army, c. 1815 to c. 1860.' *JSAHR* 84 (2006) 349-61.]
3   The East India Company authorised garrison libraries for European troops in 1821. These were to include religious works, 'instructive and amusing tales,' histories, natural history, poetry, biography, and Hindustani grammars and dictionaries. Despite some prejudice amongst officers (one remarked ' ... the fewer men that read or write in a company or troop, the better behaved the men.'), individual British regiments also established libraries, and the War Office finally approved the purchase of books in 1839. In the 9th Lancers, further books were purchased from a subscription got up from amongst all ranks, and the library stock was further supplemented by purchases using the Canteen Fund. Sergeant MacMullen described the library of the 13th Light Infantry in the 1840s as consisting mainly of ' ... books treating of abstruse, ethical, and doctrinal topics, and much better for the perusal of metaphysics and divines, than of soldiers. There was a host of old novels and romances, the large part of the last century.' Examination of soldiers' records indicate that cavalry soldiers had a high literacy rate, higher indeed than the comparable

civilian population.

[Regulations for the use of the 9th Lancers' library are set out in the DM Regimental Order Book p. 102, Wuzeerabad 20 July 1849. A complete list of books to be purchased for libraries in India in 1821 is contained in BL L/MIL/5/391 (135) p. 42. See also A C T White, *The Story of Army Education 1643-1963* (London, 1963) p. 30; F J Huddeston, 'A Barrack Library of 1839.' *JSAHR* 2 (1923) 37-8; MacMullen, *Camp and Barrack Room*, pp. 35, 154-5; Peers, 'Imperial Vice,' p. 42.]

4   Gilling's assertions are supported by the statistics. The death rate for soldiers serving in Britain in the early nineteenth century was about fifteen per thousand, compared with 9.2 for civilians living in towns. The figure for soldiers serving abroad was 57 per thousand. In 1843 in Bengal, where the 9th Lancers were stationed, it rose to 80 per thousand amongst the East India Company's troops. [Wynter, 'The Lodging, Food and Dress of Soldiers.' 155-76; BL L/MIL/5/427 (397) Letter to Bengal 3 October 1849.]

5   General Sir Charles Napier (1782-1853) was a veteran of the Napoleonic Wars, the conqueror of Scinde, a holder of radical views, and a strong advocate of improvements in the living conditions of the ordinary soldier. He became Commander-in-Chief India in 1849, but resigned less than a year later after his controversial suppression of a mutiny by an Indian *sepoy* regiment. [W N Bruce, *Life of General Sir Charles Napier G.C.B.* (London, 1885).]

6   These two men were probably Privates 1227 Alfred Moody and 1360 Frederick Smith, listed as deserted on 10 January 1845 in the Muster Roll. [TNA WO 12/891.]

7   Drowning was a surprisingly common cause of death amongst soldiers in India, although some at least were probably suicides. For example, 508 Thomas Allen and 868 William Earnshaw of the 9th Lancers were reported drowned in 1842. Therefore such a disappearance would not cause much suspicion. [TNA WO 25/3251.]

Chapter 7 (pp 67–72)

1   In 1848, 16th (The Queen's) Regiment of Light Dragoons (Lancers); later 16th (The Queen's) Lancers.

2   This was probably Lieutenant Colonel Alexander Campbell.

3   Field Marshal Hugh, First Viscount Gough (1779-1869) was born in Limerick, and first saw service, aged thirteen, in his father's militia regiment. He joined the regular army at the age of sixteen, seeing extensive service at the capture of the Cape of Good Hope in 1795, and in the Iberian Peninsula, where he was twice wounded. He was commander of the expeditionary force in the First China War in 1842, and commanded the British army at the Battle of Maharajpore in 1843. His 'white fighting coat' which he wore during battle to make himself conspicuous, was a familiar sight to his troops in the Sutlej and Punjab campaigns. However, his tactics against the Sikhs, mainly consisting of frontal attacks against prepared positions, were much criticised by the army and at home, where politicians were shocked by the high casualties. Moves to replace him after the Battle of Chillianwallah were forestalled by his victory at Gujerat.

4   The Battle of Mudki, fought on the 18 December 1845, was the first pitched battle between the Sikhs and British. The encounter was unexpected by the British, and was fought by Gough in a confused manner. Although the British could claim a victory, since they remained on the battlefield, they had lost heavily, especially from the Sikh artillery.

5   The Battle of Ferozeshah, fought on the 21 and 22 December 1845, was not the clear-cut victory that Gilling suggests. Although the British managed to capture part of the entrenched Sikh camp on the first day, they sustained many casualties, and were left that night exhausted, without water, and running out of ammunition. Nor were they 'out of reach of cannon' during the night. After they withdrew slightly, the Sikhs reoccupied some of their original positions. Shortly before dawn, Sir Harry Smith's division arrived, but this was off-set by the approach of Tej Singh with a large fresh Sikh force. He attacked the British with

cavalry and a heavy artillery bombardment, but just as it seemed that Gough would have to retreat or be destroyed, Tej Singh drew off his troops and abandoned the field – an act interpreted by many as treachery.

6 'Regimental necessaries' included clothing, cleaning equipment and other articles necessary for the soldier to perform his duties efficiently. Men often sold their necessaries, or bought cheaper, non-regimental kit, in order that they 'should have a large balance at the end of the Month to drink which too frequently sends him either to the Hospital or the Guard Room.' 734 Pte Daniel Driscoll was born in Skibereen, Co Cork, and was a labourer when he enlisted in 1841. He shot himself on 27 December 1845. [DM Regimental Order Book pp. 79-80, Cawnpore 16 August 1843; TNA WO 25/3251.]

7 Exact casualty figures vary, but in the two battles of Mudki and Ferozeshah the 3rd Light Dragoons lost approximately sixteen officers and 214 men, killed, wounded and missing, nearly half their strength. The 50th Foot lost ten officers and 234 men. [Cook, *The Sikh Wars*, pp. 223-4.]

8 The Governor General's Bodyguard, a native cavalry regiment of the East India Company; raised in 1773, it mutinied in 1857.

9 The lance had in fact been carried in battle by the 16th Lancers at the siege of Bhurtpore in 1825-6, in Afghanistan in 1838-9, and at the Battle of Maharajpore in 1843. However, in none of these campaigns had the regiment been closely engaged in a pitched battle as it was at Aliwal. [H Graham, *History of the Sixteenth, the Queen's Light Dragoons (Lancers), 1759 to 1912* (Devizes, 1912) pp. 67-114.]

10 The Battle of Aliwal was fought on 28 January 1846 between a detached force under Sir Harry Smith, and a Sikh army under Runjur Singh drawn up with its back to the River Sutlej. Smith, a very experienced officer, launched co-ordinated attacks by his infantry and cavalry, supported by the artillery, which dislodged the Sikhs from their fortified positions, and forced them back across the river with heavy losses, including sixty-seven guns. The 16th Lancers particularly distinguished themselves, charging in turn cavalry, artillery and several regiments of *Aieen* infantry, although they sustained heavy losses. An officer of the 9th Lancers, Lieutenant Thomas John Francis, who had been escorting recruits from Calcutta, and had not yet joined the 9th, attached himself to the 16th, amongst whose officers he had several friends. Alone of the 9th, he took part in the Battle of Aliwal, which he described in a letter:

> ... we were ordered to charge their cavalry. They came on with a horrid yell, which we replied to by a hearty cheer and on our meeting they went about firing at us in all directions. We formed again and went back through them and found ourselves opposite to two large squares of infantry, which we went through, lances down. I went through the first ... On reaching the centre of the square my horse fell from a shot in the leg, but the gallant Arab rose, received two sabre cuts from a man I cut down (my first) and carried on through ... So far, I have scored off the 9th as I have been in action before them, although they started before me.

[QRLA, T J Francis, Letter 31 January 1846 (typed copy); 'With the 16th Lancers in India, 1846: an extract from a private notebook of Major T J Francis, 9th and 16th Lancers.; *The Scarlet and the Green* (Journal of the 16th Queen's Lancers) 2 (9) (1933) 54-7; TNA WO 76/538.]

11 This is apparently a reference to the Arctic explorer, Sir John Franklin (1786-1847). He set out to discover the North-West Passage between the Atlantic and Pacific oceans in 1845, and was never seen again. His fate was the subject of much public speculation. *The Voyages and Travels of Captains Parry, Franklin, Ross and Mr Belzani, etc* by John F Dennett, was published in 1826; Gilling may have read it in the regimental or cantonment library.

Chapter 8 (pp 73–88)

1 These were the Nasiri and Sirmoor Battalions, raised in 1815 immediately following the Anglo-Nepalese War. The Nasiri Battalion became in 1850 the 66th (Gurkha) Bengal Native Infantry, and from 1861 the 1st Gurkha Rifles. The Sirmoor Battalion became in 1858 the Sirmoor Rifle Regiment, and from 1861 the

2nd Goorkha Rifles.

2   One company in each line infantry regiment was designated as the Grenadier Company. Originally the men of this company had been required to lead attacks on fortifications, and were trained to throw hand grenades. Although grenades had gone out of use by the 1840s, the grenadiers were still chosen from the tallest and strongest men, and were considered the regiment's élite.

3   961 Pte Samuel Day was born in London, and was a clerk when he enlisted on 30 June 1841. The Punniar Star, and a similar star for the Battle of Maharajpore, were awarded for the 'twin' battles fought on 23 December 1843, during the campaign that led to the annexation of Gwalior. The Stars were made of bronze from the guns captured during the campaign, some years before a similar source was utilised for the Victoria Cross. Strangely enough, Day's Star must have been retrieved from his body, as it was forwarded, along with £1 13s 11¼d, to his father, as next-of-kin. The other fatal casualty was 1421 Trumpeter Frederick Elphinstone. He was born in Brighton, Sussex, and like Day was a clerk when he enlisted on 21 March 1842. He died of wounds on 13 March 1846, leaving £2 9s 11d to his next-of-kin. [TNA WO 25/3251.]

4   A camel swivel, or *zamborruck*, was a small cannon, firing a ball of about a pound weight. It was fixed to a swivelling mount on the saddle of a camel.

5   In 1848, 31st (The Huntingdonshire) Regiment of Foot; in 1881 it became 1st Battalion The East Surrey Regiment.

6   This impression almost certainly was erroneous. Although the regiments might be going home, many of the men would volunteer to stay in India; thereby the army kept experienced and acclimatised soldiers in India, and saving the East India Company the expense of their passage home.

7   Lieut Col Fullerton not only promoted 610 Patrick Nugent to corporal, but took the unusual step of praising Nugent's actions in a Regimental Order:

> The Commanding Officer is much pleased to notice the gallant conduct of Private Patrick Nugent in the late Battle on the 10th instant who having had his horse shot under him, and not being able to get another, obtained permission to join HMs 50th Regiment proceeding to the Attack, and gallantly entered the entrenchments of the enemy with that Regiment thus rendering much good service and showing an example well worthy of being followed …

Nugent, as his actions at Sobraon might suggest, had a distinguished career in the ranks, despite an unsteady start. He was born at Keady, Newton Hamilton, Co Armagh, on 10 August 1823. He enlisted in the 9th Lancers at Newry, Co Down, stating his age as eighteen (he was in fact fifteen). The shock of army life led him to desert a month later, and he remained at large for twenty months before rejoining. A district court martial sentenced him to two months in prison. He had served in the Gwalior campaign before the First Anglo-Sikh War, and went on to serve again against the Sikhs in the Punjab campaign. In the Indian Mutiny he served as sergeant and troop sergeant major, being severely wounded at the Battle of Badli-ke-Serai. After seventeen years in India he was discharged at Dublin in April 1865. However, the following year he was back in uniform, as a Yeoman of the Guard. He died on 23 May 1892, having during his career been awarded the Punniar Star, Sutlej Medal (for Sobraon), Punjab Medal (with clasps for Chillianwallah and Goojerat), Mutiny Medal (with clasps Delhi, Relief of Lucknow and Lucknow), Long Service and Good Conduct Medal and Jubilee Medal 1887. [DM Regimental Order Book p. 94, Camp Kussore 13 February 1846; I McInnes, *The Yeoman of the Guard, including the Body of Yeoman Warders, HM Tower of London, Members of the Sovereign's Body Guard (Extraordinary) 1823-1903* (Oldham, 2002) pp. 140-1.]

8   1223 Pte James Firth is recorded as being wounded at Sobraon. [London Stamp Exchange, *The Army of the Sutlej 1845-6: Casualty Roll* (London, nd) p. 30.]

9   Presumably a reference to Lord Gough.

10 When selected for discharge, a man attended a Pension Board consisting of three officers, who had in front of them papers setting out his full service record, including dates of enlistment, promotions and overseas service, wounds, conduct and medical record. Up to 1829, a private soldier awarded a pension received sixpence a day regardless of service. After that date, the length of service was taken into account. The rate for a private was one shilling a day for twenty-one years' service, with an additional halfpenny a day for each extra year served. From 1833, a man's good conduct was also considered. [Regulations of 1829 set out in *USJ* 1830 (1) pp. 106-15; see also Anglesey, *British Cavalry 1*, p. 148.]

11 A reference to *Don Quixote*.

12 Sir Henry Hardinge was Governor General of India from July 1844 to January 1848. In a private account of these proceedings, Hardinge described Gulab Singh as 'the ablest man and the greatest rascal in the East.' [Bawa Satinder Singh (ed), 'The Letters of the First Viscount Hardinge of Lahore to Lady Hardinge and Sir Walter and Lady Jones 1844-1847.' *Camden Fourth Series* 32 (1986) p. 147.]

13 This treaty was signed at Lahore on 9 March 1846. There were sixteen articles altogether. Gilling refers to Article 8: 'The Maharaja will surrender to the British Government all the guns, thirty-six in number, which have been pointed against the British troops and which ... were not captured at the battle of Sobraon.'; Article 3, conceding the country between the Sutlej and Beas (not Ravee) rivers; and Article 4, ceding further territory plus half a *crore* of rupees. The full text of the treaty is printed in Cunningham, *History of the Sikhs*, pp. 371-4.

14 Gilling shows his knowledge of the Bible, referring to Mount Nebo, where Moses is said to have died (Deuteronomy 34:1). The summit gives extensive views over the Holy Land and the Jordan Valley.

15 This was the heavy curved knife, called a *kukri*, which was (and is) the unique national weapon of the Gurkhas.

16 Hudibras: the eponymous hero of a mock-heroic satirical poem written by Samuel Butler (1612-80).

17 *Batta* was an extra allowance paid to all ranks, originally as compensation for extra expenses occurred on active service beyond the East India Company's territories. If the men came under fire, they automatically received twelve months' *batta*, even if the whole campaign did not last a year. For this reason the men of the Bengal Horse Artillery raised a cheer 'for the 12 months' *batta*' as they came into action at the Battle of Mudki. The amount received by Gilling and his comrades was worth very roughly the equivalent of twenty days' pay. [P Mason, *A Matter of Honour: An Account of the Indian Army, its officers and men* (London, 1974) pp. 110-6; N W Bancroft, *From Recruit to Staff Sergeant* (2nd edn, Simla, 1900) p. 40.]

18 The cold season at Meerut was reckoned to last from November to March. The only artilleryman recorded as having died in this period in 1847 was Farrier John Graves of the Bengal Horse Artillery, who was buried on the 16 March. [Harfield, *Meerut*, pp. 3, 119.]

19 In India each regiment had a cell-block, named after the bread and water diet of the prisoners, *congee* being the water in which rice had been boiled. Sentences to the congee-house ranged from one week to twelve months, sometimes with hard labour or solitary confinement. [Yule and Burnell, *Hobson-Jobson*, p. 245; typical sentences are recorded in TNA WO 27/158, 174.]

20 Gilling's memory appears to be at fault here. 1041 Pte William H H Collins committed suicide at Meerut on 27 October 1846, aged 28. Unfortunately the Casualty Rolls for the 9th Lancers at this date are not extant. [Harfield, *Meerut*, p. 119.]

21 In 1848 32nd (The Cornwall) Regiment of Foot; in 1881 it became 1st Battalion The Duke of Cornwall's Light Infantry.

Chapter 9 (pp 89–97)

1 This insubordination was widespread in the Bengal military stations after the First Anglo-Sikh War. For example, in 1847 six men at Lahore had been transported for seven or fourteen years for striking NCOs,

and a similar number had received one or two years' imprisonment. As Gilling makes clear, the penalty for striking an officer or NCO was death, but this was normally commuted to transportation to the Australian colonies. Many men who disliked soldiering in India saw convict life in Australia as the better option, especially if they could earn a 'ticket of leave.' Under this system, a convict who had served part of his term was allowed to support himself by earning wages, engaging in business or a trade, or working the land. Some convicts became prosperous citizens in this manner. [TNA WO 90/2; Malcolm, *Barracks and Battlefields*, p. 35; J Hirst, 'The Australian Experience: The Convict Colony.' In N Morris and D J Rothman (ed), *The Oxford History of the Prison* (Oxford, 1998) pp. 242-3, 248.]

2   Richard Riley Atkins. [Waterfield, *Memoirs*, p. 31.]

3   John Ryder of the 32nd Light Infantry reported that Atkins 'did not believe that he should be shot. He thought that he should at the last moment get his reprieve, for he believed he was sentenced for an example.' [Ryder, *Four Years' Service*, p. 27.]

4   The firing party was provided by the 32nd Light Infantry, none of whom had ever witnessed a military execution before, which may account for their failure to kill Atkins at the first volley. [Waterfield *Memoirs*, p. 31.]

5   For Major Grant's own account of this affair, and a description of Palmer's background and character, see Appendix 1.

6   Major Grant was commanding officer of the 9th at this time due to the absence of the two senior lieutenant colonels. Later General Sir James Hope Grant GCB (1808-75), he came from a family of gentry in Perthshire. After being educated at Edinburgh High School and in Switzerland, he was commissioned as cornet in the 9th Lancers in 1826. His family was not wealthy, and he almost left the army at one point because of the expenses of serving in a cavalry regiment. This situation was relieved, at least temporarily, when he was appointed brigade major to Major General Lord Saltoun (with whom he shared an interest in music) in the expeditionary force to China in 1842. Having been awarded a CB for this service, he rejoined the Ninth in India in 1844. He was promoted major without purchase, and commanded the regiment at various times in the absence of the lieutenant colonels. Grant served with the Ninth in both Anglo-Sikh Wars, and again received promotion, to lieutenant colonel, without purchase, an important factor in his career as he could not have afforded to purchase his 'steps.' After three years' leave in England, he returned to the Ninth in 1854, and commanded them in the Indian Mutiny 1857-58, during which the lancers gained a formidable reputation as 'The Delhi Spearman.' He was promoted major general and awarded the KCB for this service. As lieutenant general he commanded the British troops in the second China War in 1860, being advanced to GCB. After a further sojourn in India, and promotion to general, he took over the command at Aldershot. He died 7 March 1875 and was buried in Edinburgh. His brother Francis painted a magnificent portrait of him (now in the National Galleries of Scotland) in the full dress of the Ninth Lancers.

[A McK Annand, 'General Sir James Hope Grant, G.C.B.' *JSAHR* 43 (1965) 44-8; Knollys, *Life of Grant*; C Wills, *High Society: The Life and Art of Sir Francis Grant 1803-1878* (Edinburgh, 2003) Plate 50.]

7   786 Pte William Henry Fulcher Palmer (not John as Gilling has it) was born in Whitechapel and was a twenty-two-year-old clerk when he enlisted in London on 30 March 1842. He was shot at Meerut on 23 October 1847. He left a debt of 17s 10d, as well as his Sutlej Medal. His next-of-kin were recorded as his brother George, and uncle Henry Fulcher. [TNA WO 12/890, 893; WO 25/3251; BL L/MIL/5/12.]

8   The man's name was Pte Thomas Jardine. Cpl John Ryder, a man of the same regiment who witnessed the execution, confirms Gilling's description. [Ryder, *Four Years' Service*, pp. 29-30.]

9   Julius Jakob Baron von Haynau (1780-1858), an Austrian general, was appointed dictator of Hungary after the revolt of 1849. He was already notorious for his brutal repression of a revolt in the Austrian-held provinces of northern Italy. When he visited England in 1850, he was attacked by brewery workers,

causing a diplomatic incident.
10 Capital punishment could be awarded for purely military crimes, such as mutiny, desertion and violence to superior officers, as well as for offences that also carried a capital sentence in civilian courts, such as murder. However, military executions were rare. Of 76 death sentences handed down between 1826 and 1835, 35 were commuted to transportation. It seems that the determined way in which these sentences were carried out, and the concentration of several close together, were what provoked the impact amongst soldiers. [Spiers, *Army and Society*, p. 62.]
11 Nero: Roman emperor AD 54-68; Tiberius: Roman emperor AD 81-96; Lucius Aelius Sejanus (20 BC – AD 31): Roman general and confidant of Tiberius, executed for plotting to seize the imperial throne; Maximilien Robespierre (1758-94), French revolutionary leader; Marshal Emmanuel Grouchy (1766-1847), French general known amongst other actions for his suppression of the Spanish revolt of 1808. Once again Gilling shows off his wide historical reading, in choosing examples of tyrannical behaviour.
12 Halberts, or spontoons, were spears carried by infantry sergeants. Three could be tied together in a tripod, and a fourth fastened as a cross-piece, to act as a frame on which the offender was tied. Cavalry regiments sometimes used a ladder fastened at an angle to a wall. Although halberts were abolished in 1830, the phrase obviously lingered as a metaphor for flogging. Alexander Somerville of the 2nd Dragoons (Scots Greys) described his own flogging in his *Autobiography of a Working Man* (London, 1951; originally published 1848) p. 187.
13 Between 1844 and 1850, 223 courts martial took place in the 9th Lancers. Although records of sentences handed down by these trials do not survive, comparison with other records for regiments in India suggest it is very unlikely that as many as 200 of those tried were flogged. Gilling may be including men of other regiments in the same cantonments that he saw flogged, or he may simply be exaggerating. [TNA WO27/342-398; WO 90/2.]
14 This was Pte Frederick John White, who died, apparently from the effects of a flogging at Hounslow Barracks, on 11 July 1846. Subsequent publicity, exacerbated by the army's attempts to hush the matter up, caused a renewed public outcry against army flogging, although flogging of civilian criminals never attracted the same attention. The affair is examined in Harry Hopkins' *The Strange Death of Private White* (London, 1977).
15 The number of lashes allowed to be inflicted by regimental or general courts martial was reduced to fifty in 1837, before the White affair. In 1868 flogging was severely limited in peacetime, but it was not finally abolished until 1881. [A S White, 'Flogging in the Army.' *JSAHR* 20 (1941) 114-5; E M Spiers, *The Late Victorian Army 1868-1902* (Manchester, 1992) pp. 73-4.]
16 The French army had indeed abolished the lash, but had more capital offences than the British. The Prussian army limited corporal punishment to forty strokes with a light cane on the clothed back. Russia still used flogging and other savage punishments at this date. [S Claver, *Under the Lash – a history of corporal punishment in the British armed forces* (London, 1954) pp 241-3; Hopkins, *The Strange Death*, p. 21, 195.]
17 *The Diverting History of John Gilpin*, by William Cowper (1731-1800), tells the comical tale of a would-be heroic draper whose horse runs away with him.

Chapter 10 (pp 98–107)

1 First Lieutenant Sir Peter Colnett Lambert (1821-1845) was serving with the Company's 3rd Troop, 3rd Brigade, Bengal Horse Artillery when he was killed on the second day of the Battle of Ferozeshah. [G W De Rhé-Philipe and I M Irving, *Soldiers of the Raj* (1910 and 1912, one volume reprint, London, 1989) p. 199.]
2 Charles Robert Cureton (1789-1848) had indeed known life as a private soldier. He was the son of a

Shropshire gentleman, and had served as an young officer in the militia of that county. However, having got into debt through gambling, he faked his own death by drowning at the seaside, went to London, and enlisted under an assumed name in the 14th Light Dragoons. He served with distinction in the Peninsular War from 1809 to 1814, including ten pitched battles, and in 1814 was granted a commission for his bravery and ability. He served in the 16th Lancers from 1819, seeing action in India at Bhurtpore, Afghanistan, Maharajpore and the Sutlej Campaign. When the 16th came home in 1846, he stayed on in India as adjutant-general, with the rank of colonel. Gilling was not alone in his admiration of Cureton. Senior officers recognised his professional skill, the following being a typical comment, from Major General Sir Robert Arbuthnot, inspecting the 16th Lancers in 1841:

> I have seen few Regts in my long service in such excellent order as this Corps. I cannot express the high estimation in which Lieut Col Cureton is regarded by me as a zealous sound practical officer, and possessing every quality to make himself respected and liked by Officers and men. If I was called on to submit an Officer for any service requiring the highest qualifications I should not hesitate to name Lieut Col Cureton.

Pte Tookey of the 14th Light Dragoons echoed the opinion of Gilling and other ordinary soldiers:

> General Cureton is a fine looking old man formerly a private in ours. You have read of his romantic life at the time of the Sutledge [sic] battles. He is considered the finest Cavalry Officer in the world.

Cureton's medals are now part of the collection of his old regiment, the 14th Hussars, in Preston, Lancashire.

[E Neale, *'Risen from the Ranks,' or, Conduct versus Caste* (London, 1853) pp. 9-29; A McK Annand, 'Brigadier-General C R Cureton, CB, ADC.' *JSAHR* 47 (1969) 157-160; TNA WO 27/304; Inspection report, 16th Lancers, 8 Dec 1841, NAM 6405-61; G Tookey, Letter 10 Nov 1848, .]

3   I.e. Brigadier Pope, not Brigadier Cureton.
4   *Doctor Syntax in Search of the Picturesque* was the first of three volumes of comical verse describing the adventures of a clergyman, written by William Combe and published in 1812-21. They were extremely popular, especially due to the accompanying illustrations by Thomas Rowlandson.
5   In 1848, 53rd (The Shropshire) Regiment of Foot; in 1881 it became 1st Battalion The King's (Shropshire Light Infantry).
6   In 1848, 14th (The King's) Regiment of Light Dragoons; in 1861 it became an Hussar regiment.
7   5th Bengal Light Cavalry was raised in 1800, and mutinied in 1857.
8   In 1848, 24th (The 2nd Warwickshire) Regiment of Foot; in 1881 it became The South Wales Borderers.
9   This was Lieutenant George Ellis Lloyd Williams, who entered the army as an Ensign by purchase in April 1841. He was promoted Lieutenant in August 1844, and Captain in January 1849. He left the army soon afterwards, probably as a result of his wounds. [Hart, *Army List*.]
10 This refers to Captain John Forster Fitzgerald, who was in fact an officer of the 14th Light Dragoons, not the 5th Bengal Light Cavalry. Fitzgerald was from a Co Clare family, and the son of a Field Marshal. He had joined the army in March 1837, as a Cornet in the 4th Light Dragoons, with which regiment he had seen action during the First Afghan War in 1838-9. After transferring to the 14th Light Dragoons he saw more service against insurgent Mahrattas in 1844. He died of wounds received at Ramnuggar on 26 November 1848. [De Rhé-Philipe and Irving, *Soldiers of the Raj* p. 109.]
11 Far from being impetuous at Ramnuggar, Cureton was apparently trying to stop Havelock's precipitate charge, exclaiming 'My God! This isn't the way to use cavalry!' He was shot dead by a matchlock ball shortly afterwards. [Anglesey, *British Cavalry 1* pp. 274-5.]
12 Lieutenant General Sir John Moore was killed at the Battle of Corunna, in northern Spain in January 1809. General James Wolfe was killed at Quebec in September 1759.

13 'Europeans' was the conventional term for British soldiers in India, to distinguish them from 'Native' or Indian troops. The East India Company maintained several regiments of 'Europeans,' a considerable proportion of which were Irish.
14 Beads for counting the number of prayers recited, as used in many religions.
15 Gilling's book was published two years before the outbreak of the great 'Indian Mutiny' or, as it is often regarded in India, the 'First War of Liberation.' However, there had been several outbreaks of mutiny amongst Indian troops before 1857, notably at Vellore in 1806 and Barrackpore in 1824. [Mason, *A Matter of Honour* pp. 220-46; S L Menezes, 'Race, Caste, Mutiny and Discipline in the Indian Army, from its origins to 1947.' in A J Guy and P B Boyden (ed), *Soldiers of the Raj: The Indian Army 1600-1947* (London, 1997).]
16 The fort at Attock was strategically important, as it commanded the point where the main route from Peshawar to Lahore crossed the Indus River. Its seizure by the British prevented Sikh reinforcements under Chuttar Singh from marching on Lahore. The fort was actually held by Lieut Herbert; Major James Abbott was similarly defending a fort at Srikote controlling the Hazarians. Attock fell on 2 January 1849, its Muslim garrison having had their loyalty undermined by Sikh threats against their families. [Cook, *The Sikh Wars*, pp. 127, 154, 163.]
17 General Sir Joseph Thackwell (1781-1859) was a cavalry commander of great experience. Born into a family of Worcestershire gentry, his first military service was as a teenage officer in the Worcestershire Provisional cavalry. He received a regular commission in the 15th Hussars in 1800, and served with them in the Corunna Campaign 1808-09, in Spain and France 1813-14, and at Waterloo, where he lost his left arm. After a period on half-pay, he exchanged into the 3rd Light Dragoons in 1837 in order to go to India. He held senior cavalry commands in Afghanistan, the Gwalior Campaign and in both Anglo-Sikh Wars. His eldest son Edward served as his aide-de-camp in the Punjab, and wrote a valuable account of the campaign.
[J Thackwell, *The Military Memoirs of Lieut.-General Sir Joseph Thackwell GCB, KH, Colonel 16th Lancers* ed H C Wylly (London, 1908); H C Wylly, *XVth (The King's) Hussars, 1759 to 1913* (London, 1914) p. 457.]
18 *Kubberdaur*: Take care! *Bobbery wallahs*: noisy fellows. [Yule and Burnell, *Hobson-Jobson*.]

Chapter 11 (pp 108–113)
1 Ammunition limbers.
2 The indecisive combat of Sadoolapore.
3 On the 11 December 1839, whilst returning from the first phase of the Afghanistan campaign, the 16th Lancers attempted to cross the Jhelum river by a poorly-marked ford. The safe path was missed, and most of one squadron was washed away by the strong current. Captain William Hilton, one corporal and nine privates were drowned. [Graham, *History of the Sixteenth*, p. 93.]
4 Lieutenant Colonel James Alexander Fullerton joined the 9th Lancers as a Cornet in August 1822. He served at the Battle of Punniar, and in the Sutlej and Punjab campaigns. He died of heart disease in Kashmir on 28 April 1850. In his reminiscences, Colonel J Anstruther Thomson paints an entertaining picture of the then Captain Fullerton, who was only 5 feet 4 inches tall, on a foot parade standing between his two subalterns, one 6 feet 1 inch and the other (Thomson himself) 6 feet 3 inches. [De Rhé-Philipe and Irving, *Soldiers of the Raj* pp. 179, 118; Thomson, *Eighty Years' Reminiscences*, p. 48.]
5 In the 1820s a letter to or from a soldier in India might take up to six months to arrive. By the mid-1840s this had been reduced to two months by the introduction of steamships. From 1806 soldiers up to and including sergeants could send and receive letters at the special reduced rate of one penny. At this time it was common for recipients to have to pay the postage, rather than the sender. Such letters had to

be endorsed by the commanding officer. In cantonments letters were placed in the ordinary post. On campaign an officer was appointed as Postmaster, attached to the Headquarters staff. The job paid well, but could be onerous, as all unpaid mail had to be paid for on delivery, sorted, delivered, and payment collected. During campaigns deep in enemy territory, such as Afghanistan and the Punjab, the post was often ambushed and destroyed.

The regulation of handing in post for endorsement by the commander could promote suspicion. Samuel West, a discontented private of the 16th Lancers, wrote to his parents explaining why he had put his letter (unpaid) directly into the ordinary post rather than take advantage of the soldiers' cheap rate: 'I believe in giving all the information I can. The letters you receive will cost you rather high as I don't have them franked as the Colonel is entitled to read them but he shall never have the chance to read one from me.' At the time of the Battle of Chillianwallah, there was a rumour that the post was being held back to prevent people at home from hearing bad news about the campaign. [*The King's Regulations for the Army* (London, 1837); P B Boyden, *Tommy Atkins' Letters: The History of the British Army Postal Service from 1795* (London, 1990); D S Virk, *Army Post Offices and Philately* (New Delhi, 1980); J Murray, 'Field Surgeon at the Battle of Aliwal.' Ed J Fraser *JSAHR* 67 (1989) pp. 89, 91; L C Stewart, 'A Surgeon in the Second Sikh War: Ludovick Stewart's account of the Battle of Chillianwallah.' Ed M Nicholls *JSAHR* 71 (1993) p. 225; NAM 9604-220 Pte Samuel West, Letter 27 May 1823.]

Chapter 12 (pp 114–124)

1. So called from the flags they set up to mark the position of each regiment's camp ground.
2. The 6th Bengal Light Cavalry was raised in 1800, and mutinied in 1857.
3. Gilling's troop was with the two squadrons of the 9th which, with three or four squadrons of native cavalry and eight guns, were detached as a guard to the extreme right flank of the British army. The other two squadrons of the 9th (which Gilling refers to as the 'left wing') remained with Pope's brigade. [Anglesey, *British Cavalry 1* p. 279.]
4. This was Brevet Lieutenant Colonel J T Lane, commanding 2nd Troop, 2nd Brigade, Bengal Horse Artillery, reinforced by two guns from 3rd Troop, 2nd Brigade. Lane also had overall command of the whole force, artillery and cavalry. [B P Hughes, *The Bengal Horse Artillery 1800-1861* (London, 1971) p. 119.]
5. The 8th Bengal Light Cavalry was raised in 1805, and mutinied in 1857.
6. Captain Walter Unett purchased his first commission as Cornet in August 1833. He had previously served with the 3rd in the First Afghan War in 1842. In this charge he received a sword cut across the shoulder, a spear thrust along his ribs, and a blow from a matchlock. The jacket he wore in the charge is now in the Regimental Museum. [Hart, *Army List*; J Pearman, *Sergeant Pearman's Memoirs* ed Marquess of Anglesey (London, 1968).]
7. One sergeant and twenty-two other ranks were killed, and Captain Unett, Lieutenant Stisted and several men were wounded. The fact that more men were killed than wounded grimly illustrates the Sikh custom of giving no quarter: any man who fell from his horse was immediately hacked to death. [G E F Kauntze, *Historical Record of the Third, or the King's Own Regiment of Light Dragoons ... to 1857* (London, 1857) p. 219.]
8. This was Gilling's phonetic spelling of the name of Lieutenant Colonel John Pennycuick CB KH. Pennycuick's first commission as an Ensign was in 1807, and he was indeed a veteran, having served in the attack on Java in 1811, when he was wounded, at the capture of Balli and Macassar in 1814, the Burma War of 1824-5, the First Afghan War in 1838-9, and in Arabia and Aden in 1841. His son, Ensign (not Lieutenant) Alexander Pennycuick, had only been commissioned in July 1848. He was aged seventeen when he was killed. [De Rhé-Philipe and Irving, *Soldiers of the Raj* pp. 274-5.]

NOTES 159

9   In 1848, 28th (The North Gloucestershire) Regiment of Foot; in 1881 it became 1st Battalion The Gloucestershire Regiment.
10 The 14th Light Dragoons.
11 One contemporary described the brigade commander thus:
> The officer commanding the cavalry on the right, Lieutenant-Colonel Pope, was an officer of Native Cavalry. He had earned a high reputation for personal courage in his younger days, but possessed no great knowledge of the art of war. He knew little about handling large bodies of cavalry; and was suffering from such bodily infirmity as to be incapable of mounting his horse without assistance.

[Thackwell, *Narrative* p. 132.]
12 The 14th's regimental historian diplomatically described this as 'a retrograde movement ... which was carried out at an increased pace for a considerable distance before the line was halted and reformed.' Undoubtedly the 14th had been shaken by their experiences at Ramnuggar, and the poor handling of the brigade by Pope had contributed largely to the panic. The 14th, if some accounts can be believed, were equally unsteady at the Battle of Gujerat. However, they certainly redeemed their reputation during the hard campaigning and many pitched battles of the Indian Mutiny in 1857-9. For Major Grant's account of the debacle see Appendix 2. [H B Hamilton, *Historical Record of the 14th (King's) Hussars from AD 1715 to AD 1900* (London, 1901) p. 230; J C Binkley, 'The Letters of John Curtis Binkley 1843-1849.' *JSAHR* 61 (1983) p. 36; Thackwell, *Narrative* pp. 263-6.]
13 The commander of these guns, from 3rd Troop, 2nd Brigade and 1st Troop, 2nd Brigade, Bengal Horse Artillery, Major Christie, was severely wounded. As Pope's brigade extended into its single unwieldy line, it masked Christie's guns so that they could not fire effectively on the Sikh cavalry, as Lane's guns had done on the right flank.
14 A traditional Irish war-cry meaning 'Clear the way!'
15 Possibly Gilling's (or his editor's) transcription of 'Wah! Guru ki Fath!' meaning 'Hail! Power of the Guru!' [Cunningham, *History of the Sikhs* pp. 315-6.]
16 Despite their experiences, the 9th Lancers lost only four dead and eight wounded at Chillianwallah. The dead were 1127 Cpl Richard Calcutt, 772 Pte John Cunniam, 453 Pte Robert Dalton and 1102 Pte Abraham Matthews. [TNA WO 12/89.]
17 Although the Battle of Chillianwallah is usually claimed as a British victory, and appears amongst the battle honours of many regiments, there is no doubt that the Anglo-Indian army had been repulsed with heavy losses (about 2330) The Sikhs retained their positions for some time afterwards, as well as retrieving those of their guns that had been temporarily captured. However, the Sikhs had also suffered heavy casualties, although the exact number is unknown.
18 The 30th Bengal Native Infantry was raised in 1748, and mutinied in 1857.

Chapter 13 (pp 125–140)

1   Lieutenant Augustus John Cureton, the youngest son of Brigadier Cureton, became a Cornet in the 14th Light Dragoons (his father's old regiment) in March 1847. He became a Lieutenant in July 1848. He was eighteen years old when he was killed. Two other sons of Brigadier Cureton distinguished themselves in India. Edward Burgoyne Cureton (1822-94) served in the Anglo-Sikh Wars, the Kaffir Wars in South Africa and the Crimean War, reaching the rank of Lieutenant General. Charles Cureton (1826-91) raised a regiment of cavalry during the Mutiny, known as Cureton's Multanis (later the 15th Bengal Lancers). He reached the rank of General. [De Rhé-Philipe and Irving, *Soldiers of the Raj* pp. 74-6.]
2   There were several men named Johnson in the 9th Lancers at this time.
3   This was probably 1310 Pte George Hunt. He had also fought in the Sutlej campaign. He embarked as an

invalid for England on 15 February 1856. [TNA WO 25/3251.]

4 'Sinclair' was probably 1004 Pte Charles Sinclair, although he is not listed as being wounded. He served in the Gwalior campaign and both the Anglo-Sikh Wars, and embarked for England for discharge on 5 March 1857. There were two men named Walter serving at this time. They were 901 Pte Lemon H Walter and 1476 Pte Charles Walter (promoted Corporal 1 February 1849). [TNA WO 25/3251; WO 12/893.]

5 Sinclair and Walter's adventures became common knowledge in the army. Lieut Sandford of the 2nd Bengal European Regiment entered the version he had heard in his journal for 20 January:

> Two of the 9th Lancers who were taken prisoners the other day, were sent back this morning with Shere Singh's compliments. They seemed rather sorry to come back, as they had been treated like princes, *pilawed* with champagne and brandy to the masthead, and sent away with ten rupees each in his pocket. Shere Singh is evidently providing for the worst, and making as favourable an impression as he can.

[D A Sandford, *Leaves from the Journal of a Subaltern during the Campaign in the Punjaub Sept. 1848 to March 1849* (London, 1849) pp. 118-9.]

6 The city of Multan provided the flashpoint that started the Second Anglo-Sikh War, when two British envoys were murdered by mutinous Sikh troops in April 1848. Precipitate action by Herbert Edwardes and other British officers made matters worse, and a full-scale rising by Sikhs under Mulraj took place. The first attack on Multan by an inadequate Anglo-Indian force failed. The siege was renewed in early December after the British were reinforced. The town was captured by storm on 3 January, and Mulraj surrendered the citadel on 22 January 1849.

7 This phrase was apparently of nautical origin (sailors were organised in numbered messes for their meals), and was presumably picked up by soldiers travelling on troopships. It is also used by Pte George Tookey of the 14th Light Dragoons in a letter of 13 December 1848 (NAM 6405-61); Tookey was killed at the Battle of Chillianwallah. [E Partridge. *A Dictionary of Slang and Unconventional English* ed Paul Beale (London, 8th edn., 1984) p. 733.]

8 Amongst the last troops from Multan to join were the baggage guard of the 32nd Light Infantry, including Cpl John Ryder, who noticed the poor morale amongst Gough's men:

> The men of Lord Gough's army were glad to see us, being before very low spirited. They told us that they expected the enemy would attack them every day, for that they were very superior in numbers, and were daily receiving fresh reinforcements; that they had become very bold since the battle of Chillianwallah, where our army got the worst of it; and that the enemy was quite sure of victory.

[Ryder, *Four Years' Service* p. 168.]

9 General Sir Joseph Thackwell commanded the whole of the cavalry (four brigades, consisting of three British and eleven Indian regiments), but also took command of the left of the army, as second in command to Lord Gough. For Thackwell's own account of the role of the cavalry at Goojerat, see Appendix 3. [Thackwell, *Military Memoirs* pp. 332-3.]

10 Carbines were short muskets designed for use by cavalry. These two squadrons must have been from the Indian regiments. The 9th Lancers had no carbines, their only firearms being one pistol per man. Major Yule, with his experience in the 16th Lancers' use of carbines in the Sutlej campaign, had petitioned the War Office for reissue of carbines to skirmishers, but was rebuffed by the Duke of Wellington, presumably drawing on his own Indian experience of over forty years before:

> His Grace is surprised, that Troops of this arm [lancers] should ever have been employed with matchlock men, under any circumstances, and to express his doubts whether such antagonists would have any more respect for Carbines than they have for Pistols.

In fact, the smoothbore, muzzle-loading pistols issued to cavalry were extremely inaccurate at anything other than point-blank range, and carbines were little better, and even more difficult to load and fire on horseback. [TNA WO 27/242-398; Inspection reports, 9th Lancers, 1844-50, Yule, 'Letters' *JSAHR* 64 p. 152; TNA WO 3/112 p. 136; Horse Guards Letter 27 March 1851, D F Harding, *Smallarms of the East India Company 1600-1856 Vol III: Ammunition and Performance* (London, 1999) p. 331.]

11 The Scinde Horse was a regiment of irregular native cavalry, raised in 1839, with a second regiment being raised in 1846. In 1860 they became the 5th and 6th Bombay Cavalry, and in 1903 the 35th Scinde Horse and 36th Jacob's Horse.

12 This officer was Captain Arthur Scudamore. He entered the army as a Cornet in 1835, and served with the 4th Light Dragoons in the First Afghan War, and with the 14th in both Anglo-Sikh Wars, being wounded at Ramnuggar. Gilling is mistaken in believing Scudamore died of his wound at Gujerat. He went on to command the 14th in numerous actions during the Indian Mutiny, for which he was awarded a Brevet Lieutenant Colonelcy and CB. He died a Major General in 1880. [Hamilton *Historical Record of the 14th* pp. 239-40, 497-8.]

13 984 Pte William Budgen served with the 9th Lancers in the Gwalior campaign and in both Anglo-Sikh Wars. He died on 18 August 1849. [TNA WO 25/3251.]

14 The *mohur* was a large gold coin, worth fifteen silver rupees at this time. The monthly pay of a lancer of under ten years' service, like Gilling, was eleven rupees, so his share of the loot was equivalent to nearly three months' pay. [Yule and Burnell, *Hobson-Jobson* pp. 573-4; BL L/MIL/5/400 (188) Pay of Soldiers in India.]

15 Those most concerned about caste were Hindus. In theory at least, both Sikhism and Islam rejected notions of caste, although both religions at this period recognised similar divisions in society. [Cunningham, *History of the Sikhs* pp. 304-5, 313-4.]

16 The generally accepted figures are 96 killed and about 700 wounded. The 9th Lancers had no casualties in this battle. [Cook, *The Sikh Wars*, pp.190-1; Bruce, *Six Battles for India*, p. 318.]

17 Gilling is recorded in the Regiment's Muster Roll as being discharged on 30 September 1850. The amount soldiers paid for their discharge depended on their service. If they had served under seven years the price was £30. As Gilling had served about seven years and three months he would have paid £25. Presumably the *mohurs* he had obtained on the battlefield of Gujerat, and the *batta* received for the Sutlej and Punjab campaigns all contributed towards this large sum. The twelve months' *batta* for Sutlej was paid in June 1846 and came to £7 15s 2d. Only six months' *batta* was paid for the Punjab campaign, because the Punjab was not considered to be 'foreign' territory any more. Therefore the men received only £3 17s 7d. This gave Gilling a total of £14 12s 9d; either he had saved the rest, or friends at home helped him. [TNA WO 12/895; WO 25/3251.]

Bibliography

Abbreviations
BL   British Library
DM   Derby Museums (Ninth Lancers Regimental Collections)
JSAHR Journal of the Society for Army Historical Research
JRUSI   Journal of the Royal United Services Institute
NAM   National Army Museum
QRLA   Queen's Royal Lancers Archives
TNA   The National Archives

Unpublished sources
British Library
L/MIL/5/12 Sutlej Medal Roll, 9th Lancers.
L/MIL/5/13 Punjab Medal Roll, 9th Lancers.
L/MIL/5/391 (135) p. 42 Libraries in India.
L/MIL/5/400 (188) Pay of Soldiers in India.
L/MIL/5/419 (355) Papers on Cholera.
L/MIL/5/427 (397) Letter to Bengal 3 October 1849 re. death rates of soldiers.
L/MIL/17/1/1968 Compilation of Standing Orders which have been issued to Her Majesty's Forces in India 1814-1850.
49116 ff 160-2 Papers relating to the suicide of Lieut Col J W King.

Ninth Lancers Regimental Collections, Derby Museums
912L: 2088/3 9th Lancers Regimental Order Book 1816-1877.
912L: 2089/3 Papers relating to Indian Mutiny Prize Money, 9th Lancers.
Punniar Star Roll, 9th Lancers 1843.
Pair of lances formerly owned by Captain Robert Cooke, Adjutant 9th Lancers 1827-42.

National Army Museum
6405-61 Pte George Tookey, 14th Light Dragoons, Letters from India 1846-48.
7201-45.1-5 Narrative and Papers of Pte Frederick Potiphar, 9th Lancers, India 1845-60.
8301-38 Captain Charles Abbot Delmar, 9th Lancers, Letters from India 1848-49.
9604-220 Pte Samuel West, 16th Lancers, Letters from India 1822-26.

Queen's Royal Lancers Archives, Grantham
Lieut T J Francis, 9th Lancers, typescript copy, Narrative of Battle of Aliwal 31 Jan 1846.
Sgt J Thomas, 16th Lancers, Diaries, India c. 1840-1846.

The National Archives
WO 3/100/362 Horse Guards Letter 28 Dec 1843 re Tablecloths etc.
WO 3/112 p. 136 Horse Guards Letter 27 March 1851 re Carbines for 9th Lancers.
WO 12/889-898 Muster Rolls, 9th Lancers 1841-55.

WO 25/3251 Casualty Rolls, 9th Lancers 1842-58.
WO 27/342-408 Inspection Reports, Cavalry 1821-51.
WO 76/538 Officers' Services, 9th Lancers 1842-60.
WO 90/2 Summary of Courts Martial abroad 1839-50.

University of Leeds
J H Rumsby, *The Sixteenth Lancers 1822-1846: the Experience of Regimental Soldiering in India* (PhD Thesis, 2004).

Contemporary published sources
An Act for Punishing Mutiny and Desertion; and for the Better Payment of the Army and their Quarters. Also, Rules and Articles for the Better Government of All His Majesty's Forces. (London, 1831).
O H St G Anson, *With H.M. Lancers during the Indian Mutiny: the Letters of Brevet-Major O. H. St G. Anson* ed H S Anson (London, 1896). [9th Lancers]
N W Bancroft, *From Recruit to Staff Sergeant* (Simla, 2nd edn 1900). [Bengal Horse Artillery]
P Beattie (ed), 'The Letters of John Curtis Binkley 1843-1849.' *JSAHR* 61 (1983) 30-7. [61st Foot]
M Brander (ed) 'Pte Charles Godward: Indian Journal and Letters 1842 and 1846.' In *The Sword and the Pen* (London, 1989) pp. 87-109. [16th Lancers]
J H Burton, 'The Soldier and the Surgeon.' *Blackwood's Magazine* 84 (1858) 1-24.
J D Cunningham, *A History of the Sikhs* ed H L O Garrett (Lahore, 1915).
D Dighton, *The Lance Exercise, in Three Divisions* (London, 1825).
E Eden, *Up the Country: Letters written to her Sister from the Upper Provinces of India* ed E Thompson (Oxford, 1930).
F Eden, *Tigers, Durbars and Kings: Fanny Eden's Indian Journals 1837-1838* ed J Dunbar (London, 1988).
I Fane, *Miss Fane in India* ed J Pemble (Gloucester, 1985).
G Farmer, *The Light Dragoon* ed G R Gleig (2 vols, London, 1844). [11th Light Dragoons]
T J Francis, 'With the 16th Lancers in India, 1846. An extract from a private notebook of Major T J Francis, 9th and 16th Lancers.' *The Scarlet and Green* (Journal of the 16th Lancers) 2 (9) (1933) 54-7.
J Gilling, *The Life of a Lancer in the Wars of the Punjaub, or, Seven Years in India* (London, 1855).
H G Hart, *The New Annual Army List, and Militia List* (London, 1840-1906).
R Heber, *Bishop Heber in Northern India: Selections from Heber's Journal* ed M A Laird (Cambridge, 1971).
Horse Guards, *Regulations for the Instruction, Formations and Movements of the Cavalry* (London, 1833, 1844, 1851).
Horse Guards, *Instructions for the Carbine Exercise; the Pistol Exercise; and the Lance Exercise* (London, 1844).
W W W Humbley, *Journal of a Cavalry Officer, including the Memorable Sikh Campaign of 1845-1846* (London, 1854). [9th Lancers]
Iowa State Gazetteer (ND, c. 1865).
The King's Regulations for the Army (London, 1837).
H Knollys (ed), *Life of General Sir Hope Grant with selections from his correspondence* (2 vols,

Edinburgh, 1894).
H Lawrence, *The Journals of Honoria Lawrence: India Observed 1837-1854* ed J Lawrence and A Woodiwiss (London, 1980).
[A C Lowe], *The Diary of an Officer of the 16th (Queen's) Lancers June 16 1822 to June 16 1840* (Calcutta, 1894).
W L Macgregor, *Practical Observations on the Principal Diseases affecting the Health of the European and Native Soldiers in the North-Western Provinces of India* (Calcutta, 1843).
J MacMullen, *Camp and Barrack Room; or the British Army as it is, by a late Staff Sergeant of the 13th Light Infantry* (London, 1846).
T Malcolm, *Barracks and Battlefields in India; or, the Experiences of a Soldier of the 10th Foot – North Lincoln in the Sikh Wars and Sepoy Mutiny* ed C Caine (London, 1891).
H Marshall, *Hints to Young Medical Officers of the Army on the Examination of Recruits* (London, 1828).
H Metcalfe, *The Chronicle of Private Metcalfe* ed F Tuker (London, 1953). [32nd Foot]
E Mole, *A King's Hussar, being the Military Memoirs for Twenty-five Years of a Troop-Sergeant-Major of the 14th King's Hussars* ed H Campton (London, 1897).
J Murray, 'Field Surgeon at the Battle of Aliwal.' ed J Fraser *JSAHR* 67 (1989) 80-93, 167-83; 72 (1994) 35-48. [Bengal Horse Artillery]
Naval and Military Almanack (London, 1841).
J M B Neill, *Recollections of Four Years' Service in the East with H. M. Fortieth Regiment* (London, 1845).
H A Ouvry, *Cavalry Experiences and Leaves from My Journal* (Lymington, 1892). [3rd Light Dragoons and 9th Lancers]
J Pearman, *Sergeant Pearman's Memoirs* ed Marquess of Anglesey (London, 1968). [3rd Light Dragoons.]
J Pearman, *The Radical Soldier's Tale: John Pearman 1819-1908* ed C Steedman (London, 1988).
J Ryder, *Four Years' Service in India (1844-48)* ed J Thompson (Burton, 2nd edn, 1854). [32nd Foot]
D A Sandford, *Leaves from the Journal of a Subaltern during the Campaign in the Punjaub Sept 1848 to March 1849* (London, 1849). [2nd Bengal European Regiment]
Bawa Satinder Singh (ed), 'The Letters of the First Viscount Hardinge of Lahore to Lady Hardinge and Sir Walter and Lady James 1844-1847.' *Camden Fourth Series* 32 (1986).
A Somerville, *The Autobiography of a Working Man* ed J Carswell (First published 1848. London, 1951). [2nd Dragoons]
G C Stent, *Scraps from my Sabretasche, being personal adventures while in the 14th (King's Light) Dragoons* (London, 1882).
L C Stewart, 'A Surgeon in the Second Sikh War: Ludovick Stewart's Account of the Battle of Chillianwalla.' ed M Nicholls *JSAHR* 71 (1993) 216-25.
W Taylor, *Scenes and Adventures in Affghanistan* (London, 1842). [4th Light Dragoons]
E J Thackwell, *Narrative of the Second Seikh War in 1848-1849* (London, 1851).
J Thackwell, *The Military Memoirs of Lieut-General Sir Joseph Thackwell GCB KH, Colonel 16th Lancers* ed H C Wylly (London, 1908).
J A Thomson, *Eighty Years' Reminiscences* (London, 1904). [9th Lancers 1836-42] *United States Census* (1860, 1870).
War Office, 'Warrant regulating the Pensions and Allowances to be granted to soldiers after

long service, or when discharged as wounded, disabled, or invalided, 14 Nov 1829.' *United Service Journal* 30 (Part 1) 106-112.

R Waterfield, *Memoirs of Private Waterfield* ed A Swinson and D Scott (London, 1968) [32nd Foot]

A Wynter, 'The Lodging, Food, and Dress of Soldiers.' *Quarterly Review* 105 (1859) 155-76.

R A Yule, *Notes on the employment of cavalry and horse artillery, with instructions for the evolutions of a brigade* (Calcutta, 1856).

R A Yule, 'The Letters of Brevet Lieutenant-Colonel Robert Abercromby Yule.' ed J Fraser *JSAHR* 61 (1983-4) 129-41, 215-27; 62 (1984) 36-46; 64 (1986) 152-72. [16th and 9th Lancers.]

Modern books and articles

Marquess of Anglesey, *A History of the British Cavalry 1816 to 1919 Volume 1: 1816 to 1850* (London, 1973).

A McK Annand, 'General Sir James Hope Grant, GCB.' *JSAHR* 43 (1965) 44-8.

A McK Annand, 'The 9th Lancers, 1820.' *JSAHR* 44 (1966) 63-8.

A McK Annand, 'Brigadier-General C R Cureton, CB, ADC.' *JSAHR* 47 (1969) 157-60.

M Barthorp, *British Cavalry Uniforms since 1660.* (Poole, 1984).

P B Boyden, *Tommy Atkins' Letters: The History of the British Army Postal Service from 1795* (London, 1990).

'British Recipients of the Indian Mutiny Medal.' *Family History in India* website (http://users.rootsweb.com/~indwgw/medalpage.htm. January 2007).

A P C Bruce, *The Purchase System in the British Army, 1660-1871* (London, 1980).

G Bruce, *Six Battles for India: The Anglo-Sikh Wars 1845-6, 1848-9* (London, 1969).

W N Bruce, *Life of General Sir Charles Napier GCB* (London, 1885).

J Burnett, *Useful Toil: Autobiographies of Working People from the 1820s to the 1920s.* (London, 1974).

N Carleton, *Lion's Teeth: The Artillery of Maharaja Ranjit Singh* (www.sikhspectrum.com/112005/artillery_maharaja_ranjit_singh.htm, January 2006.)

W Y Carman, *Dress Regulations 1846, with a new introduction* (London, 1971).

W Y Carman, 'The 9th Lancers c.1829.' *JSAHR* 73 (1995) 221-4.

S Claver, *Under the Lash – a history of corporal punishment in the British armed forces* (London, 1954).

R M Collins, 'Lieut-Colonel Reymond Hervey De Montmorency.' *JSAHR* 46 (1968) 97-106.

H C B Cook, *The Sikh Wars: The British Army in the Punjab 1845-1849* (London, 1975).

D Crystal, *The Cambridge Encyclopedia of the English Language* (Cambridge, 1995).

G W De Rhé-Philipe and M Irving, *Soldiers of the Raj* (1910 and 1912, one volume reprint London, 1989)

R Elias, 'Lancers and Lances.' *JRUSI* 33 (1889) 751-67.

C ffoulkes and E C Hopkinson, *Sword, Lance and Bayonet* (Cambridge, 1938).

H Graham, *History of the Sixteenth, the Queen's Light Dragoons (Lancers), 1759 to 1912* (Devizes, 1912).

H B Hamilton, *Historical Records of the 14th (King's) Hussars from AD 1715 to AD 1900* (London, 1901).

D F Harding, *Smallarms of the East India Company 1600-1856 Vol III: Ammunition and Performance* (London, 1999).

D F Harding, *Smallarms of the East India Company 1600-1856 Vol IV: the Users and their Smallarms* (London, 1999).
A Harfield, *Meerut: The First Sixty Years (1815-1875)* (London, 1992).
J Hirst, 'The Australian Experience: The Convict Colony.' In N Morris and D J Rothman (ed), *The Oxford History of the Prison* (Oxford, 1998).
H Hopkins, *The Strange Death of Private White: A Victorian Scandal that Made History* (London, 1977).
F J Huddeston, 'A Barrack Library of 1839.' *JSAHR* 2 (1923) 37-8.
B P Hughes, *The Bengal Horse Artillery 1800-1861* (London, 1971).
B P Hughes, *Firepower: Weapons Effectiveness on the Battlefield, 1630-1850* (London, 1974).
L James, *Raj: The Making and Unmaking of British India* (New York, 1998).
G E F Kauntze, *Historical Record of the Third, or the King's Own Regiment of Light Dragoons ... to 1857* (London, 1857).
London Stamp Exchange Ltd, *The Army of the Sutlej 1845-6: Casualty Roll* (London, ND).
W M Lummis and K G Wynn, *Honour the Light Brigade* (London, 1973).
J Lunt, *Scarlet Lancer* (London, 1964). [Life of John Luard, 16th Lancers]
Amandeep Singh Madra and Parmjit Singh, *Warrior Saints: Three centuries of the Sikh Military Tradition* (London, 1999).
P Mason, *A Matter of Honour: An Account of the Indian Army, its Officers and Men* (London, 1974).
C B Mayne, 'The Lance as a Cavalry Weapon.' *JRUSI* 49 (1905) 118-40.
I McInnes, *The Yeoman of the Guard, including the Body of Yeoman Warders, HM Tower of London, Members of the Sovereign's Body Guard (Extraordinary) 1823-1903* (Oldham, 2002).
S L Menezes, 'Race, Caste, Mutiny and Discipline in the Indian Army, from its origins to 1947.' In A J Guy and P B Boyden (ed), *Soldiers of the Raj: The Indian Army 1600-1947* (London, 1997) 100-117.
E Neale, *"Risen from the Ranks" or, Conduct versus Caste* (London, 1853). [Biography of Brigadier General C R Cureton, pp. 9-29.]
C B Otley, 'The social origins of British Army Officers.' *Sociological Review* 18 (1970) 213-39.
E Partridge, *A Dictionary of Slang and Unconventional English* ed P Beale (8th edn., London, 1984.)
D M Peers, 'Imperial Vice: sex, drink and the health of British troops in North Indian cantonments, 1800-1858.' In D Killingray and D Omissi (ed), *Guardians of Empire* (Manchester, 1999).
F H Reynard, *The Ninth (Queen's Royal) Lancers 1715-1903* (Edinburgh, 1904).
B Robson, *Swords of the British Army: the Regulation Patterns 1788 to 1914* (London, 2nd edn 1996).
D J J Rowe and W Y Carman, *Head Dress of the British Lancers 1816 to the Present* (Atglen, PA, 2002).
J H Rumsby, 'Suicide in the British Army, c. 1815 to c. 1860.' *JSAHR* 84 (2006) 349-61.
E W Sheppard, *The Ninth Queen's Royal Lancers 1715-1936* (Aldershot, 1939).
Patwant Singh, *The Sikhs* (London, 1999).
D Smurthwaite, 'A recipe for discontent: the Victorian soldier's cuisine.' in M Harding (ed), *The Victorian Soldier* (London, 1993).
J Spencer-Smith, *Portraits for a King: The British Military Paintings of A-J Dubois Drahonet*

(1791-1834) (London, 1990).

E M Spiers, *The Army and Society 1815-1914* (London, 1980)

E M Spiers, *The Late Victorian Army 1868-1902* (Manchester, 1992).

H Strachan, *Wellington's Legacy: The Reform of the British Army 1830-54* (Manchester, 1984).

S Stronge (ed), *The Arts of the Sikh Kingdoms* (London, 1999).

M Trustram, *Women of the Regiment: Marriage and the Victorian Army* (Cambridge, 1984).

G Tylden, *Horses and Saddlery* (London, 1965).

D S Virk, *Army Post Offices and Philately* (New Delhi, 1980).

A C T White, *The Story of Army Education 1643-1963* (London, 1963).

A S White, 'Flogging in the Army.' *JSAHR* 20 (1941) 114-5.

C Wills, *High Society: The Life and Art of Sir Francis Grant 1803-1878* (Edinburgh, 2003). [Portrait of James Hope Grant, pl 50.]

H C Wylly, *XVth (The King's) Hussars, 1759 to 1913* (London, 1914).

H Yule and A C Burnell, *Hobson-Jobson: The Anglo-Indian Dictionary* (First published 1886. London, 1996).

Index

People
Abbott, Major James, 157
Atkins, Private Richard Riley, 89, 91, 94, 154
Atkinson, George, 64-65
Auckland, Lord, 33-34
Aurangzeb, Emperor, 31

Bahadur, Tegh, 31
Budgen, Private William 'Bill', 138, 161

Campbell, Lieutenant Colonel Alexander, 20, 67, 150
Chunder, of Lahore, Ranee, 59, 71
Collins, Private William H. H., 88, 153
Cooke, Sergeant Major Robert, 16, 24
Cornwallis, Lord, 57, 149
Cureton, Lieutenant Augustus John, 125, 159
Cureton, Brigadier General Charles Robert, 99, 101-103, 125, 155-156, 159
Cureton, Lieutenant General Edward Burgoyne, 159

Dalton, Private Robert, 159
Day, Private Samuel, 75, 152
Delmar, Lieutenant Charles Abbot, 24, 35
Driscoll, Private Daniel, 151

Eden, Emily, 34
Edwardes, Herbert, 160

Fane, Miss Isabella, 33
Farmer, George, 19, 30
Firth, Private James, 77, 152
Fitzgerald, Captain John Forster, 103, 156
Franklin, Captain Sir John, 72, 151
Fullerton, Lieutenant Colonel James Alexander, 29, 152, 157

Gilbert, Major-General, 101, 109, 119, 134, 139
Gillespie, General, 88
Godward, Private Charles, 19, 37-38
Gough, Lord, 67-68, 112, 114-115, 127, 129, 132, 150-152, 160
Grant, G.C.B., General Sir James Hope, 20, 26-28, 36, 92, 141, 143, 145, 154
Graves, Farrier John, 153

Hardinge of Lahore, First Viscount Sir Henry, 83, 153
Hardinge, Lady, 153,
Havelock, Colonel Henry, 102-103
von Haynau, Julius Jakob, Baron, 154

Herbert, Lieutenant, 157
Higginson, Private Samuel, 45
Huish, Captain, 146
Humbley, Captain William Wellington Waterloo, 27

Jackson, Corporal George F., 147
Jahangir, Emperor, 31, 100
Jindan, Rani, 33, 149
Jones, Sir Walter, 153

Kemp, Lieutenant Philip, 25
King, Lieutenant Colonel J. W., 25
King, Cornet Robert William, 147

Lambert, First Lieutenant Sir Peter Colnett, 99, 155
Lane, Brevet Lieutenant Colonel J. T., 158-159
Luard, John, 16

Moore, Lieutenant General Sir John, 103, 156

Nanak, Baba, 30
Napier, General Sir Charles, 65, 150
Nugent, Patrick, 76, 152

Ouvry, Captain H. A., 27, 147

Palmer, Private William Henry, 154
Pearman, Sergeant John, 19, 38, 158
Pennycuick, Ensign Alexander, 158
Pennycuick, Lieutenant Colonel John, 158
Pope, Brigadier, 24, 35, 99, 120, 144, 156, 158-159
Pratt, Captain E. J., 25

Ryder, Corporal John, 37, 154, 160

Saltoun, Major General Lord, 154
Sandford, Lieutenant, 160
Singh, Chuttar, 157
Singh, Dhyan, 33
Singh, Duleep, 33, 83, 149
Singh, Dyem, 82
Singh, Gulab, 33, 81-82, 153
Singh, Kharak, 33
Singh, Lal, 33, 71
Singh, Narain, 82, 112
Singh, Ranjit, 31, 33-35, 59, 71, 84, 149
Singh, Runjur, 151
Singh, Shere, 33, 98, 101, 103-105, 108-110, 114, 118, 121, 127, 146, 160

INDEX 169

Singh, Tej, 33, 81, 150-151
Singh, Shere, 98, 101, 103-105, 108-110, 114, 118, 121, 127
Slone, Private Joseph, 62, 149
Smith, Sir Harry, 71, 151
Smith, Private Frederick, 150
Stisted, Lieutenant, 158
Sumroo, Begum, 68

Thackwell,K.C.B., Major-General Sir Joseph, 105, 108-109, 118, 133, 144, 146, 157, 160
Thomson, Colonel J. Anstruther, 23, 26, 157
Thonger, Captain Richard Freer, 27, 93
Tookey, Private George, 19, 156, 160
Trower, Lieutenant, 25

Unett, Captain Walter, 118, 158

Walter, Private Charles, 160
Walter, Private Lemon H, 160
Duke of Wellington, 18, 26, 160
Wheeler, Brigadier, 100-101
Williams, Lieut, 102, 105
Wolfe, General James, 103, 156

Yule, Major R. A., 22, 25-27, 146, 160

Places
Attock, 31, 105, 157
Afghanistan, 21, 23, 25, 31, 37, 151, 156-157, 158
Agra, 100
Aliwal, 35, 71, 85, 136, 151, 158
Allahabad, 56, 59, 96
Arroyo dos Molinos, 15

Barrackpore, 50, 157
Balaclava, 26
Benares, 57
Bengal, 14, 16, 18, 20-21, 26, 28, 38, 41, 58, 79, 147-148, 150, 153
Bhurtpore, 68, 151, 156
Birmingham, 35
Bombay, 134, 140, 161
Boston, Lincolnshire, 27, 93
Budiwal, 70, 81

Calcutta, 16, 48-50, 52, 55, 92, 142, 147-148, 151
Canada, 15
Cape of Good Hope, 46, 93, 143, 150
Cashmere, 82, 110
Cawnpore, 16, 19, 25, 29, 57-61, 63, 67, 70, 86
Chenab River, 31, 37, 101, 103, 105, 109, 112, 140
Chillianwallah, 21, 24-25, 35-36, 65, 101-102, 114, 116-117, 119-121, 123, 129, 134, 136, 144, 150, 152, 158-160

China, 18, 92, 150, 154
Chinsurah, 50, 52-53
Chunar, 58-59, 149
Coruckpoor Hills, 57

Delhi, 81, 152, 154
Dinghee, 112, 124, 129-130
Dublin, 152
Dum Dum, 52-54

Edinburgh, 154
Egypt, 119

Ferozepore, 67, 76, 78, 98-99
Ferozeshah, 39, 67, 69, 98-99, 104, 136, 150-151, 155

Ganges River, 16, 49, 56, 59, 66, 79, 147
Ghazeepore, 23
Gravesend, 16, 42-43, 49
Gujerat, 35, 101, 125, 132, 135-137, 146, 150, 152, 159-161
Gwalior, 25, 152, 157, 160-161

Himalayas, 31, 112

Iberian Peninsula, 15, 150
Indus River, 31, 105, 157

Java, 158
Jetch Doab, 109-110
Jhelum River, 31, 139, 157

Kashmir, 31, 33, 157
Kussoor, 80-81, 84

Lahore, 14, 31, 35, 37, 59, 65-67, 71, 79, 80-85, 99-100, 126, 149, 153, 157
Liverpool, 14
Lussoorie, 1322
Loodiana, 39

Macassar, 158
Maharajpore, 150-152, 156
Mahrattas, 31, 156
Maidstone, 14, 29, 42
Meerut, 16, 19-20, 67-68, 85-86, 88-89, 98, 141, 149, 153-154
Monghye, 56-57
Mudki, 67, 69, 76, 98, 104, 136, 150-151, 153
Multan, 31, 35, 127-128, 132, 160

New Ross, 15
New South Wales, 23, 141-143
New York, 14
North-West Passage, 151

Peer Pinjal Range, 110
Persia, 21, 31, 38
Peshawar, 31, 157
Pimlico, 16
Punjab, 15, 20-21, 28, 30-31, 33, 38, 40, 45, 59, 65, 71, 79-81, 84, 86, 92-93, 98-99, 103, 112, 136, 138-139, 147, 149-150, 152, 157-158, 160-161

Quebec, 156

Ramnuggar, 14, 35, 37, 39, 98-99, 101-103, 156, 159, 161

Shropshire, 156
Sirdhana, 68
Sirhind, 81
South Africa, 23, 159
Srikote, 157
Sutlej River, 31, 33, 67, 70, 74-75, 78-79, 81, 84-85, 89, 98-99, 140, 151, 153

Umballa, 16, 67

Vellore, 157

Walcheren, 15
Whitechapel, 154
Worcestershire, 157
Worksop, 14-15, 39
Wuzeerabad, 16, 28, 105, 139

Military Units
Listed in numerical then alphabetical order.

Bengal Horse Artillery, 153, 155, 158-159

1st Gurkha Rifles, 151
2nd Bengal European Regiment, 160
2nd Dragoons (Scots Greys), 155
2nd Goorkha Rifles, 152
3rd Light Dragoons, 25, 27, 38, 47, 70, 83, 101, 118, 147, 151, 157-158, 164, 166
4th Light Dragoons, 16, 25, 156, 161
5th Bengal Light Cavalry, 156
5th Bombay Cavalry, 161
5th Light Cavalry, 101, 103, 110-111, 118
6th Bengal Light Cavalry, 115, 144, 158
6th Bombay Cavalry, 161
6th Dragoon Guards, 45
8th Bengal Light Cavalry, 118, 146, 158
9th Queen's Royal Lancers, 14-16, 19-30, 35-37, 4145, 62-63, 67, 87, 93, 134, 142, 144, 146-147, 149-155, 157-161
11th Light Dragoons, 19
13th Light Infantry, 148, 149
14th King's Hussars, 38, 156, 159
14th King's Light Dragoons, 23, 25, 38, 101-102, 110, 120, 137, 156, 159, 160-161
14th Light Cavalry, 111
15th Bengal Lancers, 159
15th Hussars, 157
16th The Queen's Lancers, 16, 18, 25, 27, 29, 34-35, 37, 65, 67, 70-71, 109, 150-151, 156-158, 160
24th (The 2nd Warwickshire) Regiment, 102, 118, 125
28th The Gloucestershire Regiment, 159
30th Bengal Native Infantry, 122, 159
31st The East Surrey Regiment, 152
32nd The Duke of Cornwall's Light Infantry, 37, 88, 90, 93, 142-143, 153-154, 160
35th Scinde Horse, 161
50th (The Queen's Own) Regiment, 54, 75-77, 119, 148, 151
50th The Queen's Own (Royal West Kent Regiment), 148
53rd The King's (Shropshire Light Infantry), 156
62nd The Duke of Edinburgh's (Wiltshire Regiment), 149
75th The Gordon Highlanders, 148

Other
Afghan Wars, 14, 25, 156, 158, 161
Anglo-Sikh Wars, 14, 16, 19, 27, 30, 32-33, 35, 149, 151-153, 154, 157, 159-161
Burma War, 158
Corunna Campaign, 157
East India Company, 18-19, 22, 34-35, 89, 139, 147, 149-153, 157, 161
First China War, 92, 150
Gwalior Campaign, 152, 157, 160-161
Indian Mutiny, 16, 27, 38, 45, 92-93, 152, 154, 157, 159, 161
Kaffir Wars, 159
Long Service and Good Conduct Medal, 45, 152
Napoleonic Wars, 15-16, 150
Peninsular War, 156
Punjab Campaign, 20, 28, 92, 98, 147, 150, 152, 157, 161
Punjab Medal, 45, 93, 138, 152
Punniar Star, 45, 87, 152
Second China War, 92, 154
Sutlej Campaign, 27, 67, 78, 156, 159-160
Sutlej Medal for Sobraon, 45, 87, 152, 154

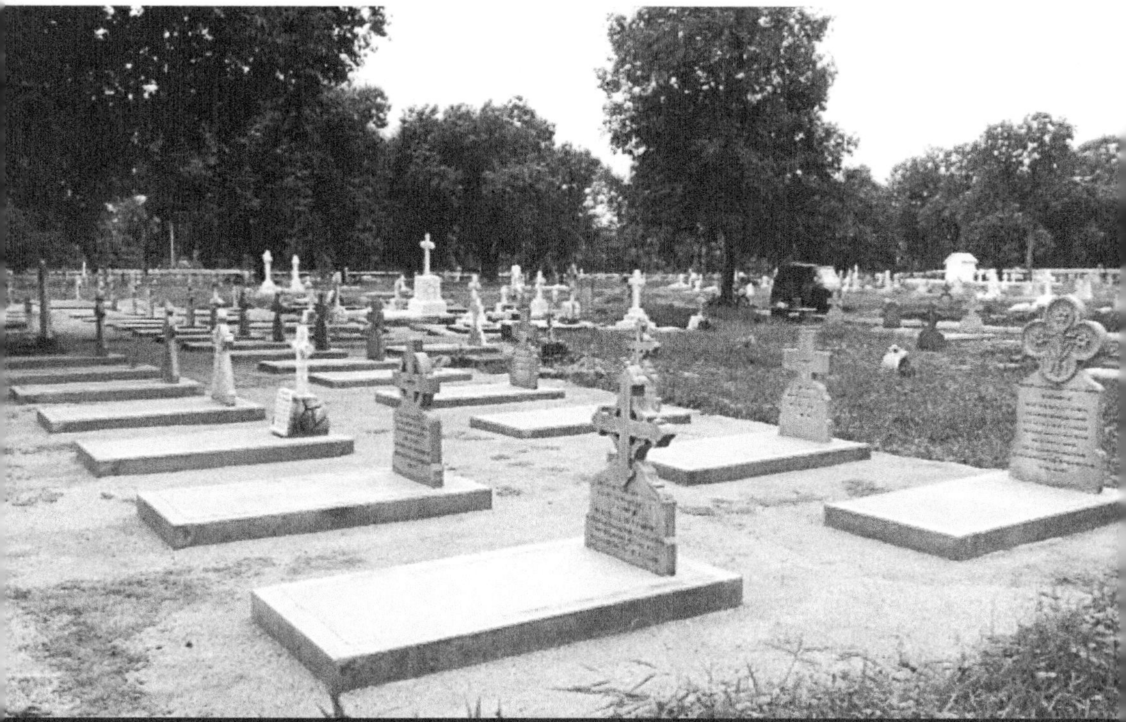

Jhansi Cantonment Cemetery, central India, restored with BACSA's help

BACSA – the British Association for Cemeteries in South Asia – brings together people with a concern for the many hundreds of European cemeteries, isolated graves and monuments in South Asia. It is the only established organisation that helps to record and restore these witnesses to centuries of European residence. An estimated two million Europeans and Anglo-Indians – mainly British administrators, soldiers, merchants and their families – are buried in the Indian subcontinent alone.

A charity, BACSA, records and publishes the locations of cemeteries and monuments, and the inscriptions on headstones. It supports local people active in the restoration and conservation of European graveyards. Well over 100 projects have benefited from BACSA funding.

www.bacsa.org.uk

Related titles published by Helion & Company

Fred. The Collected Letters and Speeches of Colonel Frederick Augustus Burnaby Volume 1:1842-1878
Edited and introduced by
Dr John W Hawkins
ISBN 978-1-909384-51-4 (hardback)

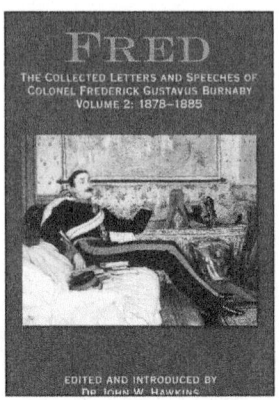

Fred. The Collected Letters and Speeches of Colonel Frederick Augustus Burnaby Volume 2:1878-1885
Edited and introduced by
Dr John W Hawkins
ISBN 978-1-909982-13-0 (hardback)

The Thinking Man's Soldier. The Life and Career of General Sir Henry Brackenbury 1837-1914
Christopher Brice
ISBN 978-1-907677-69-4 (hardback)

'Theirs Not to Reason Why'. Horsing the British Army 1875-1925
Graham Winton
ISBN 978-1-909384-48-4 (hardback)

HELION & COMPANY
26 Willow Road, Solihull, West Midlands B91 1UE, England
Telephone 0121 705 3393   Fax 0121 711 4075
Website: http://www.helion.co.uk
Twitter: @helionbooks | Visit our blog http://blog.helion.co.uk